OVERVIEW

Overview

Albert Einstein, a man known for his wisdom, was correct when he said, "The significant problems we face cannot be solved at the same level of thinking we were at when we created them."

The first step on the journey to solving these problems has to be made in your head. That is, you must examine and modify the way you think about problems today if you want to achieve success in the future.

It's hard to overestimate the power of effective thinking. Every thought you have today is in some way determining your future.

The goal of this course is to give you the tools necessary to turn yourself into a mental superhero. This change won't happen quickly. But with time and effort, you'll be able to solve problems you once found almost impossible. In this course, you'll learn to:

- think effectively about mental shortcuts,
- overcome biases and flawed assumptions,

- refine your problem-solving mind-set and decision-making style,
- cultivate the right state of mind.

Thomas Watson was chairman of IBM in 1943 when he said, "I think there is a world market for maybe five computers."

Watson certainly wasn't the only person to have ever made an inaccurate assumption about a business problem. What is an assumption? It's any facet of a business problem that you take for granted or assume to be true without calling it into question.

Roughly seven out of ten new businesses fail within three years. That failure rate often hinges directly on faulty business assumptions. Examine your assumptions and you're more likely to beat the odds.

Just as businesses receive benefits when employees examine their assumptions about given business problems, you as an individual reap personal rewards.

See each advantage to find out about the benefits of examining your assumptions about a given problem.

Greater insight into your problem-solving mind-set

When you unearth your assumptions about a business problem and examine them in the light of day, you get a better understanding of how your business mind ticks. You get a glimpse of how your brain works when left unsupervised by your conscious mind.

More confidence in your eventual decision

Your notions and opinions about a problem usually change for the better after you examine your assumptions. You think about the business problem in a more effective way. This can't help but build your confidence in the decision you eventually make.

Increased chances of enhanced career success

Once you've gained more insight into your problem-solving mind-set and upped your confidence level, it naturally follows that you will have an increased chance of succeeding in your career.

You should fully examine your assumptions about a business problem early in the decision-making process. Doing so sets the stage for success. In this lesson, you'll learn how to:

- get a better handle on your assumptions,
- recognize team assumptions,
- prioritize your problem-solving objectives.

In most Tarzan movies, you could count on one or two hapless explorers to fall into a pit of quicksand. No one ever died, of course. At the last minute, Tarzan or one of his friendly apes always came to the rescue.

Today's business world mirrors Tarzan's jungle in that pitfalls and hazards seem to await the problem solver at every turn.

Joel, a bond trader, had trouble moving past his initial stress and lack of inspiration and on to trading success. He then took direct measures to remove those roadblocks. Select each comment to receive Joel's insight.

Confidence

"The strategies I used to eliminate obstacles really worked. Once I overcame a few initial failures, I was much more confident in my ability to bounce back."

More time, less stress

"Those strategies were especially valuable because they gave me more time to focus on other business matters. I even noticed less stress in my personal life."

Question

Once you remove problem-solving roadblocks, you're well on your way to success. Choose the statements that reflect the values of using dynamic strategies to successfully move past roadblocks.

Options:

1. You'll find your personal life will probably be less stressful.
2. You'll be more confident in your ability to recover from setbacks.
3. You'll have more time to concentrate on other business issues.
4. You'll find that many important business problems will seem to solve themselves.

Answer:

Actually, you'll have a less stressful personal life, be more confident in your "bounce-back" ability, and have more time to focus on other business issues. On the other hand, business problems usually require work on your behalf to solve them.

Option 1: Correct. Successfully overcoming problem-solving roadblocks at work will build your confidence, and that confidence can spill over into your personal life, reducing stress overall.

Option 2: Correct. The confidence you develop after overcoming the first few problem-solving roadblocks will make you better able to deal with setbacks that arise in the future.

Option 3: Correct. If you are not spending large amounts of time struggling with problem-solving roadblocks because of your new-found ability to deal with them, you'll have more time to focus on other business issues.

Option 4: This option is incorrect. Business problems rarely solve themselves, and it is a mistake to wait for that to happen. It is your ability to apply effective problem-solving techniques that will solve the business problems.

Olympic hurdlers will tell you success boils down to one thing: technique. In this lesson, you'll learn effective strategies for leaping past roadblocks:

- using creative visualization,
- handling problem overload.

To sail his fishing boat safely into harbor, Jason had to consider many factors--wind, hidden reefs, tidal currents--all the while maintaining his balance on the deck. With any luck, Jason brought his "sea legs" on the outing.

After you generate solutions to a business problem, it's time to haul in the net and get your catch to shore. In business, you too have to earn your "decision-making legs."

As with sailing, many factors influence the decision or decisions you eventually make, such as timing, focus, and mind-set. This lesson will help you understand those factors and effectively prepare you for the decision implementation stage.

Understanding and mastering the various factors that influence decision making is both valuable and crucial.

See each image of Maggie, a production manager, to discover the value she realizes from carefully considering decision-making factors before implementing business solutions.

Maggie explaining

"Unforeseen complications after I implement a decision frustrate me. Recognizing decision-making factors beforehand helps me avoid these hidden snags."

Maggie pleased

"And as you can imagine, I save a lot of time as a result. Both of those factors enhance the confidence my colleagues have in my decision-making abilities."

You're about to focus on the ingredients that comprise skillful decision making. In this lesson, you'll learn to factor the following aspects into your business decisions:

- the mechanics of effective decision making,
- the various decision-making styles.

Here's a trivia question for you: Who invented the first working telephone?

Question

The inventor of the first telephone patented many inventions during his lifetime. Do you know who it was?

Options:

1. M. Charles Bourseul
2. Paul la Cour
3. Johann Philipp Reis
4. Antonio Meucci

Answer:

Actually, each of these inventors is credited with inventing early versions of the telephone.

Option 1: M. Charles Bourseul, a French telegraphist, published a plan for conveying sounds and speech by electricity.

Option 2: Poul la Cour, a Danish inventor, experimented with audio telegraphs on a line of telegraph between Copenhagen and Fredericia in Jutland.

Option 3: In 1860 Johann Philipp Reis produced a device which could transmit musical notes. It is best known as the "musical telephone".

Option 4: Antonio Meucci was recognized as the first inventor of the telephone by the United States Congress on June 11, 2002.

But Alexander Graham Bell filed the first patent, demonstrated his invention in public, and formed a company to produce the telephone.

Before good inventions gain value, they have to be implemented and evaluated.

For example:

- A toy manufacturer implements changes in its production process, reducing inventory costs.
- A department store conducts a customer survey to evaluate the attractiveness of its latest merchandising effort.

In this course, you'll learn how to take your decisions from idea to reality.

You'll learn how to:

- plan the actions required to implement your decisions,
- manage the action as your plan unfolds,
- assess the outcomes of your decisions.

"Never doubt that a small group of committed people can change the world. Indeed, it's the only thing that ever has." --Margaret Mead, anthropologist

You won't find the most valuable assets of any problem-solving organization on a balance sheet.

In the end, capital and technology amount to nothing if your organization doesn't establish a thriving network of people committed to decision-making success.

Question

And note that in this sense, "people" refers to a collective: groups and teams of colleagues whose problem-solving efforts combine and recombine to form an innovative whole. Experts sometimes refer to this resultant business mind-set as a "creative hive mentality."

How experienced are you with solving problems and making decisions in groups?

Options:

1. not experienced at all
2. a little experienced
3. somewhat experienced
4. relatively experienced
5. very experienced

Answer:

People who have solved business problems in groups often prefer teamwork to individual effort. Joint accomplishments often lead to a more marked sense of fulfillment.

In order to capture that feeling of group achievement, a problem-solving team must be designed and built properly.

See each team type to find out the different approaches to problem solving.

Information-sharing team

On an information-sharing team, people pass around data at the behest of an authority figure. After an essentially gratuitous examination of the material, members hand it back and watch the "ruler" make a decision. This type of team could be viewed as being similar to a dictatorship.

Participative team

On a participative team, the leader encourages input from and a joint decision by all group members. This type of team operates in a democratic fashion.

In fact, participative teams--not those run by corporate dictators--are far more effective. Sometimes this participation happens effortlessly.

But more often than not, it requires taking risks.

By the end of this course, you'll be ready to go out on the decision-making limb with the rest of your team.

You're about to learn how to avoid falling prey to inefficient group problem-solving habits. You'll also learn specific ways to improve overall group decision making.

CHAPTER ONE

Fundamentals of Effective Thinking

Thinking Effectively about Mental Shortcuts

It's rush hour, and the traffic on the highway is at a standstill. The radio announcer identified the problem as a major accident ahead. You exit the highway and end up in an unfamiliar neighborhood, trapped in a dead end.

Have you ever been in that kind of situation? If so, you've already learned that shortcuts don't always save you time. And sometimes they lead to dead ends.

Mental shortcuts, when used ineffectively, also can lead to dead ends--and headaches, lost productivity, and bad decisions.

You would feel cheated if you bought a microwave oven or a computer and it came without instructions. It's too bad your most important possession--your mind--came with no such guide.

When you drive a car or operate a computer, your orders are carried out exactly as you command. The machine doesn't talk back or have an agenda of its own.

However, if you tell your brain to think without taking shortcuts of any kind, it will continue on its merry way, perhaps following a less-than-optimal course. Your brain, for better or worse, is not an obedient servant.

If you're trying to decide where to raise your children, you might consider moving to the fictional town of Lake Wobegon. That's the locale popular radio host and author Garrison Keillor talks about on his show and in his books.

According to Keillor, Lake Wobegon is a place "where all the children are above average." Now wait a minute. Doesn't that sound like your own hometown?

Odds are you believe most people in your hometown are above average in most ways: neighborliness, civic pride, and so on.

Engineers need to be detail-oriented. The sheer complexity of their jobs makes it tempting for them to take mental shortcuts when evaluating problems and making decisions. So why are so many of them the picture of success?

It's because successful engineers know how to head off those unproductive mental shortcuts and instead think effectively about a problem. In this topic, you'll explore ways to productively think through problems by:

- avoiding cognitive laziness,
- gathering more information about a problem,
- taming the ego.

Counterproductive mental shortcuts

It's rush hour, and the traffic on the highway is at a standstill. The radio announcer identified the problem as a major accident ahead. You exit the highway and end up in an unfamiliar neighborhood, trapped in a dead end.

Have you ever been in that kind of situation? If so, you've already learned that shortcuts don't always save you time. And sometimes they lead to dead ends.

Mental shortcuts, when used ineffectively, also can lead to dead ends--and headaches, lost productivity, and bad decisions.

David and Ann, two financial managers, recently made some bad decisions in eliminating certain stocks from their portfolios.

See each manager to gain their insights into hindsight.

David

"I guess I got caught up in all those dot-com companies failing. I dumped all my Internet stocks, but a couple are still making huge profits."

Ann

"The information was available, but I didn't take the time to complete the research. I had a bad experience in a similar situation recently, and I just reacted by reflex."

David and Ann made their decisions based on what was fresh in their minds--a downturn of technology stocks--rather than doing thorough research and looking at the big picture. Have you ever made a decision you regretted because you used a mental shortcut instead of thoroughly thinking about and exploring the situation? Take a minute to write down that decision and what went wrong. Consider how you thought about the problem. What kinds of ill-advised shortcuts did you take?

Now look over your notes and evaluate them. Did you make a decision based on one person's recommendation? Did a recent occurrence influence your decision more than it should have?

What did you learn from this experience? If you had to do it over again, what would you do differently?

Now consider what that decision cost you: Did it cost you money? Time? A relationship that needed to be repaired?

And what did it cost others: Did someone else have to pay for your mistake? Did that person have to rework her efforts?

Question

When you use misleading mental shortcuts to think about and solve a problem, you assume some risk. But that's a negative approach to the problem. Identify what you think are benefits of avoiding counterproductive mental shortcuts.

Options:

1. You'll save time in the long-term.

2. You'll enjoy better results by thinking through decisions.

3. You'll be able to justify your decisions to interested parties.

4. You'll be able to get your work done more quickly.

Answer:

In fact, by avoiding mental shortcuts, you can save time by not having to redo work, you can achieve better results, and you can justify your decisions to others.

Option 1: Correct. By finding the right solution to a problem more often, you will not have to spend as much time fixing problems caused by poor solutions.

Option 2: Correct. By thinking things through, you will find that the quality of your solutions to problems will begin to rise, ending up with better results.

Option 3: Correct. As a result of giving proper thought to an issue, you will find that you have clearly sorted and backed up your thoughts, allowing you to support them when relating them to others.

Option 4: Incorrect. Thinking through problems isn't about accomplishing your work faster. It's about accomplishing your work better, with higher quality and levels of efficiency.

Mental shortcuts can be costly. In this lesson, you'll explore two types of shortcuts: rules of thumb and thinking traps. Note that "rules of thumb" are useful principles which have a wide application, but are not intended to be strictly accurate or reliable in every situation.

Once you've explored these two shortcuts, you'll learn ways to productively think through a problem.

Mental rules of thumb

You would feel cheated if you bought a microwave oven or a computer and it came without instructions. It's too bad your most important possession--your mind--came with no such guide.

When you drive a car or operate a computer, your orders are carried out exactly as you command. The machine doesn't talk back or have an agenda of its own.

However, if you tell your brain to think without taking shortcuts of any kind, it will continue on its merry way, perhaps following a less-than-optimal course. Your brain, for better or worse, is not an obedient servant.

Processing every bit of information about a problem is a huge task. Your brain, with or without your approval, uses rules of thumb to make its job easier. These rules of thumb, or "heuristics," can be useful tools. But they also can impair your judgment. In this topic, you'll learn about these rules of thumb:

- the availability heuristic,

- the representativeness heuristic,
- the anchoring heuristic.

Question

Consider a problem you're now encountering at work. This problem could be anything from sagging sales to communication difficulties.

Do you feel that you have the capacity to perceive, and understand, every single aspect of this problem?

Options:

1. never
2. rarely
3. sometimes 4. often
5. definitely

Answer:

Option 1: Every problem, no matter how simple, has subtleties and contingencies that are hard to account for. People must use heuristics to reduce the complexity of a problem.

Option 2: Every problem, no matter how simple, has subtleties and contingencies that are hard to account for. People must use heuristics to reduce the complexity of a problem.

Option 3: Every problem, no matter how simple, has subtleties and contingencies that are hard to account for. People must use heuristics to reduce the complexity of a problem.

Option 4: Every problem, no matter how simple, has subtleties and contingencies that are hard to account for. People must use heuristics to reduce the complexity of a problem.

Option 5: Every problem, no matter how simple, has subtleties and contingencies that are hard to account for.

People must use heuristics to reduce the complexity of a problem.

Although rules of thumb are necessary to reduce the time and effort needed to make decisions, some of these heuristics can negatively affect your judgment. The first of these potentially harmful rules of thumb is the availability heuristic.

See each of Kathleen's statements to learn more about the availability heuristic.

Statement 1

"Psychologists define the availability heuristic as the tendency to most easily recall those events that are the most "available" or vivid in our memories."

Statement 2

"This heuristic usually works quite well. By relying on their most vivid memories to estimate frequency and probability, people are able to simplify decision making"

The availability heuristic becomes misleading only when it distorts your perception of the frequency and probability of a given event. When you're solving problems and making decisions, unconsciously using the availability heuristic just because it's handy can warp your assessment of the situation.

See each example for more details on how the availability heuristic can lead you astray.

cause of death

Are you more likely to be killed by falling airplane parts or by a shark? Most people side with the shark because shark attacks get more media attention. Shark attacks are more vivid and available in their minds. In actuality, you're 30 times more likely to be killed by falling airplane parts.

performance reviews

Managers conducting performance reviews often use the availability heuristic. Vivid instances of the employee performing well or poorly are easy for the managers to remember. They also recall recent examples of high or low performance more readily than older ones.

gambling

Say a friend just returned from Las Vegas after winning big in craps. On your trip to Vegas, you may overestimate the likelihood of coming out ahead in a similar game because your buddy's story is vivid in your mind. Your perception of the odds is distorted.

The key to avoiding poor usage of the availability heuristic when making decisions is to always consider the true odds of the event at hand.

Beware of wishful thinking, and maintain accurate records of the various aspects of the problem you aim to solve.

The second rule of thumb is the representativeness heuristic. This heuristic is a mental shortcut in which people classify something according to how similar it is to a typical instance.

In other words, you use the representativeness heuristic when you judge probabilities by the degree to which A is representative of, or resembles, B. If something waddles and quacks like a duck, it's probably a duck, right? Not necessarily. The representativeness heuristic may make you ignore "base-rate information," the actual statistics concerning an event. That waddler and quacker may very well be the person in the cube next door.

See each problem and its solution for details.

Problem 1

John just got his Masters in Business Administration (M.B.A.). He loves the arts. In fact, at one time he considered becoming a musician.

Is he more likely to accept a job as a manager of the arts or as a generic management consultant?

Solution 1

Most people think John will take the arts management job. However, this ignores base-rate data. A larger number of M.B.A.s take jobs in management consulting than in arts management. With this in mind, it's only reasonable to predict John will more likely become a management consultant.

Problem 2

In Edith's industry, 50 percent of all new products fail. But Edith has marketed five successful products in a row.

What's the likelihood her latest innovation will succeed?

Solution 2

Based on her track record, it seems that she'd have a better than 50-50 shot.

But because the 50 percent success rate applies to all marketers, good and bad, Edith's true chances really can't be better than that.

Problem 3

An ad spokesman tells you to buy a pain-relief product. He's not a doctor, although he plays one on television.

Are you likely to trust this fellow more than a another actor?

Solution 3

You might not, but most people do. The actor who plays the doctor seems more representative of a medical professional than a regular actor.

His knowledge of medicine, however, is likely to be the same as any other actor's.

To counter the adverse effects of the representativeness heuristic, you have to pay attention to actual probabilities. The same holds true for the third rule of thumb, the anchoring heuristic.

Answer this: Has the mighty Cincinnati Reds baseball team won more than ten World Series, or fewer?

Anchoring is a mental shortcut in which you use a certain idea as a starting point and adjust your perception of the new event away from that anchor. In the case of the Reds, the number ten is the anchor by which you adjust your perception and estimate of the answer. You'll probably guess that numbers far away from ten are less likely to be correct, even though the Reds have actually won only five.

See each step, in order, to learn more from Terry, a statistician.

Setting a mental anchor

If you, as a novice runner, are told that most people run four-minute miles, you're going to use that time as an anchor, or measurement, for success. If you run much slower than four minutes, you're likely to feel you performed poorly.

Measuring against the anchor

But what if, instead of running a four-minute mile, you actually ran an average time? You would still feel bad because you based, or anchored, success on four minutes. You didn't adjust your expectations to the actual average time.

A faulty perception

Say you're a customer service representative making $27,000 a year. You're told that, based on your good performance, you'll get a $15,000 raise. You think: "Wow. I must be the best representative in the whole world."

Resetting the anchor

Then you find out you'd been grossly underpaid to begin with. After your raise, you're simply making the average rate. You're not so impressed with yourself now because your anchor of $27,000 was misleading.

Be aware of extreme anchor values when thinking about problems. Extreme numbers usually aren't realistic. And the key to improved judgment in general is distinguishing between the effective and ineffective uses of heuristics.

Question

Rules of thumb can be effective problem-solving tools, but not in all instances. Identify the rules of thumb and their descriptions.

Options:

1. The availability heuristic involves bringing to mind what's most available or vivid in memory.
2. The representativeness heuristic means classifying something by its resemblance to another instance.
3. The anchoring heuristic involves making vivid and emotional events of the past the foundation of memory.
4. The adjustment heuristic means using a mental anchor as a reference and adjusting to a new instance.

Answer:

Actually, the availability heuristic involves recalling those events that are the easiest--that is, the most vivid. Using the representativeness heuristic, people classify something according to how similar it is to a typical instance.

Option 1: Correct. The availability heuristic employs the most recent or plain memory for problem solving. It can, however, become misleading if it distorts your perception of the frequency and probability of a given event.

Option 2: Correct. People use the representativeness heuristic when they judge probabilities by the degree to which choice A resembles choice B.

Option 3: Incorrect. Anchoring is a mental shortcut in which you use a certain idea as a starting point and adjust your perception of the new event away from that point.

Option 4: Incorrect. There is no adjustment heuristic. Using a mental anchor is indicative of the anchoring heuristic.

As with most titles, the names of the three heuristics give you clues to their descriptions. For example, the availability heuristic concerns first recalling what is most available in your memory. Representativeness heuristics entail classifying something by how closely it represents another instance.

Finally, the anchoring heuristic involves using an idea or value as a starting point, or anchor, and adjusting away from that anchor for the new instance.

All three heuristics may prompt you to think about using misleading information.

Rules of thumb are sometimes made to be broken, especially when they cause you to misperceive a problem. In this topic, you learned about the following rules of thumb:

- the availability heuristic,

- the representativeness heuristic,
- the anchoring heuristic.

Thinking traps

If you're trying to decide where to raise your children, you might consider moving to the fictional town of Lake Wobegon. That's the locale popular radio host and author Garrison Keillor talks about on his show and in his books.

According to Keillor, Lake Wobegon is a place "where all the children are above average." Now wait a minute. Doesn't that sound like your own hometown?

Odds are you believe most people in your hometown are above average in most ways: neighborliness, civic pride, and so on.

Because nearly everyone feels this way, however, does it follow that below-average people must have attended rival high schools? Or perhaps that they don't exist at all?

No. Below-average folks live everywhere. It's just that most people fall into thinking traps when assessing the merits of their own hometown. In this topic, you'll explore the following thinking traps:

- selective perception,

- the contrast effect,
- rationalization.

Keillor may be falling prey to the first thinking trap: selective perception. Selective perception causes you to perceive what you expect and hope to find rather than what is true and accurate.

Lillith and Tommy, two accountants, talked about why they reversed a recent decision.

Lillith: Have you seen the president's new boat? Or maybe we should call it a yacht.

Tommy: Yeah, times seem to be pretty good, Lillith. Have you taken a close look at the recent revenue figures, though?

Lillith: Not as close as I should. Our business situation is so strong right now, the revenue figures almost seem like an afterthought, Tommy.

Tommy: Hmm. Well, it's time to look again. I was under the same assumption as you, Lillith--that everything was great. I mistook the appearance of company affluence for actual wealth. I started to allocate huge capital improvement funds and salary increases.

Lillith: What, no big pay increases? Your reputation as a benefactor is now at stake, Tommy.

Tommy: Better to be a man with a secure job than an unemployed benefactor. Once I took a serious look at the actual revenue stream, along with the economic forecasts, that perception of wealth was quickly gone.

Lillith: Well, you're right, Tommy. We accountants have to allocate money using hard numbers, and not simply using hopes and dreams.

Tommy: Exactly. The second look is one of our most valuable tools.

Lillith and Tommy knew that perceptions, by their very nature, are selective. Even associating the president's new boat with impressive corporate wealth was dictated by their mental and emotional expectations.

That's why, before making a judgment of any kind, it is often beneficial to stop and question your motivation. Are you motivated to see things in a way that doesn't correspond to the actual situation?

Selective perception is similar to the second thinking trap: the contrast effect. A contrast effect occurs when you compare, or contrast, two different situations, and each one distorts your perception of the other one.

When you let the contrast effect cloud your perception while solving problems, you get a distorted view of reality.

Select Celia, a sports announcer, to find out her view of the contrast effect. Then select Larry, a real estate agent, to find out how he takes advantage of this effect.

Celia

"I'm about 5 foot 6--average height. When I talk to basketball players, I look tiny in comparison. But when I interview racehorse jockeys, I look like a giant."

Larry

"When I'm showing homes to someone, I first take him to an overpriced and run-down house. In contrast, the average home he sees next looks like a real value."

Question

Most people are affected by the contrast effect when thinking about problems and their circumstances. The key is to be aware of this effect and take it into account when making judgments.

Say you've made a poor decision. With or without the contrast effect coming into play, would you be likely to rationalize your bad decision in some way to make it seem like a better decision than it actually was?

Options:

1. no chance
2. probably not
3. maybe
4. probably
5. definitely

Answer:

Option 1: No matter how you rated yourself on this question, it's often a natural and subconscious reflex to rationalize choices. After all, you've got your self-perception to uphold.

Option 2: No matter how you rated yourself on this question, it's often a natural and subconscious reflex to rationalize choices. After all, you've got your self-perception to uphold.

Option 3: No matter how you rated yourself on this question, it's often a natural and subconscious

reflex to rationalize choices. After all, you've got your self-perception to uphold.

Option 4: No matter how you rated yourself on this question, it's often a natural and subconscious reflex to rationalize choices. After all, you've got your self-perception to uphold.

Option 5: No matter how you rated yourself on this question, it's often a natural and subconscious reflex to rationalize choices. After all, you've got your self-perception to uphold.

Rationalization, the third thinking trap, is like the others in that it leads you to deny or skew some aspects of a problem. Denial doesn't help you solve problems. It's beneficial to look at all aspects of an issue clearly.

See each step of a problem solving process to learn how rationalization affected Larry in his real estate job.

identifying a problem

"I realized the other day that I'm having a problem marketing my services. My first instinct was to justify my lack of creative efforts in this area by thinking that my customers didn't want innovation. Then I thought about the problem a little more and realized I was just being lazy."

making a decision

"Last year, I decided not to fight my company's decision to reduce my territory. I based that on the notion that management just wouldn't listen to my protests. Well, I found out that Robert, my associate, raised his voice and got some trade-offs from management."

reviewing a decision

"It's been a few months since I made up my mind to buy a small sports car, even though a bigger car would have carried my clients more comfortably. But, hey, when I'm out on the open road alone, I'm in heaven. It's then that I rationalize that my decision wasn't that bad after all."

Rationalization doesn't affect only your appraisal of past decisions. You've seen that rationalization has an impact on every aspect of the problem-solving process. Avoid the rationalization trap by:

- paying attention to your feelings when deciding,
- getting feedback on your reasoning from others,
- never rushing to judgment about a problem.

Question

Some thinking traps are like quicksand: They're a real struggle to free yourself from. If you don't avoid them, however, you may end up with more problems. Match each thinking trap with one or more statements that show how that thinking trap affects problem solving and decision making.

Options:

A. rationalization

B. selective perception

C. the contrast effect

Targets:

1. That newer car looks like a bargain in comparison.

2. I think the students at my college are smarter than that.

3. After hearing so many terrible singers, that singer really sounds good.

4. Yeah, I distorted the truth, but I'm not a liar. I just made a mistake.

Answer:

Actually, mental discomfort often leads to rationalization, hopes and expectations affect selective perception, and contrast effects exaggerate differences.

When you let the contrast effect cloud your perception while solving problems, you get a distorted view of reality and accept things that aren't necessarily true.

Selective perception causes you to perceive what you expect and hope to see, rather than what is true and accurate. This person views those who surround him in a selective sort of way.

In the context of several bad singers, an average singer might sound better than he actually is. Contrast effect such as this can affect any area of a person's life.

Rationalization has an impact on every aspect of the problem-solving process. Through it, people tend to make excuses for themselves in order to ease a mental burden.

Selective perception, the contrast effect, and rationalization are shortcuts that, once taken, alter your perception of a problem. And when you begin solving a problem when you're in one of these thinking traps, it's hard to regain momentum toward success.

Ever wonder why thousands of small children can easily beat you at your favorite video game? It may

be that, rather than knowing exactly what to do, those naive minds quickly learn exactly what to avoid-- the traps that lay in wait for the hero.

In this topic, you learned that you should become like the child and avoid the thinking traps that hamper your problem-solving ability.

You first found out how selective perception can lead you astray. Then you discovered that both the contrast effect and rationalization have a tendency to distort your thinking.

Strategies used in a problem-solving scenario

Engineers need to be detail-oriented. The sheer complexity of their jobs makes it tempting for them to take mental shortcuts when evaluating problems and making decisions. So why are so many of them the picture of success?

It's because successful engineers know how to head off those unproductive mental shortcuts and instead think effectively about a problem. In this topic, you'll explore ways to productively think through problems by:

- avoiding cognitive laziness,
- gathering more information about a problem,
- taming the ego.

The first strategy for productively thinking through a problem is to avoid cognitive laziness. In general, people tend to do as little thinking as possible. Thousands of years ago, less thinking meant more time spent on survival.

In other words, humans are genetically wired to "think in a way that is easiest." This strategy was beneficial in the ancient past, but times have changed. In today's world, it is often necessary to take the time to think hard about a particular problem in order to solve it.

How can you tell if someone has resisted the impulse to be mentally lazy when thinking about a problem? Hillary heads a team that's trying to solve a problem promoting its new digital microdisplay unit.

See each indicator to learn how Hillary determines whether team members have avoided cognitive laziness.

Indicator 1

"The effective people on my team don't make premature decisions, even when it's tempting. They insist on thinking a problem through before deciding."

Indicator 2

"When these team members present information to the others, they also talk about the short- and long-term consequences of any action. That's a sure sign of studied thought."

Refusing to reach quick, easy decisions and fully exploring the ramifications of a decision are both signs that you--or someone else--have resisted the urge to be cognitively lazy.

The second strategy for productively thinking through a problem is to gather more information. In today's information society, knowledge is power. Here are examples of types of information to gather about a problem:

- reliable statistics about the problem,
- the risks associated with potential solutions,
- the people affected by the problem,
- the resources available to solve the problem.

Gathering information differs from avoiding cognitive laziness in that the former concerns the acquisition of concrete facts and figures, whereas the latter involves taking the time to think through a problem. It's usually not hard to tell who's taken the time to gather information about a problem and who's taken shortcuts. Ask questions about the situation, and listen for the details in the replies.

See each statement by Hillary or one of her managerial colleagues to find out more.

"Ask and you shall receive."

"Ask and you shall receive. I constantly ask my colleagues for their ideas about how to fix a problem. If they've done their homework, they usually provide me with a lot of numbers and multiple angles on how to approach the problem."

"I gather information about the risks."

"I gather information about the risks involved in making a certain decision. Hillary appreciates that. I usually state the risks in the form of probabilities. I expect others to have an understanding of our chance for success as well."

"Hillary is always thorough."

"Hillary is always thorough. And that's a good thing. She urges me to gather information about the impact of our decisions on customers. By getting data on customers, you're not as likely to settle for whatever is easiest internally."

"Money, money, money."

"Money, money, money. So many decisions revolve around financial constraints. It's easy to solve a problem if you think you've got unlimited funds. Hillary has taught me the value of assessing our resources rather than assuming we've always got enough."

As you saw, Hillary's team members were effective at solving problems because they gathered a lot of information, much of it statistical. They examined risks, financial constraints, and the impact of their decision on others.

Question

It's easy to become emotionally invested in your decisions or identify too much with a given problem. Which reasons are important reasons not to let your ego get in the way of solving problems and making decisions?

Options:

1. You might avoid making any decision that involves risk.
2. You might rely on others to solve difficult problems for you.
3. You might give up on a problem because it seems insurmountable.
4. You might let your own need for success lead to overly risky choices.

Answer:

Actually, all the options are correct. Letting your ego get in the way might make you shun risk altogether or assume too much risk. You may also give up on difficult problems or let others make hard decisions for you.

Option 1: Correct. If your ego is involved, you won't want to be wrong. That means that you will gravitate to solutions that involve the least amount of risk.

Option 2: Correct. When your ego is in the way, relying on others takes some of the from you. It is less risky to let others solve the problems, because if things go wrong, then it isn't your fault!

Option 3: Correct. If your ego is working hard, you will be more likely to give up on a problem quickly. If the only choices are between giving up and taking a long and uncertain road, giving up might seem like the best option.

Option 4: Correct. If your ego is in the way, you are more likely to base your choices on your own aggrandizement, rather than on finding the best solution.

Follow along as Marty and Dana, two of Hillary's colleagues, talked about a recent decision they made.

Marty: You know, Dana, when we had to decide how to market those new microdisplay circuits, I really felt like that project was mine. That feeling may have gotten in the way.

Dana: How so, Marty?

Marty: Well, I felt too close to the decision, like my entire reputation depended on its success. Sure, I had some ego at stake. But being so emotionally involved in the decision really affected my thinking.

Dana: Tell me about it. I felt my ego was at stake when I put together that proposal last week. I pretty much froze up. I just couldn't make the tough choices. I left those for the rest of the team.

Marty: Hmm. I guess we had opposite reactions. I wanted so badly to look good that I didn't think the problem through. My decisions were way too risky.

Dana: Strange when your ego gets in the way. You either stop thinking altogether or think too big.

Marty: True. Our decisions should not define who we are.

Marty and Dana suffered from the same malady--an overinvestment of ego--but displayed different symptoms.

Instead of thinking about the problem in a clear way, Marty assumed that more risk would pay off in higher returns. Dana, however, felt she had to protect her ego, so she avoided risk and passed on her decision-making responsibility to others.

Question

Practice what you've learned about taming the ego while thinking through a problem. What are the reasons you shouldn't invest too much of yourself in a problem or decision?

Options:

1. You might assume too much risk.
2. You could end up giving up on a problem and letting others solve it for you.
3. You'll probably avoid taking the kinds of mental shortcuts that facilitate problem solving.
4. In an attempt to avoid risky decisions, you may settle for an easy way out of a problem.

Answer:

In fact, too much ego may lead you to give up on a problem and let others do the hard work instead. You may also either avoid or take on too much risk when making a decision.

Option 1: Correct. One symptom of letting your ego get in the way is taking on too much risk in a situation. Other symptoms include both the avoidance of risk, and allowing others to solve your problems.

Option 2: Correct. This could be what happens when you let your ego get in the way. Two other symptoms include the seemingly contrasting ideas of taking on too much risk, or simply avoiding risk altogether.

Option 3: Incorrect. Our mental shortcuts don't facilitate problem solving; they compound it. One such shortcut is letting our ego get in the way of making decisions. This results in the misuse of risk and poor problem management.

Option 4: Correct. If your ego is in the way, your reaction to risk could go either way. You could either take on too much risk, or avoid it as much as possible. Also, you will be more willing to give up and let others make the decisions.

You've learned how to productively think through a problem, but how do you tell whether your colleagues have failed to use effective strategies to do so?

You need to really listen to what your co-workers say when talking about a problem or circumstance. The extent of their knowledge is usually betrayed by the amount of detail and the kinds of details they provide.

Select each sign of mental shortcuts to get further tips from Hillary about how to determine whether thinking strategies were used effectively.

premature decisions

"If someone says, 'Look, let's just make a decision here and move on,' it immediately raises a concern. There's a good chance this person hasn't gathered enough information about the problem. He's being cognitively lazy."

easy decisions

"In a meeting last week, a co-worker said: 'Aren't we making this decision too hard? Let's just do what's going to be easiest for all of us.' That, my friend, is short-term thinking at its finest. He preferred to take a mental shortcut and avoid the effort of thinking through the problem."

consequences

"Deidre is good about coming up with possible solutions, but she never looks at the possible consequences. Once she comes up with a few decent options, she stops gathering information. Talking about consequences is a sure sign of thinking a problem through."

long-term outlook

"'Hillary, I really think this decision will give us what we need for now until we can regroup,' Bob told me last month. I told him that once we lose sight of the long-term outlook, it's as if we've just stopped thinking about the problem. Bob might have had too much ego at stake or just been mentally lazy."

statistics

"When a colleague peppers her descriptions of a problem with a lot of numbers, I know she's really explored the situation. If she doesn't have figures to back up her ideas, there's a good chance she's just settled for a surface analysis."

personal involvement

"Ever hear a co-worker say, 'But if I decide to do this, how will I look to the others?' or 'I've put so much into this decision, I just can't seem to let it go'? When a person refers to himself when talking about a business problem, it's a potential sign he's got too much ego invested in it."

You, too, can learn from Hillary. By listening both to what your co-workers say and do not say, you can analyze the degree to which they've avoided taking ineffective mental shortcuts.

How detailed are their explanations? Do they seem to be in a rush to arrive at a speedy and obvious decision? Are they too focused on the decision's impact on themselves? These are a few of the questions to ask.

Case Study: Question 1 of 2

Scenario

Howard and Tina, two project managers at a Global 2000 agribusiness, were having problems keeping a project on schedule. The line workers refused to work the hours required to meet the deadline. Suppliers were late with their shipments. Howard felt they had been set up to fail because their bosses should have solved the problem. He worried about how this decision would reflect on him. He and Tina had a couple of weeks to propose a solution to their supervisor. While Tina was examining statistics on the long-term effects of schedule rewrites and alternative suppliers, Howard suggested they make a tentative decision to hire new workers and then get input from senior staff. Tina asked Howard to investigate some other options by contacting the human resources department regarding the labor shortage and the engineering department concerning ways to eliminate the need for the delayed chemicals.

Consider the different strategies by answering the questions in order.

Question:

Were Howard and Tina effective at using strategies to avoid counterproductive mental shortcuts?

Options:

1. Howard wasn't effective because his cognitive laziness caused him to seek a quick and easy solution.

2. Tina was effective because she examined statistics on the long-term effects of schedule rewrites and alternative suppliers.

3. Howard was effective because he thought about how the problem related to him before trying to look for potential solutions.

4. Tina wasn't effective because she had too much ego involved in the problem and insisted on gathering more information.

Answer:

In fact, Tina was effective because she didn't take any mental shortcuts and instead gathered more information. Howard wasn't effective because he rushed to a decision.

Option 1: Correct. Howard opted for the quick fix to the problem rather than the best solution. Also, his ego was involved because he became worried about how their decision would reflect on him.

Option 2: Correct. Tina did a great job of gathering information in order to help her know the best course to follow.

Option 3: Incorrect. Thinking about himself first is a sign of Howard's ego being in the way. He was actually ineffective at finding solutions to the problem.

Option 4: Incorrect. Tina gathered lots of information and deliberately thought through the issue in order to find the best resolution. If her ego was involved in the problem, she likely would have opted for the quickest, most obvious answer.

Case Study: Question 2 of 2

What kinds of questions did you need to ask when assessing this situation?

Options:

1. When discussing the problem, did Howard and Tina refer to themselves instead of the situation at hand?
2. Did Howard and Tina examine the potential consequences of potential solutions?
3. Did Howard and Tina look at the data regarding their labor and supply shortage to further explore the problem?
4. Did Howard and Tina pay attention to the corporate policies about the chain of decision-making command?

Answer:

Actually, you needed to ask whether Howard and Tina had examined the numbers and considered the consequences of possible solutions. You also needed to ask whether they had referred to themselves when talking about the problem.

Option 1: Correct. The answer to this question tells you that while Howard let his ego step in, Tina was more interested in trying to find the best solution to the problem.

Option 2: Correct. By answering this question, you learned that Howard went for the quick, but more likely to be ineffective, fix, while Tina sought out as much information as possible in order to make a good decision.

Option 3: Correct. Answering this question taught you that while Howard opted for the quick and easy option, Tina committed herself to doing research, thus avoiding potential future pitfalls.

Option 4: Incorrect. Paying attention to corporate policies is important, but it doesn't determine how effective a person is at avoiding counterproductive mental shortcuts.

As you saw in the case study, Tina didn't rush to judgment and gathered more information. Howard, however, thought about himself before he thought about the problem. He also demonstrated cognitive laziness.

In this topic, you discovered strategies to productively think through a problem:

- avoiding cognitive laziness,
- gathering more information about a problem,
- taming the ego.
-

Overcoming Biases and False Assumptions

Biases and assumptions can become obstacles when you're trying to solve a problem. Biases are mental leanings, or inclinations, that can distort thinking. Biases can be deadly because they're so well- camouflaged by habit and repetition.

Assumptions are factors about a problem that are taken for granted, often mistakenly. Assumptions often go unnoticed because, you're accustomed to them and often don't realize you're making an assumption.

Did you hear about the latest scientific study? Kids who wear really big trousers read at a higher level than children who wear smaller sizes. Who could have predicted?

You could have made this prediction, provided you were aware of the real correlation between the two measures.

Did you think, after reading about the study, that wearing big trousers caused kids to read at a more accomplished level? If so, you need to take measures to "redress" your thinking.

In a dispositional attribution, the causes of behavior are assigned to dispositions or traits within the individual. In a situational attribution, the causes of behavior are assigned to the circumstances and not to the individual.

The hindsight bias is the false belief that past events were more predictable than they really were. It leads to inaccurate thinking. For example, if you think you could have seen the drop in morale before workers went on strike, you'll likely overestimate your ability to solve a similar problem now.

The confirmation bias makes you pay attention to evidence that confirms your beliefs while ignoring evidence that does not. For example, you may want a certain car badly. You might ignore all the reports of consumer dissatisfaction and heed only your friend's advice that it's a good buy.

The consistency bias leads you to stand by your poor ideas even when there's evidence against them. It's caused by a social pressure to be consistent. Say you've made a poor decision at work. This bias will make you think there's less need to change course than there really is.

Minimizing biases and false assumptions

Edward had high hopes of winning the pie-eating contest. But when the judge told him he could only use one side of his mouth to chew, while the other contestants could use both, he knew he was at a disadvantage.

Edward was doomed because he was at a disadvantage from the start. When you're solving problems, you'll suffer the same disadvantage if you're mentally hampered by unexamined assumptions and damaging biases.

Select each of Maria's statements about Rich to find out how unexamined assumptions and biases also affected her.

Statement 1

"Rich, my contact person at the company, was a little, well, "rustic." Right from the start, I felt our services would be too sophisticated for his purposes."

Statement 2

"Rich had no experience with direct-mail marketing. I took it for granted he would need a lot of support and direction from me."

Question

Without knowing anything more about Maria's story, can you spot the flaws in her thinking?

Options:

1. She assumed, automatically, that Rich needed more training in direct-mail techniques.
2. She was apparently biased by her notion that less-polished people require only simple solutions.
3. She took for granted that she was more intelligent than Rich.

Answer:

Actually, Maria made false assumptions about her clients. She later learned her assumptions and biases were incorrect.

Option 1: Correct. Maria did not do her research before deciding what Rich's abilities and disabilities were. This is an example of an assumption that may put Maria at a disadvantage.

Option 2: Correct. Without gathering enough information, Maria made judgments about Rich. These judgments led to biased, or distorted, thinking.

Option 3: Correct. Maria assumed that she was more intelligent than Rich, and this assumption led to biased thinking. Assumptions and biases damaged her ability to see the situation clearly and make effective decisions.

Biases and assumptions can become obstacles when you're trying to solve a problem. Biases are mental leanings, or inclinations, that can distort thinking. Biases can be deadly because they're so well- camouflaged by habit and repetition.

Assumptions are factors about a problem that are taken for granted, often mistakenly. Assumptions often go unnoticed because, you're accustomed to them and often don't realize you're making an assumption.

When solving problems and making decisions, examine your assumptions and minimize your biases as much as possible. If you do, you'll have more:

- confidence in your ability to solve problems,
- assurance that you're addressing the true problem,
- understanding why others have failed at problem solving and decision making.

Question

Assumptions and biases, if not recognized and corrected, hamper your ability to think about a problem. Identify benefits of minimizing biases and false assumptions when solving problems and making decisions.

Options:

1. You'll be more sure of your ability to solve problems.
2. You'll be more likely to make decisions that entail more risk.
3. You'll be more sure that you're working on the real problem.
4. You'll be more proficient at obtaining the funding needed for a project.
5. You'll be more understanding when others have failed to solve a problem.

Answer:

Actually, you'll be more confident that you're addressing the actual problem and have more confidence in your ability to solve that problem. You'll also have more empathy for others.

Option 1: Correct. Without assumptions and biases distorting your thoughts and judgments, you will be able to make better decisions. Your clear thinking will give you confidence in problem solving and other important skills.

Option 2: Incorrect. Removing biases and assumptions will lead to thinking more clearly, but it does not change how you view risks.

Option 3: Correct. One of the benefits of reducing biases and assumptions is a reassurance that you're addressing the true problem.

Option 4: Incorrect. The benefits of the clear thinking obtained by minimizing biases and false assumptions are all related to the decision-making process. Funding is an extraneous issue.

Option 5: Correct. Examining your assumptions and eliminating your biases as much as possible will assist you in seeing a situation clearly. This clear picture leads you to understand other people better.

Examining assumptions and minimizing biases takes practice and know-how. In this lesson, you'll acquire that knowledge by learning how to:

- determine correlation strength,
- avoid attribution-making biases,
- recognize biases,
- overcome biases.
-

Correlation among variables

Did you hear about the latest scientific study? Kids who wear really big trousers read at a higher level than children who wear smaller sizes. Who could have predicted?

You could have made this prediction, provided you were aware of the real correlation between the two measures.

Did you think, after reading about the study, that wearing big trousers caused kids to read at a more accomplished level? If so, you need to take measures to "redress" your thinking.

In fact, donning larger britches doesn't cause better reading. The only reason those two variables are associated is that kids who wear big trousers are usually older. They obviously read more proficiently than younger, smaller children.

Determining the relationship between two things, or variables, is key to actually understanding the degree of influence each has on the other. You'll explore four types of relationships, or correlations:

- true causation,
- positive correlation,
- negative correlation,
- nonexistent correlation.

When there's an association, or relationship, between two variables, it's called a correlation.

It's your goal to solve business problems. In other words, you'd always like to know what caused a problem in the first place. But you need to be aware that there's a difference between causes and associations.

See each kind of relationship for an explanation and an example.

true causation

True causation means that one variable is the only reason another variable occurs. In other words, the first variable is the one true cause of the other. True causation also rules out the possibility that the event took place because of chance.

true causation - example

If you step on a glass with just enough force to smash it (the first variable) the resulting breakage (the second variable) is caused by your action--and your action alone. No other factors are involved, and no other forces influence the breaking of the glass.

positive correlation

A positive correlation means that the value of one variable increases at the same time the value of the other variable increases. Here, "value" can be synonymous with either frequency or amount. In other words, the first variable has a discernible influence on the other variable.

positive correlation - example

If a certain flower grows taller as it gets more sunshine, there is a positive correlation between

growth rate and sun exposure. Notice that in this case both variables--growth and sunshine-- increase at the same time, although not necessarily at the same rate.

negative correlation

When there's a negative correlation between two variables, the value of one variable increases as the value of the other variable decreases, indicating a negative relationship between the two variables.

negative correlation - example

Say you take a training course on problem solving and, afterward, the time it takes you to solve problems decreases. That's a negative correlation because as the amount of training increased, your problem-solving time decreased.

nonexistent correlation

A nonexistent correlation means there is no relationship between two variables whatsoever. The first variable has no influence on the other, and vice versa.

nonexistent correlation - example

Say you lose a tooth at the same time the price of barley in China rises. There's obviously no relationship between these two variables, and they did not influence each other in any way. The fact that they occurred at the same time can only be explained by pure chance and randomness.

Question

A product manager for a large clothing manufacturer thought making the logos on her jackets larger was related to increased sales. She did some research to test her theory. Which are valid statements about correlations?

Options:

1. A confirmed relationship between increased logo size and increased sales is a positive correlation.
2. A confirmed relationship between larger logo sizes and decreased sales has to be a result of pure chance.
3. A strong relationship between sales and larger logos must add up to true causation.
4. A confirmed nonexistent relationship between sales and logo size means one doesn't influence the other.

Answer:

Actually, in positive correlations, both variables increase at the same time. If two variables occur simultaneously but are not related at all, it can be explained only by randomness. Strong relationships don't necessarily imply causation.

Option 1: Correct. Considering that both the sales and the logo size increased in this case, the relationship is said to be a positive correlation.

Option 2: Incorrect. This is an example of a negative correlation, which is when one variable (logo size) increases, the other (sales volume) decreases.

Option 3: Incorrect. True causation means that one variable is the only reason another variable occurs. A strong relationship doesn't eliminate all other potential variables that could be impacting the sales volume.

Option 4: Correct. A nonexistent correlation means that the two variables, sales and logo size, had no effect upon each other.

Now that you know the various types of correlation, it's time to explore valuable techniques to gauge correlations among problem variables. You'll learn how to skillfully use the following strategies:

- focusing on evidence that argues against a correlation,
- asking whether your expectations affected your judgment,
- always factoring in the possibility that chance was involved.

The first strategy for determining the correlation between problem variables is to focus on evidence that argues against the existence of a correlation. In other words, you believe a correlation exists but try to prove it doesn't.

Fredrick, an employee at a large waste management company, talked to his boss, Ellen, about a recent change in procedure.

Fredrick: Ellen, I've noticed that since we altered our drivers' routes, they're less able to get the industrial waste collected on time.

Ellen: So you think there's a correlation there, huh? The route changes lead to less productivity.

Fredrick: Well, yeah. Doesn't it just make sense that a relationship exists there?

Ellen: Maybe. What you should really be interested in is the strength of that relationship. Do you think the route changes were the only reason productivity fell?

Fredrick: Hmm. Hadn't given it much thought. I guess saying that the route changes were the only cause of the productivity loss may not be correct.

Ellen: Good thinking, Fredrick. If we want to determine the correlation between these two things, we need to first look at evidence that points away from a relationship.

Fredrick: I think I see what you're getting at, Ellen. There could be other factors involved here, like higher waste output or increased traffic levels.

Ellen: Exactly. If we find that other factors play a role, we get a clearer picture of the real correlation between route changes and productivity levels.

Ellen pointed out that Fredrick may have been seeing a stronger correlation between route changes and productivity loss than actually existed. She later gave him these tips for focusing on evidence that contradicts a correlation:

- Gather as much opposing proof as you can, and then evaluate its merits.
- Consider that the further apart the events, the less likely there's a relationship.

The second strategy for determining a correlation between two variables is to ask whether your expectations affected your judgment about the relationship.

Fredrick had other reasons to overestimate the relationship between route changes and productivity loss. He examined them after his conversation with Ellen.

See each consideration, to reveal how Fredrick used the second strategy.

My expectations

"When our team originally decided to implement the route changes, I was opposed. I thought they would be counterproductive in the beginning and would continue to be in the future."

Was my judgment affected?

"Now, as I try to determine the real tie between those two variables, I'm wondering if my thinking led to the expectation that this measure would fail. And maybe my expectations led me to overestimate the correlation here."

Did my emotions play a role?

"There's another thing. I was a little bitter because I didn't get my way. I guess I secretly hoped the route changes would foul things up. So now I see that my emotions affected my expectations as well."

What really happened

"I've heard it said that the head and the heart follow different rules. In this case, they don't. Both increased my expectation that changing routes was bad. When there was a loss of productivity, I overestimated the correlation between them."

Fredrick did some real soul-searching, and it was beneficial. He examined his expectations and realized they caused him to misjudge the strength of the relationship between route changes and decreased productivity.

Fredrick studied both his thoughts and feelings about the situation. He was then able to counteract his biased thinking and use more accurate assumptions when handling other problems.

Question

Practice what you've learned about the first two strategies. Which statements are valid descriptions of a strategy for determining the correlation between two problem variables?

Options:

1. Examining your expectations means determining whether your emotions and thinking biased your estimation of a correlation's strength.

2. Focusing on evidence against a correlation entails checking to make sure that chance played a role in the relationship.

3. Examining your expectations means re-establishing your goals about a business problem.

4. Focusing on evidence against a correlation entails also looking at the timing of two events and gathering opposing proof.

Answer:

The given strategies will help you eliminate potential biases in the way you think about a problem.

Option 1: Correct. You can do this by gathering as much opposing proof as you can, and then evaluating its merits.

Option 2: Incorrect. In order to focus on evidence against a correlation, you are attempting to discount a correlation that you believe to be right. This can be done in many ways, not just checking into the possibility of chance.

Option 3: Incorrect. Examining your expectations helps you to counteract your biased thinking and use more accurate assumptions when handling other problems.

Option 4: Correct. This involves getting as much evidence as you can and then evaluating its merits. Also, it is necessary to consider that the further apart the events are, the less likely there's a relationship.

To accurately determine the actual relationship, it's crucial to examine both your expectations about a correlation and the evidence against its existence.

The third strategy for judging the correlation between two variables is to always factor in the possibility that pure chance was involved. Keep in mind that pure chance is the same thing as randomness.

Ellen discussed the correlation between route changes and productivity with her team at a follow-up meeting. Across the board, the members believed there was at least a modest relationship between the two variables. But Ellen knew not to stop there if they wanted to determine the strength of the relationship.

See each of Ellen's statements to find out more about the possible correlation.

Statement 1

"I told my team that it was possible, albeit unlikely, that there was no correlation between the variables at all. Maybe the productivity drop had nothing to do with the routes."

Statement 2

"We changed one of the routes and studied the effect. Another decline in productivity meant support for our notion that there was a moderate correlation.

Notice how Ellen and her team took an active step to reveal whether the correlation was a random event. By doing so, they were able to discount the possibility that there was no relationship between the two variables at all but not rule it out completely. If Ellen and her team were unable to conduct an actual experiment, they could have listed other reasons for the productivity drop.

If you wanted to analyze whether Ellen's team, or anyone else for that matter, has effectively determined the correlation between two variables, what kinds of questions would you want to ask?

In the preceding pages, you learned that Ellen wanted her teammates to think hard about their assessments of the potential correlation. What you didn't notice was Ellen constantly asking team members specific questions about their thinking in order to evaluate their effectiveness.

You'll want to ask the same questions Ellen asked so that you can analyze people's thinking as well as Ellen did.

See each category to reveal questions that Ellen posed to evaluate the effectiveness of her team's thinking.

Evidence

"Sure, there might be a correlation there, guys, but have you really focused on evidence arguing against one? When doesn't this relationship occur? Did the events take place one immediately following the other, or were they spread out over time?"

Expectations

"Also, were you expecting to find a strong correlation between route changes and productivity? Did thoughts and emotions about the relationship bias your assessments? And did you gather any data to back up your opinions?"

Randomness

"I know it seems like there's some kind of correlation there, but is it possible that the two things are really unrelated? Did any other factors contribute to the events? If so, did one of them cause the other? Were you able to test the correlation in any way?"

Ellen was tough on her teammates but fair. Because she was the team lead, it was her responsibility to detect biased thinking and snuff it out before it led to other less-than-ideal decisions.

Select each category, in order, for some final tips. These tips will help you decide whether someone else has taken the steps to effectively determine the correlation between two variables.

evidence

If you ask someone if he's considered evidence against a correlation and he says yes, it's less likely he's overestimated the strength of the relationship. That's because he's really looked at reasons that the correlation is weaker than he originally thought.

expectations

If, after asking about a person's expectations (including thoughts and emotions), she tells you that her expectations were strong, you'll know there's a chance she overestimated the correlation's strength. She may have strongly expected there to be, or not to be, a solid correlation.

randomness

Finally, when you ask questions to determine whether someone has considered pure chance as the driving force behind the perceived correlation, you're able to see whether he's imagined a relationship between the two variables where a relationship never actually existed.

Case Study: Question 1 of 2

Scenario

For your convenience, the case study is repeated with each question.

Ian, an attorney for DoomNgloom Entertainment, was thinking about the video game company's latest product. A reporter had asked him if he was aware of a study, just released, that found a link between violent video games and increased aggression in children. The company's product was an action-packed war game. Ian had always expected there to be a causal link between violent video games and aggression in children. He hadn't looked for statistical evidence to support that expectation, but he certainly didn't believe the relationship was the result of pure chance.

After Ian read the study, he was curious whether the researchers had compared the effects of violent video games with those of nonviolent ones. That, he thought, could make a difference. He did some quick research and found that no studies addressed this factor.

Consider Ian's process of determining a correlation by answering the questions in order.

Question

Did Ian do a good job of assessing the researchers' claim that violent video games caused increased aggression in children?

Options:

1. He was effective in that he researched whether other studies examined violent versus nonviolent video games.
2. He was ineffective in that he immediately ruled out the notion that the aggression resulted from pure chance.
3. He was effective in that he sought out other statistical evidence to back up the researchers' claim.
4. He was ineffective in that he allowed his expectations of a causal link to influence his decision.

Answer:

Actually, Ian did more than wonder about other studies; he checked for them. But he was ineffective in that he dismissed the potential role of chance and he let his expectations cloud his judgment.

Option 1: Correct. By examining other related areas of research, Ian was able to find information that was useful for his purposes.

Option 2: Correct. Ian made an assumption that closed off some possibilities for him. He would have done better to continue gathering information before administering a judgment on the matter.

Option 3: Incorrect. Ian sought out other research, but he didn't seek any other sorts of evidence.

Option 4: Correct. By assuming that a causal link existed, Ian limited the possible outcomes in his own mind. If the truth happens to be due to a factor that is other than his expectation, he may not recognize or accept it.

Case Study: Question 2 of 2

What questions did you ask when assessing Ian's effectiveness at using strategies to determine the correlation between violent video games and aggression?

Options:

1. Did Ian overestimate the relationship between video games and aggression because of his expectations?
2. Did Ian seek out evidence that argued against the relationship between video games and aggression?
3. Did Ian take into account that children's aggression could be explained by pure chance alone?
4. Did Ian want to know more about the marketing strategies of different video game companies?

Answer:

Actually, you should ask if Ian considered the effects of chance and his own expectations and if he determined whether there was evidence contradicting the researchers' claim.

Option 1: Correct. By answering this, you can see that Ian allowed his own expectations to bias the possible outcomes in his mind.

Option 2: Correct. By asking this, you found that in not seeking out this evidence, he was denying himself access to information that might help him look at the issue more objectively.

Option 3: Correct. He didn't, and that shaped the judgments he ended up making on the issue. His personal bias shaped his attitude on the matter.

Option 4: Incorrect. Ian would have done well to seek out more information concerning the correlation between violence and aggression, but more information about marketing strategies would not have helped him.

Ian, as you noticed, didn't do the best job of assessing the correlation between violent video games and actual aggression. By learning from his errors, you'll become a more accomplished problem solver.

Most problems you face at work involve many variables. That's why they're often difficult to solve. You'll have a much better shot at success if you use the strategies you learned to determine the relationships among those variables. In this topic, you explored the following techniques:

- Don't focus only on positive and confirming evidence.
- Ask whether your expectations affected your judgment.
- Always factor in the possibility of chance.
-

Attribution-making biases

Jackie reached the final stage of a popular television game show, only to become flustered by a relatively simple question.

When you evaluated Jackie, you made attributions. Making attributions entails assigning the cause of an event to another thing--a person or a situation. In this topic, you'll learn about three types of attribution- making biases:

- the fundamental attribution error,
- the self-serving bias,
- the egocentric bias.

Diana supervised convention centers owned by a large company. She was viewed by the exhibitors as a meticulous planner who was quiet but stern with exhibitors who refused to follow established corporate policies.

How did the exhibitors decide about Diana's personality? What thought processes did they use? Making attributions involves explaining to yourself the causes of your own and others' behavior.

In a dispositional attribution, the causes of behavior are assigned to dispositions or traits within the individual.

In a situational attribution, the causes of behavior are assigned to the circumstances and not to the individual.

Say Diana, because of noise-restriction policies, had to firmly deny Tony, a video game exhibitor, his request to set up video stations in his booth. To what would Tony attribute Diana's refusal? One of the most common attribution biases is making the fundamental attribution error. This is the tendency to overlook the influence of the situation on others' behavior and to overemphasize personal traits.

See each statement to get Diana's insight about the situation.

My Disposition

"This exhibitor wrote my boss, saying I was an overly stern person. He interpreted my behavior in this instance as being a function of my disposition. He thought I behaved that way because I was actually that way."

Company Policy

"He didn't realize that my decision was restricted by company policy. And of course the situation dictated that I had to be firm with him. Otherwise, he would have kept pursuing unacceptable compromises."

In this case, Tony showed bias in his thinking. He underestimated the influence of the situation on Diana's behavior and overemphasized the role her personality traits played. When he did both at the same time, he committed the fundamental attribution error.

The second bias, the self-serving bias, is similar to the fundamental attribution error in that it warps your perception of a problem and leads to inaccurate thinking.

If you are affected by the self-serving bias, you attribute the cause of success or failure in an exaggerated manner. You overly attribute the cause of your own success to your traits and attribute your failures to the effects of the circumstance. When making attributions about others, you do the opposite.

See each element, in order, to find out more from Diana about the self-serving bias.

your success

"After taking care of the video game exhibitor, the convention went off smoothly. I got quite conceited, thinking the convention's success was all due to my admirable efforts. Later, I realized that it took the efforts of many people to make the conference a success."

your failure

"The next convention didn't go as well. I assumed it was because the weather was bad, the location was poor, and the crowd was a bit rude. At the same time, I conveniently forgot that I had mishandled some arrangements and made some other mistakes with the logistics."

the success of others

"The exhibitor's stock was extremely successful last year. I wondered how a company full of foolish people could do so well. Maybe it's the favorable economy. Plus, kids today buy just about any video that's out on the market."

the failure of others

"I read in the paper the other day that the video game people are adjusting their earnings projections for next year. I'm guessing they're not as bright as they imagine and that their lack of business savvy is catching up to them."

Notice how Diana overestimated her influence on her success and downplayed her personal role in her failure. When it came to the video game exhibitors, she attributed their success to the situation and their failure to their internal traits.

The last attributional bias, the egocentric bias, happens when you assume that other people experience events the same way you do--and that they make the same attributions as you.

Antonio was summoned for jury duty. He and his fellow jurors sat in judgment on an embezzlement trial.

See each of Antonio's appraisals to find out how he was first misled by, and then eliminated, an egocentric bias.

guilty

"I was sure this guy was guilty as could be. His alibi was flimsy, and he looked, well, just like I imagined a criminal would look. I thought the others would certainly agree."

not guilty

"Well, they didn't. I considered the other jurors' points of view and realized that not everyone thinks like me. In fact, I eventually changed my mind about this case."

Question

Are you able to make valid attributions about the problems you face at work? Which are examples of attribution-making biases and their corresponding descriptions?

Options:

1. The fundamental attribution error occurs when you overestimate dispositional factors and underestimate situational factors.

2. The self-serving bias involves overly attributing your success to internal traits and your failure to external factors.

3. The egocentric bias is the tendency to assume that other people experience things the same way you do.

4. The egocentric bias occurs when you think only of how problems affect you and not how they affect others.

Answer:

There is no such thing as an egocentric error. The other three are attribution errors that lead to misperceptions about events and problems. You should constantly be aware of their potential effects.

Option 1: Correct. Fundamental attribution is the tendency to overlook the influence of the situation on others' behavior, and to overemphasize personal traits.

Option 2: Correct. Self-serving bias leads you to overly attribute the cause of your own success to your traits, and attribute your failures to the effects of the circumstance. When making attributions about others, you do the opposite.

Option 3: Correct. The egocentric bias happens when you think that everyone's views and life's happenings are the same as yours, and that they make the same attributions as you.

Option 4: Incorrect. The egocentric bias is defined as thinking everyone has the same viewpoint and experiences as you.

In the previous question, you learned that the fundamental attribution error involves simultaneously underestimating the influence of the situation or an event, and overestimating the influence of people's personalities and traits. The self-serving bias entails overly attributing your success to internal traits and your failure to external factors.

Finally, you were asked about the egocentric bias: the tendency to think that others share the same attributions and experiences that you do. As you learned, this is not always the case.

Were you ever admonished by a teacher to "think straight"? At the time, you may have attributed that remark to the bad temper of your instructor. In fact, the situation may have called for your straight thinking. That stern admonition could have been good attributional advice.

In this topic, you learned about three potential missteps to avoid when making attributions about a problem or a decision: the fundamental attribution error, the self-serving bias, and the egocentric bias.

Biases that distort thinking

A frustrated Katrina remarked: "I'm lucky to work with you, Greg. You have such good judgment. How is it that you can think about our human resources problems so clearly?"

Greg's secret--one he was happy to share--was that he thought clearly because he used techniques to overcome mental biases that threatened to eclipse his view of the big picture. In this topic, you'll learn these techniques:

- List possible causes of past outcomes.
- Purposely focus on contradictory evidence.
- Examine your motives regarding the problem.

Before learning how to use the strategies to overcome bias, take a moment to update your knowledge of the biases themselves.

See each type of bias to find out more.

hindsight bias

The hindsight bias is the false belief that past events were more predictable than they really were. It leads to inaccurate thinking. For example, if you think you could have seen the drop in morale before workers went on strike, you'll likely overestimate your ability to solve a similar problem now.

confirmation bias

The confirmation bias makes you pay attention to evidence that confirms your beliefs while ignoring evidence that does not. For example, you may want a certain car badly. You might ignore all the reports of consumer dissatisfaction and heed only your friend's advice that it's a good buy.

consistency bias

The consistency bias leads you to stand by your poor ideas even when there's evidence against them. It's caused by a social pressure to be consistent. Say you've made a poor decision at work. This bias will make you think there's less need to change course than there really is.

Question

Practice what you know about the biases that distort thinking. Which biases are correctly described?

Options:

1. Hindsight bias is the tendency to overestimate your regret over past decisions that didn't succeed.
2. Consistency bias is the reluctance to change decisions even when there's opposing evidence.
3. Contingency bias is the tendency to believe that solutions are contingent on valid evidence.
4. Confirmation bias is the tendency to acknowledge supporting evidence and ignore contradictory evidence.

Answer:

Detecting the influence of these biases before you work on a problem will save you time and, possibly, embarrassment.

Option 1: Incorrect. Hindsight bias is the false belief that past events were more predictable than they really were.

Option 2: Correct. Consistency bias is caused by a social pressure to be consistent. It will make you think there's less need to change course than there really is.

Option 3: Incorrect. There is no contingency bias. Believing that solutions are based on valid evidence is not a bias.

Option 4: Correct. This bias makes you pay attention to evidence that confirms your beliefs, while ignoring evidence that does not, leading you down a path that is not based on solid data.

As you saw, the hindsight bias makes you overestimate the predictability of the past. The confirmation bias leads you to acknowledge only evidence that supports your position. And the consistency bias causes you to continue supporting ineffective ideas even when they're shown to be inaccurate.

Remember Greg's techniques to overcome mental biases? The first technique he used addressed the hindsight bias in particular. To negate the effects of this bias, he made an exhaustive list of other possible causes of past outcomes.

This list should be "exhaustive," but not in the sense that it tires you out. It should make you consider a wide range of alternative explanations for past events. For example, Bernard worked for a major airline that was experiencing problems with flight delays. The customers were furious.

See each of Bernhard's statements, in order, to find out more about overcoming the hindsight bias.

Statement 1

"At first, I thought we should have seen these delay problems coming. After all, other airlines were experiencing a similar situation."

Statement 2

"Then we made a long list of other possible causes, like pilot error, mechanical failures, increased runway construction, and air traffic controller inefficiencies."

Bernard and his colleagues listed as many other contributors to the delays as they could think of. When they investigated further, they found out something that had never occurred to them: The pilots had been secretly delaying flights because they were disgruntled about salary levels. That's when they realized that the delays were not nearly as predictable as Bernard and his co-workers had previously believed.

So when you're basing future solutions on past results, take a look at all the possible reasons for the success or failure of previous decisions. You'll decontaminate your thinking and avoid the negative consequences of the hindsight bias.

The second technique for overcoming bias centers on the confirmation bias. To avoid acknowledging only supporting evidence for your ideas, purposely focus on contradictory evidence. This is tough to do because not many people like to concentrate on reasons they may be wrong. However, this is a crucial thing to do when trying to solve a problem.

See each step of the second technique, in order, to find out how Bernard and his colleagues put this strategy to work.

Gather evidence

"When it comes to evidence about a problem, we shoot for quantity--the more information, the better. We thought the high fuel prices would drop soon, but we scoured every piece of evidence, for and against, that we could find."

Question your judgment

"After we had gathered as much information about fuel price forecasts as possible, we focused first on the reasons fuel costs would actually increase. In other words, we forced ourselves to question our own judgment."

Get feedback from outside

"As you can see, our team made a proactive effort to head off our use of the confirmation bias. As a last precaution, I got input from other people who weren't involved in solving the fuel problem. They were happy to evaluate our findings."

Bernard and his team took a methodical approach in eliminating confirmation biases by:

- gathering as much evidence as possible,
- focusing first on the evidence opposing their idea,
- seeking input from impartial third parties.

Question

Practice what you've learned about overcoming the confirmation bias. Say you're spending a lot of money fixing an old, ailing car. You're operating under the assumption that just around the corner a fix- all solution will be presented to you soon. Then you realize that you may be wasting your time. What strategies would you use to overcome the possibility of a confirmation bias?

Options:

1. I could get two or three opinions about selling the car from a trusted mechanic.

2. I could research on the Web and see whether there are consumer reports arguing against keeping the car and focus on that evidence first.

3. I could gather as much evidence as possible on the life expectancy of the car.

4. I could avoid driving the car for three months and then revisit the problem.

Answer:

Actually, you should gather as much evidence as you can, focus on contradictory evidence, and seek input from disinterested parties. Putting off the problem would have no effect on your bias.

Option 1: Correct. Seeking input from impartial third parties allows you to look at the situation more objectively.

Option 2: Correct. Focusing on the evidence opposing your idea will allow you to work past your own biases and view the issue as it really is.

Option 3: Correct. Gathering as much evidence as possible will help you to make an informed decision that is well supported.

Option 4: Incorrect. This is avoiding the problem instead of using one of the three active methods of overcoming a possible confirmation bias.

The third technique for overcoming bias addresses the consistency bias. You have to examine your motives regarding the problem. The consistency bias makes you cling to old, inaccurate ideas even when there's good reason not to. Bernard decided to have his team vote on all decisions using a secret ballot. The decision led to team conflict and hampered productivity. Bernard was reluctant to change his mind at first but eventually reconsidered.

See each factor, in order to find out more from Bernard about examining motives regarding the problem.

motivation

"The team members kept griping about the new system, but I felt a need to stand firm. But then I decided to examine my motives for being so stubborn. I listed possible reasons and concluded that I wanted to appear consistent when senior staff reviewed the situation."

emotions

"I also wondered if I had any strong emotions about clinging to the secret ballot. I thought about it and realized that I rush to make decisions to avoid the stress of additional discussion. My feelings prompted me to stand by the secret-ballot idea, even though it was harmful."

Bernard overcame his consistency bias by, in effect, taking a timeout. He knew he was being unproductively stubborn, so he made up his mind to examine his motives for continuing to use the secret ballots. He did this by:

- listing the reasons why he might be motivated to be consistent,
- examining his feelings and determining whether he had strong feelings about prolonging his bad decision.

You can't always tell when a colleague is taking steps to overcome biased thinking. By asking the right questions, you're more likely to detect whether techniques to overcome bias are being used.

Before being transferred, Bernard gave Adrianna, the new team lead, advice about how to determine if someone has used techniques to overcome bias.

Adrianna: You were great at telling whether people were biased in their thinking. That made our team so much more effective. Please share your wisdom with me.

Bernard: Wisdom? That's pushing it, Adrianna, but thanks. Your real goal is to determine if a team member has taken active measures to counter potential biases. And you do that by asking yourself questions.

Adrianna: Such as?

Bernard: Ask yourself if a team member has studied up on solutions others have used in the past. Also question whether he listens closely when others offer views that oppose his own.

Adrianna: So does that mean I need to turn into a skeptic?

Bernard: No way. I'm the picture of optimism. It's just that bias is harmful. You need to examine others' efforts to counteract it.

Adrianna: What if I can't tell from the start if they're using these techniques?

Bernard: In that case, I'd come right out and ask them to explain their reasons for thinking a certain way. Their answers usually let you know the level of effort they've put into overcoming bias.

You'd be wise to take a lesson from Bernard and use questions to analyze whether someone has taken steps to overcome bias. In his exchange with Adrianna, Bernard mentioned several ways to determine whether people are biased in their thinking.

See each intention to overcome bias for more examples of questions to ask.

overcoming hindsight bias

Has she considered other people's success rate when using the same solution? Has she thought about how the situation today differs from circumstances in the past? What about other potentially different outcomes? Did she make an exhaustive list of those?

overcoming confirmation bias

Did he gather enough evidence about the problem? Does he listen to opposing viewpoints, or does he avoid dealing with them thoroughly? Did he even ask for the opinion of others?

overcoming consistency bias

What potential motivating factors might be pushing her thinking in a certain direction? Does she have pronounced emotional involvement that might be leading her to stand by the decision?

Case Study: Question 1 of 2

Scenario:

Nolan and Susie worked as purchasing managers for a luxury hotel chain. They had decided six months ago to purchase a supply of upscale cosmetic items for the rooms. They believed the more luxurious bath items would enhance customers' opinions about the hotel chain. Surveys conducted after the fact showed no such enhancement. They met to review their decision and plan for the future. Nolan recommended continuing to buy the higher-priced toiletries. Even though he thought they should drop the upscale cosmetic line, senior staff members were pushing to keep it and he was afraid of the consequences of changing course. Susie initially agreed, but she later changed her mind. She had read some research that suggested there was no link between the quality of complimentary items and customer opinion. So she recommended purchasing less expensive toiletries instead.

Consider Nolan and Susie's techniques by answering the questions in order.

Question:

Were Nolan and Susie effective at using techniques to overcome biases in their thinking?

Options:

1. Susie was effective at beating the confirmation bias by paying attention to contradictory evidence.
2. Nolan was ineffective at avoiding the consistency bias because he didn't study his motivations and feelings.
3. Nolan was effective at beating the hindsight bias because of his effort to compare the past with the present.
4. Susie was ineffective at avoiding the consistency bias because she alienated Nolan by disagreeing with him.

Answer:

In fact, Susie overcame the confirmation bias because she heeded opposing evidence. Nolan was ineffective at overcoming the consistency bias because he didn't consider his motivations.

Option 1: Correct. Susie researched others' conclusions and allowed those conclusions to shape her own determinations. In this way, she overcame the confirmation bias.

Option 2: Correct. Nolan was allowing himself to make the decision based upon his own personal opinion, rather than relying on authoritative research.

Option 3: Incorrect. Nolan and Susie did not perform any research to determine other companies' success levels at using such a strategy. They could not overcome hindsight bias when they paid no attention to the past.

Option 4: Incorrect. Susie took the time to gather some solid information, allowing her to work past her emotions and avoid the consistency bias.

Case Study: Question 2 of 2

What questions should you have asked in order to analyze the effectiveness of the techniques Nolan and Susie used to overcome bias?

Options:

1. Did they listen closely to the opinions of others who disagreed with buying the high-priced toiletries?
2. Did they make sure that their decision wouldn't upset upper management?
3. Did they produce an exhaustive list of other reasons why customer opinion would have remained the same?
4. Did they examine whether their feelings about the purchase of the toiletries made them choose to continue buying them?

Answer:

Actually, to determine if Nolan and Susie overcame their biases, you need to examine whether they heeded contradictory evidence, considered other possible factors, and examined their feelings about the decision.

Option 1: Correct. Answering this helped you see that Nolan based his decision on emotional factors, while Susie did research and was able to base her decision on facts other than her own opinion.

Option 2: Incorrect. Some examples of questions to ask to detect consistency bias are: Are you having strong feelings about this decision that might be influencing your thinking? Are you feeling social pressure to be consistent in your decision?

Option 3: Correct. Answering this question helped you see how well Nolan and Susie did at overcoming the hindsight bias.

Option 4: Correct. Answering this question illustrated how well both Nolan and Susie did or did not overcome the consistency bias.

Susie took measures to overcome potential biases in thinking. Nolan didn't do so well. It's no wonder that Susie went on to productively solve other problems and Nolan didn't make much progress.

The "you" that practices biased thinking is the same "you" that gets up at 3:00 a.m. for a fatty snack from the fridge. Overcome your subconscious urges, and use the strategies you learned to solve problems like a lean, thinking machine. In this topic, you learned the following techniques:

- List possible causes of past outcomes.
- Purposely focus on contradictory evidence.
- Examine your motives regarding the problem.
-

Refining Your Mind-set and Decision-making Style

As a leader you're stuck with decision making. It's your job to make decisions that are in the best interest of the whole organization. And problems can be overwhelming when you don't know how to think about them.

Solving problems doesn't have to be stressful. But it will be if you adopt an ineffective mind-set and style that essentially freeze you in your problem-solving and decision-making tracks.

In the popular children's story "Three little pigs", each of the three little pigs had his own idea about effective house construction.

Only one of the pigs' thinking, however, kept the local wolf problem at bay. That was because the third pig had an effective problem-solving mind-set. In this topic, you'll learn about three of those mind-sets:

- the apathetic mind-se,
- the analytical mind-set,

- the adaptive mind-set.

Just as there are different kinds of skiers, there are different types of decision makers. The type of decision maker you are is determined by the habits and procedures you adopt when making a decision. It also is central to your impression on others.

An effective problem-solving mind-set and decision-making style

As a leader you're stuck with decision making. It's your job to make decisions that are in the best interest of the whole organization. And problems can be overwhelming when you don't know how to think about them.

Solving problems doesn't have to be stressful. But it will be if you adopt an ineffective mind-set and style that essentially freeze you in your problem-solving and decision-making tracks.

Mind-set describes the thought process you use to approach and solve problems. It's sort of like the fuel used to power a car. Style concerns the habits and procedures you adopt when making a decision, as well as the basis of your impression on others. It's similar to the design of the car itself.

See each benefit of adopting an effective problem-solving mind-set and style to get more information from Clarence.

decreased stress

"The first year I was with True/Brunt Partners, I was overwhelmed by business problems I faced on a daily basis. I was scrambling because I just didn't know how to think about the problems. Once I adopted the right mind-set and style, I wasn't as stressed out while making decisions."

career success

"When I use an effective mind-set and style, I'm able to be more productive in every aspect of business, not just in my specialty alone. I view my career advancement thus far as a direct result of the mind-set and style I use to solve problems."

better relationships

"Ever notice how much better relationships are when there's a high degree of trust present?

Because I have an effective mind-set and style when it comes to problem solving, my colleagues trust me and have more confidence in me. That always builds better relationships."

Question

Do you think this statement is true or false?

Most people use the same mind-set and decision-making style every time they solve a problem.

Options:

1. true
2. false

Answer:

Actually, it's more accurate to say that most people use the same mind-set and decision-making style most of the time. There will always be exceptions, however.

Option 1: Incorrect. It is true that a person seldom varies in their mind-set and decision-making style, but there are always exceptions; so it is not true every time.

Option 2: Correct. There are exceptions to every rule which means it is false to say that a person uses the same mind-set and decision-making style every time. But it is true to say that they use the same one most of the time.

Question

Used together, a productive mind-set and style lead to outstanding decisions. Which are benefits of adopting an effective problem-solving mind-set and decision-making style?

Options:

1. You'll feel less stress when solving problems.
2. You'll be more likely to advance your career.
3. You'll improve your communication skills.
4. You'll build better relationships with co-workers. 5. You'll always implement your choices effectively.

Answer:

In fact, you'll feel less stress when solving problems, be more likely to achieve career success, and build better work relationships.

Option 1: Correct. Problems can be overwhelming when you don't know how to think about them. Adopting the right mind-set and style will reduce stress while making decisions.

Option 2: Correct. Using an effective mind-set and style allows a person to be more productive in every aspect of business. Being more productive leads to career advancement in a person's desired direction.

Option 3: Incorrect. Improved communication skills is not one of the benefits of an effective problem- solving mind-set and decision-making style. The three benefits are: less stress, career success, and improved relationships.

Option 4: Correct. An effective mind-set and style in problem solving helps build trust and confidence between people. This builds better relationships.

Option 5: Incorrect. A productive mind-set and decision-making style will benefit and improve the decision-making process, but it does not affect implementation.

A productive mind-set is a factor internal to the problem solver, whereas the outcomes of an effective style are more readily apparent to others. Combine the two, and you will solve problems more effectively. In this lesson, you'll learn more about:

- problem-solving mind-sets,
- decision-making styles.

Problem-solving mind-sets

In the popular children's story "Three little pigs", each of the three little pigs had his own idea about effective house construction.

Only one of the pigs' thinking, however, kept the local wolf problem at bay. That was because the third pig had an effective problem-solving mind-set. In this topic, you'll learn about three of those mind-sets:

- the apathetic mind-se,
- the analytical mind-set,
- the adaptive mind-set.

Question

Consider a problem you face at work right now. When you sit down and think about that problem, how does it make you feel?

Options:

1. terrified
2. intimidated
3. no strong feelings

4. optimistic
5. excited

Answer:

Option 1: There's a strong connection between the mind-set you use to solve problems and your feelings about the problem-solving process. Pay attention to both when making decisions.

Option 2: There's a strong connection between the mind-set you use to solve problems and your feelings about the problem-solving process. Pay attention to both when making decisions.

Option 3: There's a strong connection between the mind-set you use to solve problems and your feelings about the problem-solving process. Pay attention to both when making decisions.

Option 4: There's a strong connection between the mind-set you use to solve problems and your feelings about the problem-solving process. Pay attention to both when making decisions.

Option 5: There's a strong connection between the mind-set you use to solve problems and your feelings about the problem-solving process. Pay attention to both when making decisions.

Nancy, Ricardo, and Edith, three operations managers, talked about a recent problem they wanted to solve.

Nancy: Don't you think this problem is kind of scary? I'd rather have someone higher up take it on.

Ricardo: Hey, Nancy, we can handle this one. Let's stay open to new options and try to think creatively. Have any of our competitors solved this problem effectively?

Edith: Interesting question, Ricardo. I say we start gathering as much information as we can. I think we need hard data before worrying about getting creative.

Ricardo: I hear you, Edith. There's nothing wrong with combining facts and creativity, though. It's best that we tailor our solution according to what the situation calls for.

Nancy: Well, just as long as we don't take on a lot of risk. I vote for taking a really cautious approach to this problem.

Ricardo: I disagree, Nancy. We won't assume unnecessary risk, but if the situation calls for a novel, unproven solution, then we need to consider that path too.

Edith: Enough. How about we all start analyzing this problem and planning our attack? I'll see you at the next meeting.

How effective do you think Nancy, Ricardo, and Edith will be at working together toward a solution? Could you tell from that exchange what sort of problem-solving mind-set each person had?

Nancy seemed timid and reluctant to take action. Edith urged everyone to get started but focused only on one approach to the problem. Ricardo sounded flexible and optimistic about their chances of success.

What is a mind-set? It's essentially the thought process you use to think about and solve problems. In many ways, your mind-set results from the attitude and mental habits you adopt when solving problems.

First, take a closer look at Nancy's thinking. She displayed an apathetic mind-set. People with apathetic mind-sets are a lot like jellyfish.

They simply float through the waters of decision and wait to see where the current takes them. People with apathetic mind-sets think wishfully that problems will solve themselves. They dislike risk, preferring that others do the thinking for them.

The second mind-set, the analytical mind-set, isn't as flawed as the apathetic mind-set, but it still limits your thinking. It's the mind-set Edith displayed when talking to Nancy and Ricardo.

See each of Ricardo's descriptions of Edith's mind-set to find out his thoughts on the analytical mind- set.

A real analyzer

"I like working with Edith because she's a real analyzer. But most of the time, that's the only way she contributes to the problem-solving process. She's not very creative."

Rational decisions

"She really likes getting concrete data and planning, but she insists on making only rational decisions. She thinks using creativity to solve problems is inferior to using logic."

The analytical mind-set is best used during the information-gathering stage of problem solving. Because the analytical mind-set entails only rational, lincar thinking, it's not as effective when a solution calls for creativity and novelty.

All great minds don't think alike, but many of them share the third type of mind-set, the adaptive mind- set. The adaptive mind-set is the most suitable to solving any sort of business problem that arises. Why is that?

See each aspect of the adaptive mind-set, in order, to find out what Ricardo has to say about this mind-set.

problems as opportunities

"When I first heard about the adaptive mind-set, what intrigued me most was its tendency to frame problems as opportunities. By doing just that, my outlook on problems immediately improved. My colleagues even told me that I seemed more confident and cheerful."

situational factors

"When I use an adaptive mind-set, I design solutions based on what the situation dictates. In other words, I'm flexible and not locked into one mode of thinking. I often say, 'If you're a cook, match your recipe to the diner's taste.'"

existing resources

"Being adaptive also means using what's already available. If someone else has devised a good solution, even a competitor, don't be afraid to build on his ideas. Don't feel like the solution has to be a product of your superior thinking."

combinational thinking

"With regard to flexibility, I keep my mind-set adaptable by thinking about problems in different ways. I've found that the best solutions involve both analysis and creativity. There are all kinds of music in the world, and I want to be able to dance to all of them."

Question

Mind-set is something that's within your control to change and improve. Match each problem-solving mind-set with one or more appropriate descriptions.

Options:

A. the analytical mind-set
B. the adaptive mind-set
C. the apathetic mind-set

Targets:

1. waits to see whether the problem will simply solve itself

2. considers a variety of solutions, if they are rational

3. is most effective while gathering information

4. wonders first how to turn problems into opportunities

Answer:

Try to stop yourself before you adopt either an analytical mind-set or an apathetic mind-set. Be an effective problem solver by using an adaptive mind-set instead.

People with apathetic mind-sets think wishfully that problems will solve themselves. They dislike risk, preferring that others do the thinking for them. The apathetic mind-set is marked by a wait-and-see problem-solving approach.

The analytical mind-set is marked by a strong preference for rational and linear solutions. That's usually the only way they contribute to the problem-solving process; they're not very creative.

Someone with an analytical mind-set likes getting concrete data, but they insist on making only rational decisions. They think using creativity to solve problems is inferior to using logic.

The adaptive mind-set is characterized by a tendency to view problems as opportunities. They are the most suitable to solving any sort of business problem that arises. The adaptive mind-set is both flexible and adaptive.

As you noticed, there are huge differences among the three types of mind-sets:

- The apathetic mind-set is marked by a wait-and-see problem-solving approach.

- The analytical mind-set is marked by a strong preference for rational and linear solutions.
- The adaptive mind-set is characterized by a tendency to view problems as opportunities.

In this topic, you learned about three problem-solving mind-sets. Apathetic and analytical mind-sets limit your effectiveness, whereas an adaptive mind-set optimizes your problem-solving skills.

Types of decision makers

Randy could barely keep up with June as they skied down the mountain. At the bottom, June remarked, "You didn't score many style points up there, but, hey, you made it to the bottom of the mountain in one piece."

Just as there are different kinds of skiers, there are different types of decision makers. The type of decision maker you are is determined by the habits and procedures you adopt when making a decision. It also is central to your impression on others.

In this topic, you'll learn about four types of decision makers: the despot, the waffler, the safety blanket, and the judge.

What type of decision maker you are is usually a manifestation of your problem-solving mind-set. Ineffective decision makers usually make less-than-ideal decisions. The first type is the despot. The characteristics of this type are listed here:

- The despot's core belief is "I'm better and smarter than you."
- Imposing his solutions on others, the despot rules in a dictatorial way.
- The despot squelches all opposing viewpoints.
- Think of the despot as someone forceful who steals your right to contribute.

Question

Can you think of the types of environments in which you may find despots making important decisions?

The despot will likely be found in:

Options:

1. companies that have a flat hierarchy and equal distribution of power.

2. bureaucratic organizations in which there are rigid rules to follow.

3. companies that tolerate employees who intimidate and bully others.

4. dynamic organizations that encourage teamwork and creativity.

Answer:

In fact, despots are usually found in bureaucratic organizations that have pronounced hierarchies. If allowed to, they will bully underlings with their authoritative style.

Option 1: Incorrect. A despot is most likely to be found in companies that encourage people to consider themselves higher up on the ladder of authority.

Option 2: Correct. A despot's style of decision-making includes imposing his solutions on others, and squelching all opposing viewpoints. This style fits best in a static, traditional environment.

Option 3: Correct. The despot believes in his own superiority, makes autocratic decisions, and then imposes them on others.

Option 4: Incorrect. A despot will not be able to tolerate a system that must include the opinions of others. They believe that their opinion is superior, and impose it on everyone else; they do not encourage team participation.

You have to give credit to the despot for one thing: He's proactive. The next two decision-making types, the waffler and the safety blanket, are just the opposite.

The waffler is chronically indecisive. She thinks she's ready to decide but backs out at the last minute. The safety blanket fears making decisions to the point of paralysis.

Joe manages a decision-making team for a large newspaper publisher. His team consists of six people, including two wafflers and two safety blankets.

See each decision making type to find out why Joe gets frustrated with these four team members.

Waffler

"It's tough to work with folks who have the waffler style. They're always saying, 'Well, maybe we should take another look before we decide.' And even when a decision's made, they rarely show confidence in the choice."

Safety blanket

"Two team members with the safety-blanket style hardly ever make decisions. For example, they said they had no input on the editorial changes the other day. They always defer decisions to others. And risky choices? No way."

Can you blame Joe for being frustrated? Apparently, he and two others on his team carry all the responsibility. The two wafflers never contribute because they're never willing to settle on a decision. Instead, they constantly revisit options but remain mentally stuck.

The two safety blankets on Joe's team are morale killers. They think the best action is to take no action whatsoever. Safety blankets either hope problems will magically disappear or force others to do the work of deciding.

The last decision-making type is that of the judge. Traditionally, people admire judges not only for their ability to methodically think through legal problems but also for their deftness in carrying out their judgments.

You probably want to be known for the same qualities. That's why it's important to look to the judge when deciding which type of decision maker you want to be. In the court of decision making, the judge always presides.

See each characteristic to find out how Judith, a public relations expert, uses the judge decision- making approach.

evaluates ideas based on merit alone

"It doesn't matter who comes up with an effective solution. Whether a decision comes from me, the president of the company, or an entry-level employee, if it's the best decision, I'll act on it. Ego concerns are the least of my worries."

is comfortable considering conflicting ideas

"Everything worthwhile in this world resulted from some sort of conflict. Good decisions result

from the clash of many ideas. I encourage my colleagues to come up with as many problem- solving ideas as possible. I also encourage discussion of those ideas."

is open to unorthodox solutions

"Who's afraid of the big creative idea? Not me. Make choices as risky as the situation

requires. Only by considering unorthodox ideas can you determine that the reliable and most- used method actually works better in a certain case."

champions decisions once they're made

"Optimism is infectious. Once I've made a decision, I try to inspire confidence in others. I'm always open to changes when needed. It's important, though, to show others that there's reason to believe their hard work will result in success."

Question

When it comes to making decisions, what type of decision maker do you want to be known as? Match each type of decision maker with the statement that characterizes that decision maker.

Options:

A. judge

B. safety blanket

C. waffler

D. despot

Targets:

1. It's OK to disagree about the decision. Let's talk it out.

2. Here's my solution: Let's stop talking and take some action.

3. Now I'm doubting the solution. Let's revisit our options again.

4. I'm hoping the problem will eventually solve itself.

Answer:

Actually, the judge likes to examine and discuss opposing ideas, the waffler is indecisive, the safety blanket hopes problems solve themselves, and the despot enforces his own solution.

A judge encourages as many problem-solving ideas as possible and an open discussion of those ideas. She also believes that good decisions result from the clash of many ideas.

A despot makes decisions by believing in his superior ability to make decisions, making the decision by himself, and then pushing that decision onto everyone else. Despots do not encourage discussion.

A waffler does not ever reach a decision. They just keep revisiting the options and discussing them.

A person with a safety blanket approach thinks the best decision is to not make a decision. They hope the problem will solve itself, or someone else will do the work of solving it without them.

As you have learned, the person who makes his decisions like the judge is the most reasonable decision maker. By adopting this approach, you'll be a much more effective problem-solver.

As with most aspects of life, there's a hard way to do things and an easy way. Make your problem- solving life easier by first becoming an effective decision maker. In this topic, you learned about the four decision-making types:

- the despot,
- the waffler,
- the safety blanket,
- the judge.

Cultivating the Right Frame of Mind

Writer and educator Susan Taylor said: "Thoughts have power; thoughts have energy. And you can make your world or break it by your own thinking."

Taylor nicely described the real substance of thought. Your thoughts may originate in your head, but they rarely stay there. Many events that take place, for better or worse, are the manifestation of someone's once-invisible thinking.

"The problem with most people is that they think with their hopes or fears or wishes rather than their minds." -- Walter Duranty

"Critical thinking," however, keeps you on the right mental track. Critical thinking is the scientific method applied to the everyday world. It's a reasonable, reflective, and skillful way of thinking about business problems.

Is your memory as bright as the sun or as dim as the ocean at night?

You probably can't improve your memory through willpower alone. You need to use specific strategies, especially when the information to be remembered is vital. In this topic, you'll learn about three memory devices:

- chunking,
- mnemonic devices,
- the method of loci.

"The only reason some people get lost in thought is because it's unfamiliar territory." --Paul Fix

When you first arrive in a new town, it's difficult to find your way around. But after you've had a chance to explore a little, taking the shortest route becomes a habit. The same can be said of your critical- thinking skills. As you explore different ways of solving problems and making decisions, you'll learn the quickest way to get where you need to go. But your brain is a complicated place. Forming effective thinking habits takes a lifetime of practice

Effective thinking techniques

Writer and educator Susan Taylor said: "Thoughts have power; thoughts have energy. And you can make your world or break it by your own thinking."

Taylor nicely described the real substance of thought. Your thoughts may originate in your head, but they rarely stay there. Many events that take place, for better or worse, are the manifestation of someone's once-invisible thinking.

Question

How often do you think effectively about business problems?

Options:

1. never
2. almost never
3. sometimes
4. most of the time
5. all the time

Answer:

Someone who thinks effectively all the time is the exception to the rule. However, if you strive to make effective thinking techniques a true habit, you'll increase your odds of success.

Using effective thinking techniques at work is valuable in many ways. Your self-esteem will likely increase as you think about and tackle problems that at first seemed imposing and beyond your reach. You'll also attract and deserve more respect from your colleagues because of their increased trust in your abilities.

Finally, you'll get a more accurate perspective on your business life and your personal life. That's because effective thinking techniques make you see both failure and success in a more realistic light.

Question

The advantages of effective thinking are profound. Select statements that indicate the value of using effective thinking techniques.

Options:

1. You'll likely benefit from heightened levels of self-esteem.
2. You'll likely gain increased respect from your co-workers.
3. You'll likely gain a more accurate perspective on business life.
4. You'll likely be more careful when interacting with your supervisor.

Answer:

Actually, effective thinking habits will likely result in heightened self-esteem, an accurate perspective on business life, and more respect from colleagues.

Option 1: Correct. Your self-esteem will likely increase as you think about and tackle problems that at first seemed imposing and beyond your reach.

Option 2: Correct. You will attract and deserve more respect from your colleagues because of their increased trust in your abilities.

Option 3: Correct. You will get a more accurate perspective on your business life and your personal life. That's because effective thinking techniques make you see both failure and success in a more realistic light.

Option 4: Incorrect. More effective thinking will not significantly affect how you interact with your supervisor, but it will increase your supervisor's respect for you.

Not many people would argue against the value of self-esteem, respect, and enhanced perspective. And those are benefits you'll receive when you use techniques that improve the effectiveness of your thinking.

In this lesson, you'll explore many valuable ways to help you think critically, improve your memory, and form effective thinking habits.

Techniques to think critically

"The problem with most people is that they think with their hopes or fears or wishes rather than their minds." -- Walter Duranty

"Critical thinking," however, keeps you on the right mental track. Critical thinking is the scientific method applied to the everyday world. It's a reasonable, reflective, and skillful way of thinking about business problems.

In this topic, you'll learn how to apply critical thinking to situations in which you're assessing the merit of a "claim." Sales pitches and advertisements almost always contain a claim of some kind. You'll assess those claims by:

- evaluating underlying assumptions,
- examining invited inferences.

Critical thinking doesn't entail just knowing to stop at red lights or being able to tell whether you got the correct change at the supermarket. Such low-order thinking, useful though it may be, is sufficient only in "getting along" in the world.

True critical thinking is higher-order thinking that enables a person to, for example, responsibly evaluate political candidates, serve on juries, and assess the consequences of problematic business decisions.

Rita and Hugh, two telecommunications engineers, discussed the merits of installing a certain phone system in their call center.

Rita: I wasn't too impressed with the sales representative for that telephone system supplier.

Hugh: She seemed pretty knowledgeable to me, Rita. Sounds like she's got a unique and innovative product as well.

Rita: Think about the claims she made. She said the last call center that adopted her system saw sales increase by 16 percent in the first six months. What do you think she meant by that?

Hugh: Ah, I think I see what you're getting at. She tried to make it seem like her phone system was the only factor involved in the sales increase.

Rita: Exactly. It's all in the numbers, as they say. You have to wonder whether there were other things that contributed to that figure.

Hugh: Good point, Rita. Now that I think about it, she also claimed that the employee productivity increased by an even larger percentage.

Rita: She did, didn't she? Well, I wonder what her basis of comparison was. By productivity, she might have been referring to the time it takes to dial out instead of the number of successful calls.

Hugh: Right on, detective. Numbers might not lie, but they can definitely deceive. We need to get her back in here and go over her claims one more time.

Notice that Rita and Hugh focused on the figures the sales representative gave them. They evaluated the underlying assumptions of those numbers and found those statistics to be misleading. In particular, they wanted to know whether the phone system caused the sales increase or was simply a contributing factor. They also thought to examine the basis of comparison for the representative's claim about enhanced productivity.

See each aspect of the salesperson's claims and each example, in order, to find out more from Rita.

causation

"I just didn't believe the idea that using her phone system would lead directly to higher sales. There were too many other things that could have explained the increase."

example

"Here's another example: She said the morale of the call center employees greatly improved after adopting her system. That rise in morale could have been caused by salary hikes, benefits enhancements, added training, or any number of things not related to the phone system."

examining causation

"When someone claims that X does Y, I always examine whether X actually caused Y. If there were other factors involved, I place less faith in the merits of that claim. Sure, it takes an extra mental step, but that's what critical thinking is all about."

basis of comparison

"Another thing to think about is the basis of comparison used in the claim. You can compare any number of things and come up with impressive differences. The important thing is that the difference really translates into a meaningful comparison."

example

"When I hear the phrase 'compared to,' I always ask, 'Compared to what?' When the representative said her phone system was 55 percent easier to use, what was she basing that on? If it's 55 percent easier to use than an old rotary phone system, that's a far less impressive figure."

analyzing comparisons

"Comparisons should be broken down and their separate parts analyzed. A claim may be made that most dentists say a certain toothpaste is better, but better than what? No toothpaste? And is the toothpaste better for a short time or over the long-term? What is meant by 'most'?"

Say you go to a nursery to buy a tree. You not only look at the branches and leaves, but you examine the roots as well. You do the same thing when you analyze the underlying assumptions of a claim. You look at its roots.

Question

A colleague placed a trade publication advertisement for a motivational seminar on your desk and asked you to read it. The seminar promoter claimed that 100 participants in the last seminar got an average salary increase of 24 percent afterward. What questions should you ask yourself when evaluating the underlying assumptions of that claim?

Options:

1. What is the cost of the seminar, and will it require that I devote several days to it?

2. Were the skills acquired at the seminar the only cause of the salary increases?

3. Could 99 participants have received no pay increase and one have received a huge one?

4. Could the salary increases have been measured over an extended period instead of right away?

Answer:

Actually, you should ask whether the seminar really caused the pay increases, and you should also examine the basis of comparison by questioning the 24 percent average and the time frame involved.

Option 1: Incorrect. This is important information, but it does not require the higher level of thinking that is used to critically evaluate a claim.

Option 2: Correct. Critical thinking means asking if there were other factors that could have explained the increase. If there were other factors involved, that claim loses merit.

Option 3: Correct. Another thing to think about is the basis of comparison used. You can compare any number of things and generate impressive differences. The important thing is that the difference translates into a meaningful comparison.

Option 4: Correct. It is good to examine the basis for comparison. Comparisons should be broken down, and their separate parts analyzed.

The motivational seminar promoter may or may not have made a misleading claim. Your analysis of the underlying assumptions of that claim revealed that you need more information about this promoter's motivations.

The second strategy for thinking critically about a claim is to examine the invited inferences of the claim. An invited inference is a conclusion the claim maker invites--or urges--you to draw about the benefits of the claim.

The motivational seminar promoter claimed that 100 participants in the last seminar got an average salary increase of 24 percent. He was inviting you to draw many conclusions about the results and benefits of the seminar.

Select each inference, in order, to learn how Jason, who also received the ad, thought critically about the promoter's invited inferences.

Inference #1: I need motivation

"The promoter obviously wanted me to take certain things for granted. For example, he wanted me to think I was in need of motivation in the first place. That might not be the case."

Inference #2: I need what he's offering

"The 'claimer' automatically assumes you want or need what's being offered. I always examine my own desires before I let someone tell me what they are."

Inference #3: More motivation is better for me

"And another thing: The promoter wanted me to draw the conclusion that a motivated 'me' would be a vast improvement over my normal self. Would that really be the case? Perhaps the extra motivation would skew my priorities in life."

Inference #4: I will be rich

"The seminar's slogan was 'You'll make Howard Hughes look like a pauper.' That slogan was plainly an invited inference that I would become rich after the seminar."

Inference #5:That sounds too good to be true

"Hey, who knows? I might have earned more money because of my increased motivation, but enough to make Hughes look like a poor man? That was one claim I had serious doubts about."

Jason was a tough customer--and rightly so. He considered what the promoter implied he would gain from the seminar and discovered some reasons not to blindly buy in to the invited inferences.

See each of Jason's actions to find out more details on examining invited inferences.

Action 1

"Whenever someone makes a claim, I first ask myself whether I truly desire the benefits being touted."

Action 2

"I never fail to examine the wording of claims, either. The promoter's Howard Hughes analogy was a blatant attempt to oversell the results of the seminar."

Question

The manufacturers of a controversial diet product claimed: "Spring is on its way, and you want to look sexy. With our product, you'll be as thin as a rail in three weeks." What questions do you need to ask to think critically about the invited inferences made by this claim?

Options:

1. Is the analogy being used here overinflating the real benefits?
2. Do I really want and need to lose weight enough to buy this product?
3. Has the manufacturer had more success marketing to men or women?

Answer:

Actually, you need to determine whether the analogy being used was realistic and whether you really wanted the supposed benefits.

Option 1: Correct. You need to examine the claim. Can their product really make everyone as skinny as a rail in three weeks? This is an invited inference: a conclusion the claim maker invites--or urges--you to draw about the benefits of the claim.

Option 2: Correct. The promoter wants you to take certain things for granted, like that you need to lose weight in order to be sexy. This is an underlying assumption.

Option 3: Incorrect. It is helpful to examine the company's invited inferences and underlying assumptions, but you do not need to examine their marketing strategies.

By thinking critically about the invited inferences of the "miracle" diet product, you could see that the merits of the claim were questionable. Always examine inferences and decide whether the invitation is one you want to accept.

Evaluate life using your head and your heart. When it comes to assessing claims, however, do all your thinking above the neck. In this topic, you learned to think critically about claims by:

- evaluating underlying assumptions,
- examining invited inferences.

Memory devices

Is your memory as bright as the sun or as dim as the ocean at night?

You probably can't improve your memory through willpower alone. You need to use specific strategies, especially when the information to be remembered is vital. In this topic, you'll learn about three memory devices:

- chunking,
- mnemonic devices,
- the method of loci.

The first memory device is chunking. Chunking means grouping a long series of numbers into more manageable segments.

It's been found that the brain has difficulty storing more than nine numbers in a string. So say you have 20 individual numbers to memorize. Chunk the numbers into four groups of five or five groups of four. Your brain holds on to these shorter, more memorable series a lot more readily.

Numbers representing money always get chunked. Could you remember the price of a computer if it cost "one-four-nine-five dollars and two-five cents"? Maybe, but why try? "Fourteen ninety-five and a quarter" works much better. Other common numbers that are chunked for easier recall include:

- telephone numbers,
- government identification numbers, like your driver's license or Social Security,
- credit card numbers.

The second memory aid is to use mnemonic devices to help you remember a series of objects or names. Mnemonic devices are words or chains of letters formed from the first letters of a series of objects or names to be remembered. Using mnemonic devices is like chunking in that you break large groups of information into more manageable and memorable groups.

See each tip to get examples of mnemonic devices from Elise, a neurologist.

familiar terms

"If I tell a patient I'm about to use computerized tomography to diagnose his ailment, I'll probably receive a blank stare in return. But if I tell him that I'm going to run a CT scan, he'll more likely know what I'm talking about."

acronyms

"I kept forgetting which departments were on my floor of the hospital. I made an acronym to help me remember. 'NEAR' stood for neurology, endocrinology, anesthesiology, and rheumatology."

initialisms

"If the first letters of things you want to remember don't form an actual word, try using a 'letter chain.' Take pancreas, lung, spleen, and kidney, for example. I remember them by repeating the letter chain 'PLSK' again and again in my mind. I then recall the abbreviation and have my list right there."

sentences

"That reminds me of my favorite nonmedical mnemonic device. In high school astronomy, I turned the first letters of the planet names into a sentence. 'My very excellent mother just served us nice pickles' stood for Mercury, Venus, Earth, Mars, Jupiter, Saturn, Uranus, Neptune, and Pluto."

Whereas number chunks and mnemonic devices are verbal aids, the third memory device, the method of loci, is visual.

This device entails mentally placing objects you want to remember in familiar locations--or "loci"--so that you can later revisit that place in your mind and more easily recall the targeted objects.

It was an hour before the company picnic. Attendance was high, and the food supply low. Gene was asked to go to the store and purchase these items: ice, marshmallows, watermelon, hot dogs, and sodas. He didn't have paper and pencil handy to write the items down, so he used the method of loci to remember them.

See each item and the result, in order, to find out how Gene brought back the goods.

Ice

"First, I pictured the front door of my house covered with ice and frozen shut. I mentally rehearsed pushing on the door to crack the ice. By doing this, I associated the ice I needed to buy with the front door of my house."

Marshmallows

"Next, I imagined walking into my living room and seeing my sofa. I pictured the cushions of the sofa as being marshmallows--very comfy to sit on at the end of the day. I now had the second grocery item covered."

Watermelon

"From the living room, I pictured myself walking into the kitchen and seeing a watermelon sticking out of the refrigerator. I imagined worrying that the open door of the fridge was letting out the cold air."

Hot dogs

"Next, I mentally walked into my bedroom. I pictured a giant hot dog, tucked under the covers, sleeping in on a lazy Sunday."

Sodas

"Last, I pictured going from my bedroom into the bathroom. I imagined turning on the shower and being doused by soda. I then saw myself emerging from the shower a bit stickier than I was when I went in."

It worked

"I came up with little stories, like the soda shower, as a way to help me remember the things on my list. Now all I had to do was rehearse the walk through my house a couple of times. After that, the only challenge was finding the stuff at the store."

When Gene arrived at the store, he mentally took a trip through his house to retrieve his food list. Of course, you can always "get out of the house" and use other locations with this method. For example, your loci could be:

- the route you take to work,

- the inside of your car,
- your office,
- the campus of your favorite college,
- different locations on a familiar map.

Question

A better memory often translates to more business success. Select the correct descriptions of memory devices.

Options:

1. Retrieval means organizing information into clusters so that they are more easily recalled.

2. Chunking means categorizing a series of numbers into more manageable groups.

3. Mnemonic devices are words formed from the first letters of a series.

4. Method of loci means using the spatial arrangement of a familiar place to aid recall.

Answer:

In fact, chunking involves grouping numbers into manageable segments. Mnemonic devices are formed from the first letters of objects to be remembered. The method of loci entails using a familiar place to aid in the recall of a list.

Option 1: Incorrect. The three memory devices are chunking, mnemonic devices, and method of loci.

Option 2: Correct. Chunking is grouping numbers into smaller groups to make them easier to remember. Some examples are telephone numbers, government identification numbers, and credit card numbers.

Option 3: Correct. Mnemonic devices are words or chains of letters formed from the first letters of a series of objects or names to be remembered. One example of a mnemonic device is an acronym.

Option 4: Correct. This device entails mentally placing objects you want to remember in familiar locations--or "loci"--so that you can later revisit that place in your mind and more easily recall the targeted objects.

Some philosophers believe that nothing happens in the future that hasn't already taken place. What if you're unable to picture effective solutions that worked in the past? Well, you probably won't solve many problems in the future.

By using the memory aids you learned in this topic, you'll make business decisions that are wiser and more comprehensive.

In case you've forgotten, you explored the following memory aids in this topic: chunking, mnemonic devices, and the method of loci.

Effective thinking habits

"The only reason some people get lost in thought is because it's unfamiliar territory." --Paul Fix

When you first arrive in a new town, it's difficult to find your way around. But after you've had a chance to explore a little, taking the shortest route becomes a habit. The same can be said of your critical- thinking skills. As you explore different ways of solving problems and making decisions, you'll learn the quickest way to get where you need to go. But your brain is a complicated place. Forming effective thinking habits takes a lifetime of practice

Question

Many people set aside time in their schedules for physical exercise. But what about mental exercise? How much time do you spend improving your thinking skills?

Options:

1. none
2. only when time permits

3. up to an hour each month
4. up to an hour each week
5. more than an hour each week

Answer:

Effective thinkers and decision makers set aside time for mental workouts. Improving your thinking skills requires a deliberate effort.

There are many thinking habits that can help you improve your problem-solving and decision-making skills. In this topic, you'll explore three of those habits:

- viewing problems as opportunities,
- obtaining a wide range of life experiences,
- learning from experience.

The first habit for more effective thinking is to view problems as opportunities. Claude is a regional manager for a fast-food chain. He's been grappling with a persistent problem for months.

Select each aspect of the problem to learn how Claude's failure to look for opportunities has kept him from solving a critical problem.

Aspect 1

"Our payroll costs were spiraling out of control. Why? Our young employees were leaving as fast as we could train them. We tried to keep them by raising wages."

Aspect 2

"The problem didn't go away. Our turnover rate among young employees is still way too high. And now our profitability is suffering too"

The situation is different for Claude's biggest competitor. Grace's company faced the same problems. But Grace, a human resources manager, looked at the problem as an opportunity to explore new solutions.

See each statement in order, to learn how Grace's thinking habits helped her make a sound decision.

Statement 1

"We also had a problem keeping younger workers. As soon as they were trained, they left for higher-paying jobs. We needed a new approach."

Statement 2

"Several managers mentioned how many retirees came in looking for work. We decided to offer them jobs. We found a new source of enthusiastic workers."

The second habit for effective thinking is seeking out a wide range of life experiences. Every experience, even those that seem unrelated to your work, gives you a larger pool of knowledge from which to draw.

Check each person to learn how Grace and two of her friends benefited from expanding their life experiences.

Bill

"I once took a class in computer programming to help me represent one of my corporate clients. The class taught me a lot about logic. Since then, I think I do a much better job preparing my arguments for court."

Grace

"Last year, I took a fencing class. Who would have guessed that it would help me handle difficult customers? I learned that you can't always attack problems to solve them. Sometimes it's better to let your opponent attack first, and then deflect the attack."

Mary

"When I traveled across Europe, I visited many countries where I didn't know the language. I had to rely on the graphics on road signs to find my way around.

That taught me how to use visual images to make my programs easier to use."

Grace and her two friends used their life experiences to help them solve problems and make decisions at work. Think about it: What experiences in your past help you make better decisions?

Question

Do you agree or disagree with the following statement?

Effective thinking habits can help prevent you from repeating the same mistakes again and again.

Options:

1. I agree. Effective thinkers learn from the past and avoid repeating their mistakes.

2. I disagree. Even the most effective thinkers suffer from momentary lapses in reason that doom them to repeat mistakes.

Answer:

Actually, learning from past mistakes is an important mental habit for better decision making and problem solving.

Option 1: Correct. Effective thinking sharpens many mental skills. One example is analyzing cause and effect. The ability to see clearly the cause and effect of a mistake helps to avoid repeating the mistake.

Option 2: Incorrect. Effective thinking increases a person's ability to effectively examine a situation. This aids in learning from mistakes and then not repeating them.

It's surprising how easy it is to live life by merely hopping from one experience to the next, registering fleeting sensations instead of absorbing lessons.

Effective problem solvers know how important it is to retain the important lessons they've learned. That's why they cultivate the third habit of effective thinking: learning from experience.

See each reference about experiences, in order, for more information on learning from the past.

failure

Failure is uncomfortable, but it's also a valuable teacher. You can often learn more from failure than success. Pay close attention to the reasons a problem went unsolved. But be gentle with yourself: Failure is less a reflection on you as it is on the situation at the time.

success

The same holds true for success. Take to heart the reasons a problem was successfully overcome, including the strategies, thinking, and resources behind the success. Keep your ego at bay, though, because it can distort the past, the present, and the future.

learning log

Don Burch, one of the first Americans to climb several mountains in Russia, made it a habit to record important life experiences in what he called a "learning log." He recorded details of both successes and failures. When he faced a tough problem, he would consult his log for inspiration.

Question

With practice, effective thinking strategies become habits. Which statements describe effective thinking habits?

Options:

1. Be realistic and regard problems as obstacles.
2. Be curious and seek out new life experiences.
3. Be aggressive and assume more risk at work.
4. Be wise and learn from the mistakes of the past.

Answer:

Actually, you should strive to learn from your past mistakes, which will help you become wiser, and remain curious by trying out new things. Problems don't have to be obstacles, and more risk is not always advised.

Option 1: This choice is incorrect. An effective thinking strategy is to view problems as opportunities for growth.

Option 2: Correct. Every experience, even those that seem unrelated to your work, gives you a larger pool of knowledge from which to draw. This will aid you in making the best decisions.

Option 3: This answer is incorrect. Effective thinking strategies are about the mental processes, not the actions that follow.

Option 4: Correct. Effective problem solvers know how important it is to retain the important lessons they've learned. Both failures and successes can be effective teachers. It is especially productive to keep a log of what you have learned.

The habits you learned in this topic will help you think about all problems. That's why they're so powerful. In this topic, you learned to:

- view problems as opportunities,
- obtain a wide range of life experiences,
- learn from experience.

You deserve some congratulations. After completing this course, you should be a more effective thinker. You should also make better decisions based on your improved thinking skills. The future looks bright.

In this course, you learned how to think effectively about mental shortcuts, overcome biases and false assumptions, refine your mind-set and decision-making style, and cultivate the right frame of mind.

CHAPTER TWO

Problem Framing

Gaining an Overview Perspective

Peter had seen the symptoms before. He thought he knew exactly what the problem was. Instead, he spent hours fixing a hardware circuit that didn't actually need to be fixed.

You can learn from Peter's mistake. Always identify and gather information about a problem before attempting to solve it. In this lesson, you'll learn that the value of doing so means that you'll have:

- fewer unforeseen complications down the line,
- more assurance that you'll eliminate premature decisions,
- greater confidence when generating solutions.

"It isn't that they can't see the solution. It is that they can't see the problem." --G.K. Chesterton, English journalist and literary figure

Chesterton was referring to politicians in the early 1900s. He claimed they were more interested in eliminating symptoms than in solving actual problems. In this topic, you'll learn to address the real issue by using effective techniques to identify a business problem:

- listing other problems that might be related,
- performing a utopia comparison,
- writing a simple problem statement.

One thing's for sure: A brain's capacity is finite. No one person can contain the knowledge of all the people in the world or even of colleagues in adjoining cubicles."

Knowledge is key and there are several ways of accessing knowledge and gathering information about a business problem. In this topic, you'll learn to consult valid sources of information:

- libraries and librarians,
- the Internet,
- subject-matter experts.

"See anything good in my future?" Geoff asked the crystal-ball reader. "Well, sure, if you have an extra ten bucks," was the reply.

Experts are like crystal-ball readers. You have to dig a little bit to find out their level of expertise. In this topic, you'll learn how to assess the expertise of a subject-matter expert by using these effective techniques:

- finding out how much direct experience the expert has,
- determining how immediately testable the expert's knowledge is,

- finding out if the expert has a vested interest in giving advice.

Gathering information

Peter had seen the symptoms before. He thought he knew exactly what the problem was. Instead, he spent hours fixing a hardware circuit that didn't actually need to be fixed.

You can learn from Peter's mistake. Always identify and gather information about a problem before attempting to solve it. In this lesson, you'll learn that the value of doing so means that you'll have:

- fewer unforeseen complications down the line,
- more assurance that you'll eliminate premature decisions,
- greater confidence when generating solutions.

Ruth and Lillith worked for a large bus manufacturer. Newly introduced government regulations changed the way they had to design their product.

See Ruth and Lillith to find out how they first identified the design problem and then gathered information about it.

Ruth

"I was tempted to just dive in and throw solutions at the problem. We avoided a premature decision by first doing some research on the regulations."

Lillith

"Ruth and I found an obscure clause in the laws that affected the design. By doing our homework, we avoided all kinds of hidden complications down the road."

Question

Think about a time when you had to solve a business problem quickly but didn't have much information to base your solutions on. How much confidence did you have in the solutions you generated?

Options:

1. no confidence
2. little confidence
3. neutral
4. some confidence
5. complete confidence

Answers:

Option 1: For almost all problem solvers, the equation is a simple one: The more information you have about a problem, the more confident you'll be when generating solutions for that problem.

Option 2: For almost all problem solvers, the equation is a simple one: The more information you have about a problem, the more confident you'll be when generating solutions for that problem.

Option 3: For almost all problem solvers, the equation is a simple one: The more information you have about a problem, the more confident you'll be when generating solutions for that problem.

Option 4: For almost all problem solvers, the equation is a simple one: The more information you have about a problem, the more confident you'll be when generating solutions for that problem.

Option 5: For almost all problem solvers, the equation is a simple one: The more information you have about a problem, the more confident you'll be when generating solutions for that problem.

Question

Before you can solve a problem, you have to know exactly what the problem is. Select the statements that represent values of effectively identifying and gathering information about a problem by completing the sentence You're likely to...

Options:

1. reduce the number of unforeseen complications.
2. more effectively head off premature decisions.
3. design solutions that will solve all similar problems.
4. be more confident in your ability to generate solutions.

Answers:

Actually, you'll be able to reduce unforeseen complications, be more assured that you're not deciding prematurely, and be more confident when generating alternative solutions.

Option 1: Correct. "An ounce of prevention is worth a pound of cure." An effective way to prepare for the future is to gather useful information in the present.

Option 2: Correct. With sufficient research and information, you will be able to look at decision points in an objective manner. By weighing every side of the issue you will be able to make informed, rather than emotional, decisions.

Option 3: Incorrect. Having good information about a problem doesn't guarantee that similar problems will have the same solution, but it can affect the way you look at the new problems.

Option 4: Correct. Confidence is the natural consequence of being prepared. With preparation, you will be able to move forward, believing in your ability to solve the problem.

As you saw in the previous question, there are many values of identifying a problem and gathering information about it. Other problems, even similar ones, require their own information-gathering process, but in all cases, your success rate will be much higher if you first take time to prepare for problem-solving. In this lesson, you'll learn how to spot a business problem, research a business problem, and evaluate the advice of a subject-matter expert.

Techniques to identify a business problem

"It isn't that they can't see the solution. It is that they can't see the problem." --G.K. Chesterton, English journalist and literary figure

Chesterton was referring to politicians in the early 1900s. He claimed they were more interested in eliminating symptoms than in solving actual problems. In this topic, you'll learn to address the real issue by using effective techniques to identify a business problem:

- listing other problems that might be related,
- performing a utopia comparison,
- writing a simple problem statement.

Edward and Trudy, two financial-call-center managers, were concerned. The customer service representatives had reported rumors of general customer dissatisfaction. Edward and Trudy used the first technique, listing other problems that might be related, to move past appearances and first guesses and on to a more specific view of the problem.

See each factor to find out how Edward and Trudy used this technique.

The phone system

"We started off looking at the phone system itself. Could it be that the real problem centered on our telecommunications hardware? Were customers being cut off or mistakenly rerouted?"

Employee morale

"Another problem that may have been associated with customer dissatisfaction was the professionalism and motivation of our representatives. We made a note of that possibility and decided to investigate it."

Product knowledge

"Our employees had to be knowledgeable about our products. Otherwise, customers would lose trust in our abilities. We identified that as a potential snag as well."

Software proficiency

"Finally, we realized that representatives need to be proficient at using the software system to access account and financial market information. Any lack of skill in this area would certainly leave a bad taste in customers' mouths."

Just as doctors seek to heal a patient instead of simply prescribing painkillers, Edward and Trudy looked past the symptom by listing associated problems. They were one step closer to getting their call center back to optimal health.

The next technique for identifying a business problem is to perform a utopia comparison by imagining an ideal situation. Edward and Trudy pictured and described their call center in a utopian manner and compared it with the current situation. If customers were perfectly content with their service, what reasons would the customers give for their satisfaction? How would an ideal call center be run? This comparison technique helps you identify why the problem is happening in the first place.

Edward and Trudy determined that, in a perfect world, the call-center employees would be highly motivated, extremely knowledgeable about the company's products, and proficient at using the tools of their jobs. Then Trudy and Edward compared that scenario with the current situation to better identify the problem.

See Edward and Trudy to find out more.

Edward

"Trudy and I established that our employees' motivation and product knowledge were close to ideal. Only one other factor fell short of utopia."

Trudy

"When we looked closely, we realized that performance on the software system was less than desired. Representatives weren't getting the training they needed."

After listing the problems that might be related and performing a utopia comparison, you should have more specifically identified the parameters of the given problem. Now you should use the third technique and write a simple problem statement. Simple problem statements help you identify the problem by forcing you to home in on the central issue.

See each attribute to learn more from Edward.

Brevity

"Our executive staff members have enough on their plates. They don't need managers describing problems in a long-winded, rambling way. And they don't need all the details about a given problem. That's why Trudy and I pared the situation down to its essential components."

Clarity

"The problem statement should be clear and shorn of needless detail. Senior staff members need to know what the problem is, not what it isn't. We told them about the problem without using software terms only our department was familiar with. We used clear, simple language."

Definable measure of performance

"Trudy and I made sure our problem statement contained concrete performance measures. Upper management then realized that we had identified and accounted for all aspects of the problem."

Edward and Trudy's problem statement

"We told the president at the beginning of the meeting that the proposed solution was to improve customer satisfaction by increasing worker knowledge of the software system by 33 percent within six weeks. There was no need to further identify the problem. We just had to solve it."

Question

It's time to practice what you've learned. Scattershot approaches to problem identification rarely succeed. Instead, you need to improve your aim. Which statements represent techniques to identify a business problem?

Options:

1. Identify the decision time frame.
2. Account for potentially associated problems.
3. Perform a utopia comparison.
4. Write a simple problem statement.
5. Establish several solution milestones.

Answers:

Option 1: Incorrect. At this stage, you are only identifying the problem, recognizing the goal, and recording a problem statement.

Option 2: Correct. Accounting for associated problems helps you to more completely view the problem and identify it.

Option 3: Correct. By doing this you will go beyond documenting the problem to identify where you want to be once the problem is solved. This establishes the goal toward which you will be working.

Option 4: Correct. It is important that in your problem statement you describe the problem briefly and clearly. You must also outline the performance measures that you are working toward.

Option 5: Incorrect. Milestones can be useful, but establishing them is not part of identifying the problem, outlining the goal, or writing down the problem.

The previous question illustrated that there are several valuable techniques for fully identifying a business problem. Use all three during the initial stages of problem solving and you'll know exactly which target to shoot for.

Rush past the problem-identification phase and success, in turn, will likely pass you by. In this topic, you learned to effectively identify a business problem by using these proven techniques:

- listing other problems that might be related,
- performing a utopia comparison,
- writing a simple problem statement.
-

Sources of information about business problems

One thing's for sure: A brain's capacity is finite. No one person can contain the knowledge of all the people in the world or even of colleagues in adjoining cubicles."

Knowledge is key and there are several ways of accessing knowledge and gathering information about a business problem. In this topic, you'll learn to consult valid sources of information:

- libraries and librarians,
- the Internet,
- subject-matter experts.

Question

Businessman and educator Arthur D. Little once said, "Research serves to make building stones out of stumbling blocks." His quote highlights the need to do research and gather information about all business problems so you can remain on your feet.

That said, how confident do you feel about your ability to gather information about a business problem?

Options:

1. not at all confident
2. not very confident
3. neutral
4. somewhat confident
5. perfectly confident

Answers:

Option 1: No matter what your degree of confidence is, there's always room for improvement. Gathering information in an efficient manner is key to both devising solutions and implementing your eventual decision.

Option 2: No matter what your degree of confidence is, there's always room for improvement. Gathering information in an efficient manner is key to both devising solutions and implementing your eventual decision.

Option 3: No matter what your degree of confidence is, there's always room for improvement. Gathering information in an efficient manner is key to both devising solutions and implementing your eventual decision.

Option 4: No matter what your degree of confidence is, there's always room for improvement. Gathering information in an efficient manner is key to both devising solutions and implementing your eventual decision.

Option 5: No matter what your degree of confidence is, there's always room for improvement. Gathering information in an efficient manner is key to both devising solutions and implementing your eventual decision.

The first valid source of information about business problems is libraries and librarians. Libraries are essentially storehouses of humankind's accumulated knowledge. What is perhaps most surprising is that they can usually be consulted at no charge.

There are generally two types of libraries: traditional public libraries and specialty libraries.

Traditional libraries contain information about almost everything. Specialty libraries hold material on narrower subjects, such as business and engineering. They're often found on college campuses. Ian is a marketing specialist who uses libraries and learns from the people who work in them.

See each library type to learn more.

Public library

"When I face a business problem, my first stop is the public library. The librarians there do a great job of guiding me to the best reference tools and catalogs."

Law library

"Say my problem concerns obscure marketing laws. I then consult a law library. Librarians there are often specialists who are glad to share their knowledge."

Ian also found library specialists who helped him use the second valid source of information: the Internet. The contents of the Internet change rapidly. If you aren't comfortable using the Internet to research a business problem, you may consider taking a class or seminar on its use. Many public and college libraries offer low-cost or free Internet research classes that require only a day of your time.

See each Internet feature to find out more from Camille, an online research expert.

Search engines

"There are some great search engines out there. I suggest entering your subject into some of them and then sampling the first 20 or so pages the search engine returns. That's a good way to get a high-level overview of things."

Databases

"Many governmental and research organizations post their databases on the Internet. For example, the United Nations and the U.S. Bureau of the Census provide all kinds of valuable information at no charge."

Online encyclopedias

"Talk about being fortunate. Many expensive and rare reference volumes that you once found only at colleges are now at your Internet fingertips. Consulting them saves a lot of time and even more money."

Online discussion boards

"If you look around on the Web, you'll likely find your business problem being discussed in a chat room or on a bulletin board. Don't rely completely on advice given there, though. Use it only if it's backed up by other reliable sources."

More than other sources of information, the Internet can be amazingly fruitful or wildly misleading. It's important to double-check your sources and the information they provide.

The third valid source of information about a business problem is a subject-matter expert. A subject-matter expert is well-versed in a particular knowledge area and can summarize the existing information relevant to your problem, which could make a venture to the library unnecessary. However, not all experts have solid knowledge. It's a good idea to seek advice from more than one expert.

See each professional type to find out more about several types of subject-matter experts.

Attorneys

Most business problems today involve legal ramifications of some kind. When your problem falls into this category, seek the advice of a legal expert. You may have legal counsel in your organization. If not, most business-law attorneys specialize in specific areas.

Scholars

Scholars are a great source of up-to-date information and usually enjoy sharing it. Say your business problem involves the chemical structure of an adhesive you are marketing. A chemistry professor at a local college could probably provide valuable advice.

Trade organization members

Trade organizations are composed of experts in a particular endeavor and range from services such as advertising to more product-oriented concerns such as computer software. Members join these organizations to network and often enjoy being sought out for advice.

Governmental advisers

Many government agencies are staffed by information officers. These folks can often provide you with statistics and studies that concern your business problem. They're also a good source of information about federal and state laws that might affect your eventual decision.

Colleagues

Most organizations contain a wealth of brainpower and knowledge. Your organization is probably no different. Don't hesitate to seek out colleagues within and outside your department who might have insight into your business problem.

Question

The source of information you use could very well be the source of your solution. Identify valid sources of information about business problems.

Options:

1. advertisements
2. subject-matter experts
3. libraries
4. librarians
5. the Internet

Answer:

In fact, subject-matter experts, libraries, librarians, and the Internet are all valid sources of information about business problems. Advertisements may be biased.

Option 1: Incorrect. The information contained in advertisements works toward the goals of the advertising company and is not always reliable for your needs.

2: Correct. Subject-matter experts have experience and knowledge in their areas of specialty. They can greatly aid you in your search for information relating to what they know.

3: Correct. Libraries are depositories of knowledge that has been recorded. You can use both public and specialty libraries to find out what you need.

4: Correct. Librarians can guide you to reference tools and catalogs where you might find the answers you are seeking.

5: Correct. There is a huge amount of resources on the Internet from which you can glean information. You must, however, be careful to verify any information you receive in this manner.

There are many sources from which to gather information about your business problem. Some sources of information are more reliable than others, however. The best journalists get the scoop from trustworthy sources. Like those reporters, you'll usually hear the real story only from reliable sources.

In this topic, you learned about consulting valuable sources of information about business problems, including libraries and librarians, the Internet, and subject-matter experts.

Assessing the expertise of a subject-matter expert

"See anything good in my future?" Geoff asked the crystal-ball reader. "Well, sure, if you have an extra ten bucks," was the reply.

Experts are like crystal-ball readers. You have to dig a little bit to find out their level of expertise. In this topic, you'll learn how to assess the expertise of a subject-matter expert by using these effective techniques:

- finding out how much direct experience the expert has,
- determining how immediately testable the expert's knowledge is,
- finding out if the expert has a vested interest in giving advice.

A first-rate subject-matter expert is very knowledgeable about a particular subject and can summarize the existing information relevant to your problem. Some experts, however, are more "expert" than others. Before you take any subject-matter expert's advice, you need to determine his level of expertise.

Say you needed advice about selling watches in cold-climate drug stores. The very best international watch-marketing expert may not be able to help because your need is too specific. You must match your need to the expert's true expertise.

The first technique for assessing the expertise of a subject-matter expert is to find out how much direct experience the expert's had. The emphasis here is on the word "direct." Trust the advice of experts whose insight matches your business problem's level of specificity. The more they know about your issue, that is, the more "local" knowledge they have, the better their advice will probably be.

Justin is a manager at a Web-based training company.

See each experience type to see how he uses this technique.

Direct work experience

"I sought advice about some training software from a person well known for expertise with this software. It didn't matter how much she knew about Web-based training in general. I was more interested in how much she'd worked directly with the software in question."

Direct academic experience

"Not all subjects lend themselves to actual work experience. Some issues are more abstract in nature. When that's the case, I try to determine how much direct academic experience the expert's had. Have her studies involved my problem in particular or just the broader, more general area?"

Justin also needed advice on the proper compression of audio files for his Web-based courses. He consulted an industry expert and a professor who both specialized in audio engineering.

Select each of Justin's questions to find out what he asked the experts to determine their direct experience with audio compression.

Question 1

"I asked the industry expert if he had ever compressed audio files and delivered them over the Internet. I also asked how many times he had done so."

Question 2

"I asked the professor how much he'd studied this specific issue rather than general audio issues. I wanted to determine his expertise specifically on compression."

The second technique for assessing the expertise of a subject-matter expert is to determine how immediately testable the expert's knowledge is. If knowledge is immediately testable, it means the expert has a lot of opportunities to do reality checks on his ideas by paying attention to feedback. For example, a mechanic is more likely to be reliable when he says he'll fix your car than a philosopher who says he'll show you how to lead a rewarding life.

Speaking of feedback, Justin heard that Web-based training courses that provide learners with feedback on their progress are more effective. He was concerned that his courses didn't meet that standard. He decided to ask Patricia, an expert in adult learning theory, whether increased feedback would enhance his courses.

See each heading to find out how Justin used the second technique and determined the testability of Patricia's knowledge.

Patricia's advice

"Sure enough, Patricia was vehement about the inclusion of regular feedback in Web-based courses. She was obviously confident in this notion, but I wanted to find out how immediately testable her advice was."

How valid was it

"I first asked her what she based her opinion on. Was there a way to determine how valid her idea was? Had she simply seen the benefits of added feedback with her own two eyes, or were there other, less anecdotal indicators?"

Show me proof

"I also asked if she was familiar with any reliable evidence that supported her opinion. That way, I could examine the evidence and evaluate her advice. In other words, I was looking for concrete proof that her advice had merit."

How scientific is the proof?

"As far as proof goes, the more scientific the evidence, the more testable the advice. Was there scientific proof that supported feedback enhancement? Whenever I mention scientific proof, the expert knows I'm serious about testing her knowledge."

Question

Practice what you've learned about the second technique. Which of the choices are valid questions to ask to determine how immediately testable an expert's knowledge is?

Options:

1. Has your advice yielded concrete results that I can verify?

2. In the past, how have you known your advice was reliable?

3. If I followed your advice, how confident are you that it would work?

4. Is there any scientific proof to back up your opinion on this issue?

Answer:

In fact, you should have asked about concrete results that you could verify, available scientific proof, and the expert's means of receiving feedback about his knowledge. The other question merely asked for a general opinion.

Option 1: Correct. This provides you with the ability to research your subject-matter expert's claims and support your own ideas through his statements.

Option 2: Correct. You will be able to analyze the subject-matter expert's answer to determine if the information is reliable.

Option 3: Incorrect. This reaches for the subject-matter expert's opinion, but does not establish how valid the opinion actually is. To do this, you will need to substantiate the expert's views with the statements of others.

Option 4: Correct. This provides a link between the subject-matter expert's statements and the other research that has been performed on the subject. Proper evidence will solidify your own statements on the matter.

If you're lucky, you'll find an expert who has direct experience with your business problem and whose knowledge is immediately testable. There's another thing to consider, though. The last technique for assessing the expertise of a subject-matter expert is to find out whether the expert has a vested interest in giving certain advice. For example, stockbrokers and car salespeople may have good reason to recommend one product over another.

In other words, will the expert personally gain by promoting a given opinion? Perhaps there's money at stake. Maybe if you followed the expert's advice, it would somehow enhance his career. Or perhaps he's doing friends or associates a favor by pushing you in a certain direction.

Rita, a manager at a large camera manufacturer, asked Alana, an optics expert at a local university, about a focal lens her company was thinking about using.

Rita: Thanks for speaking to me, Alana. I understand you've had some exposure to the UCWell Lens Company's new product. What do you think of it?

Alana: Great in all aspects, Rita. I truly think this lens will dominate the market in a year or so.

Rita: Wow. Those are strong words. What are your main reasons?

Alana: No other company is getting the kind of clarity from its lenses that these folks are. Besides that, they're great people to work with.

Rita: In what capacity do you work with UCWell Lens?

Alana: Well, the company supplies my department with equipment at little cost. And I'm friends with one of the vice presidents.

Rita: I see. So you might have some good reasons to recommend them. Is there any evidence against your opinion? Or other experts I can speak with who would disagree with you? Please don't be offended. I'm just wondering if you have a vested interest in giving this advice.

Alana: You're right, Rita. Because these people came through for me at the college, I wouldn't mind sending some well-deserved business their way. I should also tell you that I might even take a job there next year.

Alana had personal reasons for recommending that Rita consider using her friends' product. Rita politely found out about Alana's allegiance and questioned the reliability of her advice. To find out whether Alana had a vested interest in giving the green light to UCWell lenses, Rita asked:

- about Alana's relationship with the company,
- if there was evidence against her opinion,
- if there were other experts she could speak with who hold opposing ideas.

As you saw, it was as important to determine Hugh's level of expertise as it was to obtain his advice. When you get solid advice from reliable experts, you can proceed with confidence.

Consulting an expert is a valuable and enjoyable way to gain insight into your business problem. In this topic, you learned to assess the expertise of a subject-matter expert by using three effective techniques:

- finding out how much direct experience the expert has,
- determining how immediately testable the expert's knowledge is,
- finding out if the expert has a vested interest in giving the advice.
-

Dealing with Problem Assumptions

Thomas Watson was chairman of IBM in 1943 when he said, "I think there is a world market for maybe five computers."

Watson certainly wasn't the only person to have ever made an inaccurate assumption about a business problem. What is an assumption? It's any facet of a business problem that you take for granted or assume to be true without calling it into question.

Roughly seven out of ten new businesses fail within three years. That failure rate often hinges directly on faulty business assumptions. Examine your assumptions and you're more likely to beat the odds.

"Well, that little red light hasn't come on yet," Kyle told his wife. "I bet we have enough gas to make it to the movie theater. After all, we've never run out of gas before."

Ten miles later, Kyle ran out of gas. To avoid running out of gas, question and validate your assumptions about a business problem so you're prepared from the start. In this topic, you'll learn these techniques to identify assumptions:

- listing your initial assumptions about the problem,
- determining which assumptions are constrained by "policy",
- questioning and investigating the remaining assumptions.

"If our airline keeps losing baggage at this rate, I have a feeling the company will be packing it in as well," said a frustrated Jerome.

If you were on Jerome's managerial team, what would you assume the problem was? How would your team uncover its assumptions? In this topic, you'll learn to uncover your team's assumptions about a business problem by:

- holding an initial assumption meeting,
- assigning assumption investigation tasks,
- conducting an assumption follow-up meeting.

At an all-staff meeting, the president of a high-tech company said to employees: "I have no doubt that we have what it takes to revolutionize this industry overnight. In fact, that is our objective."

In this case, overnight turned out to be never because the president's assumptions about his objectives were way off-base. In this topic, you'll learn about constraints that affect your assumptions about objectives:

- financial constraints,
- time constraints,

- social constraints.

Examining assumptions

Thomas Watson was chairman of IBM in 1943 when he said, "I think there is a world market for maybe five computers."

Watson certainly wasn't the only person to have ever made an inaccurate assumption about a business problem. What is an assumption? It's any facet of a business problem that you take for granted or assume to be true without calling it into question.

Roughly seven out of ten new businesses fail within three years. That failure rate often hinges directly on faulty business assumptions. Examine your assumptions and you're more likely to beat the odds.

Just as businesses receive benefits when employees examine their assumptions about given business problems, you as an individual reap personal rewards.

See each advantage to find out about the benefits of examining your assumptions about a given problem.

Greater insight into your problem-solving mind-set

When you unearth your assumptions about a business problem and examine them in the light of day, you get a better understanding of how your business mind ticks. You get a glimpse of how your brain works when left unsupervised by your conscious mind.

More confidence in your eventual decision

Your notions and opinions about a problem usually change for the better after you examine your assumptions. You think about the business problem in a more effective way. This can't help but build your confidence in the decision you eventually make.

Increased chances of enhanced career success

Once you've gained more insight into your problem-solving mind-set and upped your confidence level, it naturally follows that you will have an increased chance of succeeding in your career.

Question

Don't ever assume that your assumptions are self-evident. Question yourself instead. Identify the benefits of fully examining assumptions about a given problem by selecting the correct sentence endings.

You'll gain...

Options:

1. a better understanding of how your industry really works.
2. a better idea of the mind-set you use to solve problems.
3. added confidence in the decision you end up making.
4. a better shot at experiencing success in your overall career.

Answers:

Actually, fully examining your assumptions means you'll get a better feel for your problem-solving mind-set, more confidence in your eventual decision, and a better chance at career success. Knowing how your industry works is another matter.

Option 1: Incorrect. Coming to an understanding of your own assumptions is all about coming to know yourself better, not your industry.

Option 2: Correct. As you identify how your own mind works out a problem, you will better understand your opinions and how you came to them. This can provide valuable insight in solving a decision.

Option 3: Correct. Once you have analyzed your assumptions and resolved any issues that have come up, your decision is further validated. You can now proceed with confidence.

Option 4: Correct. By analyzing your assumptions, you are coming to a greater understanding of the actual state of things, which leads to decisions that increase the chances of succeeding in your career.

You should fully examine your assumptions about a business problem early in the decision-making process. Doing so sets the stage for success. In this lesson, you'll learn how to:

- get a better handle on your assumptions,
- recognize team assumptions,
- prioritize your problem-solving objectives.
-

Validating assumptions

"Well, that little red light hasn't come on yet," Kyle told his wife. "I bet we have enough gas to make it to the movie theater. After all, we've never run out of gas before."

Ten miles later, Kyle ran out of gas. To avoid running out of gas, question and validate your assumptions about a business problem so you're prepared from the start. In this topic, you'll learn these techniques to identify assumptions:

- listing your initial assumptions about the problem,
- determining which assumptions are constrained by "policy”,
- questioning and investigating the remaining assumptions.

An assumption is any facet of a business problem you consciously or unconsciously take for granted or do not question. Lucille thought the server in her company's network would be a breeze to fix. Knowing this might not be the case, she used a strategy to see if she was operating under a faulty assumption. The first strategy Lucille used to validate her assumptions was to list her initial assumptions about the problem.

See each factor to get input from Lucille.

Scope of the problem

"How big a problem did I think this was? On my assumption list, I wrote down my thoughts about the difficulty involved in solving the server problem."

Required resources

"Next, I wrote down my assumptions about the cost of fixing the problem. How many colleagues would need to work on the server issue? I recorded that on my list as well."

Time needed to solve the problem

"How efficiently did I think I'd be able to overcome this obstacle? I wrote down my first impulse, that it would take me and one other colleague two days. I would revisit that assumption once I'd gathered more information."

Overall feasibility

"Finally, I questioned the overall feasibility of solving the problem. I examined my own thinking to see if I thought I should take incremental steps or tackle the whole problem in one fell swoop. I also listed what I thought my chance of success was in the form of a percentage."

Lucille put her list of initial assumptions into a file for future reference. If she had complications with this issue down the line, she would be able to revisit her list to see if those complications resulted from faulty assumptions.

Question

All problem solvers wish they had unlimited time and resources to engineer solutions to business problems.

However, that's wishful thinking at best. The effectiveness of all problem solvers is limited by policies regarding the use of corporate assets.

To what extent are your problem-solving actions at work constrained by corporate policy?

Options:

1. not at all
2. slightly
3. somewhat
4. more than I'd like
5. to a great extent

Answers:

Option 1: Most people encounter formidable corporate policy constraints. It's important to factor in those constraints during the initial problem-solving phase.

Option 2: Most people encounter formidable corporate policy constraints. It's important to factor in those constraints during the initial problem-solving phase.

Option 3: Most people encounter formidable corporate policy constraints. It's important to factor in those constraints during the initial problem-solving phase.

Option 4: Most people encounter formidable corporate policy constraints. It's important to factor in those constraints during the initial problem-solving phase.

Option 5: Most people encounter formidable corporate policy constraints. It's important to factor in those constraints during the initial problem-solving phase.

The second technique for validating your assumptions about a business problem is to determine which assumptions are constrained by policy.

See each resource to find out how using this technique led Lucille to question her initial assumptions.

Funds

"I assumed our company had the funds required to replace the server if necessary. But that wasn't the case. We had enough money only for a temporary fix."

Time

"I also found out my co-workers had no time whatsoever to work on this problem. Corporate policy dictated they spend their time on a different project until next year."

Corporate staffing policies affected the way Lucille thought about the server problem. She initially assumed the server fix would be easy. After her initial assumptions conflicted with corporate policy, however, she had to retool the assumption list in her problem file.

At this point, Lucille used the third technique to validate assumptions about a business problem: questioning and investigating her remaining assumptions.

Lucille now assumed she needed to temporarily patch the server rather than replace it and that it would require more time than she originally thought.

See each factor to find out how Lucille questioned and investigated these remaining assumptions.

Continue questioning

"I realized that my new assumptions were still that--assumptions. I had to continue questioning the validity of my thoughts until this problem was completely solved."

Concrete details

"I made sure those members of senior staff whose policies affected my assumptions gave me concrete details on the feasibility of the new solution."

As you can see, validating assumptions is an ongoing process, not a one-time activity. That's because your assumptions affect every aspect of your problem-solving task from beginning to end.

After using the third technique of questioning and investigating her remaining assumptions, Lucille updated her assumption list and placed it back in her file. She was one step closer to solving her server problem.

Question

Validating your assumptions about a given problem is key. You must be alert and meticulous. Which statements are strategies to validate assumptions about a given problem?

Options:

1. Write down your initial assumptions about resources and feasibility.
2. Establish the corporate policies that affect your assumptions.
3. Examine and explore remaining assumptions for realism and likelihood.
4. Motivate your team members to take on a larger share of the load.

Answers:

In fact, you should list your assumptions about the problem, establish which assumptions are affected by corporate policy, and question and explore those assumptions. Motivating your teammates is unrelated to identifying assumptions.

Option 1: Correct. By doing this you will be able to identify what you think the scope of the problem will be as well as the resources it will take. Also, you will examine your thoughts on the how long a solution will take and its feasibility.

Option 2: Correct. Corporate constraints could drastically change your options in solving the problem. You may need to reshape your assumptions.

Option 3: Correct. This method helps to question the validity and establish the feasibility of your solution.

Option 4: Incorrect. During this stage of the process, validating your own assumptions, it is not necessary to involve other team members.

As you saw in this topic, validating your assumptions requires you to think in stages. First, you expose your overall assumptions. You then analyze them to determine how they're constrained by corporate policy. Finally, you re-examine them based on those factors.

In this topic, you learned that to validate your assumptions about a problem, you must list your initial assumptions, find out which ones are constrained by policy, and question and investigate those that remain.

Uncover problem assumptions

"If our airline keeps losing baggage at this rate, I have a feeling the company will be packing it in as well," said a frustrated Jerome.

If you were on Jerome's managerial team, what would you assume the problem was? How would your team uncover its assumptions? In this topic, you'll learn to uncover your team's assumptions about a business problem by:

- holding an initial assumption meeting,
- assigning assumption investigation tasks,
- conducting an assumption follow-up meeting.

Question

Do you agree with the statement?

Unless you fully explore your team's assumptions about a business problem, team members will probably never be on the same problem-solving page.

Options:

1. yes

2. no

Answers:

Actually, teams are composed of multiple individuals. These people likely have differing assumptions about any given problem. Unless all of those assumptions are analyzed, there may be no unified perspective on the problem.

Option 1: Correct. A team is composed of individuals who each have their own assumptions which shape their outlook. To be on the same page, the team's assumptions must be clearly defined.

Option 2: Incorrect. Defining the team's assumptions allows them to be validated, allowing the problem solving process to continue unhindered.

The first step to uncovering your team's assumption about a business problem is to hold an initial assumption meeting. Don't just circulate e-mails. An official meeting lets members know how key assumption exploration really is.

Jerome, the airline manager faced with the lost-luggage problem, called his team together for an initial assumption exploration meeting. He stressed to the members that before they could proceed to generate solutions to the problem, they needed to first explore their assumptions about the lost baggage.

See each task to find out how Jerome conducted the initial assumption meeting.

List all initial assumptions

"I told my team to list all of their assumptions about the luggage problem, not just their first guesses. I had them note their assumptions about the cause of the problem, other factors that might be involved, and how long they thought it would take to solve the problem."

Don't aim to reach consensus

"Team members usually have many shared assumptions. I instruct colleagues to generate an exhaustive assumption list rather than seek agreement about the situation. In this case, the quantity of assumptions is more important than the quality."

Set up a centralized assumption file

"After all the assumptions have been listed, I deposit a comprehensive list of them into a centrally located file. I make sure the assumption file is accessible to everyone at all times. That way, we can add notes to the assumptions as more information about the problem is gathered."

During the initial meeting, Jerome took the second step to uncovering his team's assumptions: He assigned assumption investigation tasks. These tasks were a kind of homework assignment to complete before following up on team members' initial assumptions.

See each investigation task to find out how Jerome assigned and determined them.

Look for constraints

"After uncovering our initial assumptions, I reminded my colleagues that various corporate policies might put limits on or change the nature of our assumptions. I charged each team member to investigate a possible constraint or two."

Assign tasks

"I put one member in charge of checking policy constraints on funding. Another member was to explore limits on the number of people we could assign to the problem. I made every effort to cover all potential policy constraints."

A good place to start

"In this case, the team was cross-departmental. That made it easier for members to investigate policy constraints originating in their own department. Otherwise, team members would speak to other department heads about the issue."

Assess constraint flexibility

"Before I sent them on their way, I made sure they knew to ask about the flexibility of each policy constraint. After all, I wanted to know which constraints were written in stone and which might change or be altered in the near future."

Constraints that affect assumptions about objectives

At an all-staff meeting, the president of a high-tech company said to employees: "I have no doubt that we have what it takes to revolutionize this industry overnight. In fact, that is our objective."

In this case, overnight turned out to be never because the president's assumptions about his objectives were way off-base. In this topic, you'll learn about constraints that affect your assumptions about objectives:

- financial constraints,
- time constraints,
- social constraints.

"Problem solving" can be a misleading term. A problem is not only an obstacle thrown up unforeseeably, but it's also anything you want to do or accomplish. In the latter case, the "problem" you want to "solve" is how to get from here to there, or how to accomplish your objective.

When you establish business objectives and goals, you also make assumptions about their feasibility. These assumptions, if unexamined, can have the same adverse effect as the more stereotypical "problem" assumption.

The first constraints that affect your assumptions about objectives are financial constraints. No company has unlimited funds. Your business objectives must adhere to financial reality. Before setting objectives, make sure you have enough funding to:

- perform research on the feasibility of your objectives,
- acquire the material resources necessary to reach your goals,
- execute a backup plan in case your objectives prove more costly than anticipated.

Next, examine your assumptions about the time constraints affecting the feasibility of your objectives. Time and money often go hand in hand, but when it comes to assumptions, you have to examine them separately.

Sheila is a direct-mail marketing expert.

See time frame and never assume to find out how she examines her assumptions about the time factor.

Time frame

"I wanted to do a mass brochure mailing for a client. I pitched the idea and then later realized that the materials couldn't be sent out in the time frame I'd promised."

Never assume

"I learned my lesson. Now, I never assume goals can be met at the last minute. In fact, I even gauge my backup time in case there are complications."

Sheila questioned her assumptions about the time constraints on her objectives, but she also knew to examine the third restriction: social constraints. Sheila realized that business objectives aren't abstract ideas that reside only on paper. They directly affect everyone related to that issue.

See each group to find out more about Sheila's insight into social constraints.

Colleagues in your department

"One of my objectives for the department was to increase international mailings. This meant my colleagues would have to learn about an entirely new way of doing business. I assumed they would be excited about this. It turned out that some were more excited than others."

Colleagues in other departments

"My goal of enhanced global reach meant that folks in other departments would have to redirect their focuses to a certain extent. After the reaction of my department, I didn't assume that everyone would accept the new direction immediately and built more training time into the mix."

Suppliers

"I realized I'd assumed my suppliers would be able to provide heavier materials that would hold up to international shipping. I ended up having to enlist the help of specialist suppliers for that. I'm glad I didn't gloss that one over."

Customers

"I thought about how the new global objective might affect our existing clients. Would they remain pleased with our services even though we were working toward this new goal? I didn't take that for granted and made sure that measures were in place to keep those clients happy."

Unproductive assumptions about business objectives are sometimes worse than no objectives at all. Always know your goal. But never forget to examine the obstacles and constraints that might stand in your way.

By thoroughly examining the constraints that affected her assumptions about business objectives, Sheila saved herself and those around her time and aggravation.

Question

Practice what you've learned. If you don't think clearly about your objectives, you probably won't know whether they're attainable. Match the constraint that affects assumptions about objectives to one or more corresponding descriptions.

Options:

A. time constraints

B. financial constraints

C. social constraints

Targets:

1. Your objective may turn customers away.
2. Colleagues may be required to focus on other projects.
3. Your objective may take longer to reach than anticipated.
4. You may lack the funds needed to meet your objective.

Answers:

In fact, time constraints affect the time needed to meet your objective. Financial constraints concern the availability of funding. Social constraints involve both customers and colleagues.

This is an example of social constraints. It is important to consider how an objective is going to affect all the people involved. This could include colleagues within and without your department, clients, and suppliers, for example.

This is an example of a way that an assumption about an objective could be incorrect because of a social constraint. In this case, the social constraint results from the effect of the objective on a colleague.

This is an example of a time constraint. A common assumption that prevents the achievement of an objective is not budgeting enough time to achieve that goal.

This is an example of a financial constraint. The financial reality needed to achieve the goal must be known in order to avoid financial constraints. An assumption that there are enough funds can be a barrier to completing the objective.

Before you head out the door on a vacation, you can't assume you've packed everything you need to reach your destination. You need to double-check your packing list.

And as you saw in the previous question, you can't just assume your objectives are reachable. Be wise, and check your list of constraints that affect assumptions about objectives.

In this topic, you learned to identify constraints that affect your assumptions about objectives: financial constraints, time constraints, and social constraints.

Getting to the Root of the Problem

"Dad, does a volcano erupt because it's mad?" asked little Timmy. Timmy's father patiently explained that the real cause of eruptions occurred far below the surface of the earth. The volcano's feelings were another matter entirely.

Timmy will eventually become an effective decision maker. But first he'll have to learn to identify the real cause of problems.

Jessica and Ben overheard another couple arguing in a restaurant. Jessica thought they might be experiencing financial problems. Ben suggested the couple might be squabbling over household chores.

Jessica and Ben were guessing about the root cause of the argument by sorting through possible explanations. In this topic, you'll learn to take the guesswork out of identifying problem causes by using these sorting techniques:

- chronologies,

- checklists,
- problem pyramids

On the day of the big game, the reception on Craig's television set was horrible. Craig's friend Shawn suggested the cause of the bad reception was their failure to aggressively kick the TV set.

Shawn's analysis of the cause of the reception problem doesn't deserve to make the evening news. Your analysis will, after you read this topic and learn to get to the root of a business problem by using the steps of a causal flow analysis:

- determining the input factors of the problem,
- determining the output factors of the problem,
- examining the causal flow between the factors.

Addressing the root problem

"Dad, does a volcano erupt because it's mad?" asked little Timmy. Timmy's father patiently explained that the real cause of eruptions occurred far below the surface of the earth. The volcano's feelings were another matter entirely.

Timmy will eventually become an effective decision maker. But first he'll have to learn to identify the real cause of problems.

By addressing the root problem instead of peripheral issues you'll:

- avoid wasting time by concentrating only on essential problem issues,
- generate potential solutions in a more confident manner,
- be more focused when solving problems in a team setting.

Question

Answer the following question:

Have you ever been assigned a task, worked hard to complete it, and later found out your task was actually irrelevant to the real business problem at hand?

Options:

1. yes
2. no

Answers:

You're in the minority. At some point, most people waste time because their efforts are directed toward nonessential matters and not to the root of their business problems. You should always try to avoid experiencing their frustration.

Option 1: It is a common obstacle for non-essential issues to prevent forward progress on the core of a problem.

Option 2: It is a rare thing to have never experienced this kind of frustration. It stems from using resources to work on a problem which turns out to be irrelevant.

Think of it this way: If you want to reach the hardware store as soon as you can, you don't take detours. You aim straight for the store and go. In the same way, you should solve problems by heading right to the heart of the issue, to the root cause, and not get caught up on inconsequential problem concerns.

In this lesson, you'll learn how sorting techniques and causal flow analyses can be valuable techniques for addressing the root problem instead of peripheral issues.

Sorting techniques

Jessica and Ben overheard another couple arguing in a restaurant. Jessica thought they might be experiencing financial problems. Ben suggested the couple might be squabbling over household chores.

Jessica and Ben were guessing about the root cause of the argument by sorting through possible explanations. In this topic, you'll learn to take the guesswork out of identifying problem causes by using these sorting techniques:

- chronologies,
- checklists,
- problem pyramids

Sabrina, a marketing manager at a large bicycle manufacturer, was puzzled over her company's recent loss of market share. It didn't help that her colleagues held differing opinions about the cause of the problem.

Sabrina was bound and determined to find the root causes of the market share dip instead of investigating speculations. She used the first sorting technique and devised chronologies that shed light on the history of the problem. A chronology is essentially a timeline in which significant events associated with the problem are noted along with the corresponding dates.

See each item to find out how Sabrina used chronologies to sort through her market share problem.

A market trends timeline

"First, I plotted market trends of the bicycle industry in general. I listed the dates when new designs were introduced, when consumer demand increased and decreased, and when any other significant market changes took place."

A company strategy timeline

"Next, I constructed a timeline that included the dates and descriptions of my company's strategy changes. Those strategies involved everything from product innovations to promotional campaigns. This helped me get a better feel for the origins of the market share decline."

A comparison of market trends and company strategies

"I then compared both timelines to see if there were meaningful overlaps. It helped me determine whether the drop in sales had an internal or external cause. I've found chronologies to be a great way to go back in time, sort through associated events, and identify the real problem."

Chronologies help you examine the past for clues to the cause of your business problem. The next sorting technique, checklists, is oriented to the here and now. Checklists are lists of potential causes that allow you to make sure you've explored all aspects of a problem's source.

See checklist and business factors to discover how Sabrina used checklists to sort through her dilemma.

Checklist

"On my checklist, I listed key business areas, such as production capacity, market timing, financial policy, and promotional strategy."

Business factors

"I made sure I covered all business factors that might contribute to the problem. I listed issues related to each area and compared them with the other items to gain insight."

Sabrina now had a handy checklist that she could reference while tackling her market share problem. The checklist gave her confidence that she had accounted for most possible causes. She also added information to the checklist as time went by and thus kept a running record of her thinking.

Not all checklists contain the same items. Every business problem is unique, so you'll have to determine the contents. The important thing is to list as many possible contributing factors as you can.

The next sorting technique used to identify root causes of business problems is the problem pyramid. Use problem pyramids to visually represent and rank the various contributors and causes of a business problem. You arrange and rearrange the possible causes according to their dominance as you go along.

See each step to find out from Sabrina how the most likely cause of her problem, the one that dominated the others, ended up on top.

And the winner is...

"That's how lower consumer demand took command of the uppermost reaches of my problem pyramid. Simply put, it subsumed all the other potential causes. Now I could orient my problem-solving strategy toward the most likely contributing factor."

Others critiqued my ranking

"I got input from others about the significance of each possible cause of our drop in market share. Most pointed out that the low general consumer demand really determined how we approached all the other factors."

I organized the rest

"Next, I came to the conclusion that product design changes determined our promotional strategies to a great extent. I then rearranged my pyramid's hierarchy accordingly."

I put financial policy higher up

"After thinking about it, I realized that production capacity was actually a subset of financial policy. So I put financial aspects on a higher tier on the pyramid than production capacity."

Examples of potential causes

"Some of the factors included in the bottom tier were production capacity, product design changes, financial policy, promotional strategy, and overall consumer demand."

I listed all potential causes

"I started building my problem pyramid by listing all the potential causes from my checklist and chronologies around the pyramid base. That bottom tier included many factors."

As you noticed, the most likely cause or causes of the business problem wind up on top of the pyramid. The other potential causes are merely symptomatic of that dominant explanation and assume a less prominent position. Remember playing "King of the Hill" when you were a kid? The problem pyramid follows the same logic in that the most powerful explanation lords over the others.

Magicians are experts at making the audience misjudge the root causes of their tricks. Business problems can also involve sleight of hand. Take measures to look beyond the surface. The career magic you work will astound you.

Question

Practice what you've learned in this topic. Select sorting techniques to identify the root causes of business problems.

Options:

1. Checklists involve sorting potential problem causes by comparing items on the list.

2. Chronologies involve tracking associated problem events back to their source.

3. Problem pyramids are visual representations of the problem with the cause at the top.

4. Sorting involves rearranging the problem so that possible solutions become apparent.

Answers:

In fact, checklists involve sorting and comparing problems on a list. A chronology details the history of the problem. A problem pyramid visually illustrates the root causes and their associated symptoms.

Option 1: Correct. Using checklists helps you focus on the current issues, and also helps you account for the most probable causes. Remember that the checklist should be added to whenever new issues are identified.

Option 2: Correct. Chronologies help you learn from the past by looking for clues relating to the cause of your business problem.

Option 3: Correct. You can use problem pyramids to visually rank the contributors to a business problem by arranging and rearranging the possible causes according to their dominance.

Option 4: Incorrect. Sorting is not one of the three identification techniques discussed in this lesson. Rather, the techniques of creating chronologies, checklists, and problem pyramids are all part of sorting out the root cause of the problem.

Identifying the root cause of a business problem will allow you to focus on the core issue. You disregard insignificant and nonessential problem factors and then narrow your attention to the real drivers of the issue. Using sorting techniques to reach the problem's core will help you accomplish this multilayered task. And it will likely reduce the amount of obstacles you will face in the process.

You learned about three sorting techniques in this topic: chronologies, checklists, and problem pyramids.

Causal flow analysis

On the day of the big game, the reception on Craig's television set was horrible. Craig's friend Shawn suggested the cause of the bad reception was their failure to aggressively kick the TV set.

Shawn's analysis of the cause of the reception problem doesn't deserve to make the evening news. Your analysis will, after you read this topic and learn to get to the root of a business problem by using the steps of a causal flow analysis:

- determining the input factors of the problem,
- determining the output factors of the problem,
- examining the causal flow between the factors.

Most business problems have several contributing causes and a multitude of less significant symptoms. Filtering through those various problem causes and determining the truly crucial ones allows you to effectively prioritize both your solutions and your objectives.

A great way to do this is to perform a causal flow analysis. Causal flow analyses are especially powerful means to validate or invalidate initial ideas about broad and complex problems like sales declines and product deficiencies.

The first step of a causal analysis is determining the input factors of the problem. Input factors are those aspects of your company's internal policies or strategies that might contribute to the creation or existence of a business problem. Think of input factors as the ingredients that go into making a meal.

See each factor in order, to find out how Eileen, a sales manager at a large office-furniture manufacturer, determined the input factors associated with her company's recent sales decline.

Labor shortage

"We've been short-staffed for a while now. The labor pool in this area is a shallow one, to say the least. The fact that we haven't been able to hire enough people poses a real problem in producing the furniture. That's why it's an input factor in our sales drop."

Training vs. production

"The general labor shortage is tough, but the lack of trained and expert workers is even tougher. Getting new hires up to speed has taken time away from actual production. Since this factor is internal to our company, I listed it as an input factor in my causal analysis."

High production times

"Speaking of production time, our product is high-end and requires lots of time to build. It's been a problem meeting time-to-market demand."

Lack of market research

"Another problem I determined to be an input factor is our lack of market research. Most managers agree that we rush to get furniture out the door and neglect to research industry trends. I feel like we're putting the cart before the horse, and our product suffers."

Low quality materials

"Another problem is that we used some inferior materials. These substandard materials resulted in excessive repairs and returns. In this case, our furniture input was literally an input factor in my analysis."

Lack of capital funding

"Lastly, I found our company's lack of capital funding to be an input factor that affected every aspect of our business, including our mind-sets. We've been overanxious to cut corners, and our product has suffered as a result."

All the factors Eileen listed were internal to her organization and originated before the furniture went to market. Notice Eileen also considered more than one or two input factors. She examined staffing, training, market research, and production materials. It's crucial to examine all associated factors and not leave any possibilities out.

Eileen then took the second step in her causal analysis and determined the output factors. Output factors, as you may guess, are problems associated with the output of the furniture. They are problems that originate after her product was manufactured.

In this step, Eileen turned her attention to the problematic events associated with the marketing of her upscale office furniture. All of these factors occurred once her product was displayed and being evaluated.

Using Dynamic Problem-framing Techniques

Noted artist Pablo Picasso was fond of telling art patrons that the hardest part of painting was figuring what went into the frame of the picture and what had to be left out.

Picasso's notion holds true in the realm of problem solving. When you frame a business problem, your aim is to discover a new perspective, that is, a way of thinking about the problem that's more accurate and compelling.

Fishbone diagrams, being visual in nature, let you see a business problem from different angles. This helps put a problem in a more accurate frame, or perspective. In this topic, you'll learn the steps to take to construct a fishbone diagram:

- Diagram all possible causes of the problem.
- Prioritize and rearrange the associated problems.
- Reduce the remaining causes.

You should do the same thing when faced with a business problem. In this topic, you'll learn how to perform a deviation analysis in a team setting. The components of a group deviation analysis are:

- anonymously performing a deviation analysis,
- comparing and analyzing the initial results.

The second component of the problem-redefinition technique is to enlarge your picture of the problem. You do this by restating the problem in a larger context.

It's tempting to narrow a problem down and shrink it, but sometimes a business problem needs to be enlarged.

For example, if you fail to solve a problem at a departmental level, perhaps it's time to look to the divisional or overall customer pictures. Problem-solving action taken at the wrong level is worse than no action at all because it can easily lead to lost time and frustration.

Incorporating dynamic problem-framing techniques

Noted artist Pablo Picasso was fond of telling art patrons that the hardest part of painting was figuring what went into the frame of the picture and what had to be left out.

Picasso's notion holds true in the realm of problem solving. When you frame a business problem, your aim is to discover a new perspective, that is, a way of thinking about the problem that's more accurate and compelling.

Don't leave this task up to your artistic intuition, however. Instead, put the dynamic problem-framing techniques you'll learn in this lesson to work. You'll find the results to be a stroke of genius.

So what are the benefits of incorporating dynamic problem-framing techniques into your everyday business life? Tammy is the manager of a large restaurant franchise.

See each benefit type to find out what Tammy has gained from using dynamic problem-framing techniques.

The immediate benefit

"I started using these techniques a few years ago. The immediate benefit? My career really got a great boost. It was enhanced to a great degree."

Personal life benefit

"Almost without knowing it, using these techniques at work also led me to better frame issues in my personal life. I really gained a new and better perspective on things."

Question

When you know your perspective on a business problem is accurate and reliable, you can communicate more confidently with other colleagues about that problem.

Options:

1. I don't agree at all.
2. I slightly agree.
3. I'm neutral.
4. I somewhat agree.
5. I completely agree.

Answers:

Option 1: Most people agree that the more accurate their perspective on a business problem, the more confident they are when discussing it with others. Using dynamic problem-framing techniques helps promote that level of confidence.

Option 2: Most people agree that the more accurate their perspective on a business problem, the more confident they are when discussing it with others. Using dynamic problem-framing techniques helps promote that level of confidence.

Option 3: Most people agree that the more accurate their perspective on a business problem, the more confident they are when discussing it with others. Using dynamic problem-framing techniques helps promote that level of confidence.

Option 4: Most people agree that the more accurate their perspective on a business problem, the more confident they are when discussing it with others. Using dynamic problem-framing techniques helps promote that level of confidence.

Option 5: Most people agree that the more accurate their perspective on a business problem, the more confident they are when discussing it with others. Using dynamic problem-framing techniques helps promote that level of confidence.

Question

Problem framing is the first step toward picturing the accompanying solution. Which items are benefits of incorporating dynamic problem-framing techniques into everyday business life? Select the correct sentence endings.

You'll be able to...

Options:

1. enjoy enhanced career success in an overall sense.
2. communicate the problem to colleagues in a more confident way.
3. appreciate your ability to better frame personal issues.
4. greatly reduce time spent researching the problem.

Answers:

In fact, you'll more confidently communicate the problem to others, better frame nonwork issues, and enjoy enhanced career success. Framing a problem and doing research are two separate activities.

Option 1: Correct. Learning how to effectively frame a problem can lead to a real boost in your career.

Option 2: Correct. Knowing how to frame the problem correctly leads to better understanding of the problem. This, in turn, lead to more confident communication of the problem to others.

Option 3: Correct. The skill of framing a problem in order to view it more correctly can be carried over into your personal life.

Option 4: Incorrect. Researching the problem is a separate issue from framing the problem.

"If the only tool you have is a hammer, you tend to see every problem as a nail," said psychologist Abraham Maslow. The framing techniques you're about to learn will ensure that you have enough tools to frame almost any business problem.

In this lesson, you'll learn how to use fishbone diagrams, deviation analyses, and problem-redefinition techniques to accurately frame your business problems.

Constructing a fishbone diagram

On a recent hike, Eric lost his way. The terrain was rough, and the trails were confusing. His frustration melted away once he reached into his pack and found the map he thought he had left behind.

Question

A written set of instructions wouldn't have framed Eric's actual location for him. But a map, being a visual tool, was just the thing to help him recover his bearings.

Visual aids often help you gain an accurate perspective on an issue. Do you find business presentations that include visual aids to be the most effective?

Options:

1. No. I find just the opposite.
2. I rarely find that to be the case.
3. I'm neutral on that.
4. I find that most of the time.
5. Definitely.

Answer:

Most people see visual aids as an especially helpful way to absorb information. Imagine if this course had no graphic images. Your perspective on the material would probably suffer.

Fishbone diagrams, being visual in nature, let you see a business problem from different angles. This helps put a problem in a more accurate frame, or perspective. In this topic, you'll learn the steps to take to construct a fishbone diagram:

- Diagram all possible causes of the problem.
- Prioritize and rearrange the associated problems.
- Reduce the remaining causes.

In your effort to frame a business problem, the first step to constructing a fishbone diagram is to diagram all the possible causes of the problem. All business functions are interrelated, so all business problems have an effect on other aspects of your organization. Nathaniel, a vice president at a national bank, wanted a more accurate perspective, or frame, on his revenue loss problem.

See each task to find out how Nathaniel has diagrammed the problems associated with the loss of revenue.

Circle the main problem at the head of the fish

"I started my fishbone diagram by drawing a circle around the main problem, loss of revenue. That became the head of my fish."

List the major possible causes at the ends of the bones

"Then I drew the bones of the fish. At the end of the bones, I listed the major possible causes. These were the ones I thought most broad and obvious."

List the subcauses along the corresponding bones.

"Next, I analyzed each possible cause. Were there narrower, more focused causes associated with the major cause? I noted those along the corresponding bones."

See each aspect of Nathaniel's fishbone diagram to find out about how he mapped the possible causes of his business problem.

Major causes at the end

"I have plenty of other possible causes to add to my diagram. You only see my initial thoughts. Notice I wrote major potential causes at the end of the bones. They're the ones that are really overarching and apparent."

The whole picture at-a-glance

"Notice how my fishbone diagram gave me an instant, visual means of framing my initial thoughts about our revenue problem. The information is just more accessible than it would be if written out on a report of some kind."

Breakdown of causes

"See how I broke down those major possible causes into more focused explanations? For example, under the overall soft economy, I noted that banking revenues were down industry-wide."

Nathaniel added several bones to the rough diagram detailing other possible causes of the main problem. Then, as many researchers on problem solving recommend, he "slept on it." That is, he let his initial thoughts percolate for a few days. This process in turn led to other insights and ideas he'd use later.

The next step Nathaniel took to construct his fishbone diagram was to prioritize and rearrange the possible causes. Nathaniel considered which possible causes were most complex and significant.

After prioritizing the most significant and complex potential causes, he rearranged their positions along the fish's spine. He put the most important, multifaceted causes closer to the head. This enabled him to get an instant frame on the true scope of the problem. He also knew which simple problems could be eliminated because they were superseded by the others. So the layout of his fishbone diagram became slightly smaller, and Nathaniel's thoughts about the revenue problem became more focused.

The last step Nathaniel took to construct his fishbone diagram was to reduce the remaining causes. Nathaniel tried to determine whether the major causes on the bones' ends dominated the accompanying, more focused explanations listed within the bones.

See each action to get Nathaniel's insight on reducing the remaining causes.

Isolate the drivers

"I examined the remaining causes and isolated the true "drivers." For example, even though the general economy was off, the banking industry was even worse."

Eliminate

"I collapsed that bone by eliminating the soft economy and focusing my attention on industry trends instead. Then I reduced the remaining bones"

After Nathaniel reduced the remaining causes, he had a more organized, concise picture of the problem. The problem was more defined as a result of framing it effectively. He was ready to attack his revenue concerns.

Question

Fishbone diagrams will prevent you from flopping around in the problem-solving sand. Identify the steps of constructing a fishbone diagram.

Options:

1. Diagram all the possible causes of the problem.
2. Isolate the true cause of the main problem.
3. Prioritize and rearrange the associated problems.
4. Design solutions to a few associated problems.
5. Pare down the remaining problems.

Answers:

Actually, the correct steps in constructing a fishbone diagram are: Diagram all possible causes of the problem, prioritize and rearrange the possible causes, and reduce the causes that remain.

1: Correct. Getting all the possible causes of the problem on paper is the first step in creating a fishbone diagram.

2: Incorrect. The purpose of the fishbone diagram is to give a visual representation of the breakdown of problem. No analysis is performed yet except as it relates to the facets of the problem.

3: Correct. Putting the problems in a hierarchical order on the fishbone diagram gives a clear visual representation of the multi-faceted problem.

4: Incorrect. At this stage of the problem solving process the fishbone diagram is providing a visual representation of the many aspects of the problem. Generating solutions is not expedient yet.

5: Correct. Careful analysis of the problems will lead to elimination of some and consolidation of others, both of which are constructive activities that will allow for more effective problem solving.

Once your fishbone diagram is constructed and analyzed, your perspective on the problem will probably change for the better. Follow the steps outlined in this topic and you won't get hooked by ineffective problem frames.

In this topic, you learned about the components of a fishbone diagram: Diagram all possible causes of the problem, prioritize and rearrange the possible causes, and reduce the causes that remain.

Using a deviation analysis

Neil bought a new computer with a superfast processor. After setting and booting up, the computer was about as fast as a rotary telephone.

Question

Do you agree with the statement ?

It's helpful to describe Neil's problem in terms of a performance deviation, that is, the difference between how his computer should perform and how it actually performs.

Options:

1. yes
2. no

Answers:

It's often helpful to frame a problem according to its deviation from ideal performance. You're then able to picture the difference between where you are and where you really want to be.

Option 1: Correct. Defining Neil's problem this way provides clarity regarding how his computer is currently performing and how it needs to be performing.

Option 2: Incorrect. Describing a problem according to current distance from the goal helps put the problem clearly into perspective.

Neil will answer a host of deviation questions when he calls customer service about his computer. You should do the same thing when faced with a business problem. In this topic, you'll learn how to perform a deviation analysis in a team setting. The components of a group deviation analysis are:

- anonymously performing a deviation analysis,
- comparing and analyzing the initial results.

The managers at You'reThereCo, Inc., a manufacturer of professional grade camera film, wanted to frame their problem effectively. Customers who'd taken pictures with their slide film had been returning it at an alarming rate. Almost all the slides were badly overexposed.

In the first part of their group deviation analysis, team members anonymously performed a deviation analysis.

Grace, the team leader, explained to the members that a deviation analysis entailed posing four questions about the overexposure problem and having team members record their thoughts on those questions. There was to be no discussion during this activity.

See each question type to find out about the four deviation questions Grace required team members to answer.

what

"What's the problem? It sounds like a movie line, but it's one of the most important questions to ask about any problem. Team members usually have an idea in their heads. But once they have to put pen to paper, they usually realize how obscure their initial thoughts were."

where

"The "where" question is multifaceted, and its nature will change according to the problem being addressed. It may concern locating a physical problem, such as a faulty circuit. It also may involve finding where, in geographic or demographic terms, the problem is happening."

when

"The 'when' questions concern when the problem began to happen and when the problem takes place now. For example, my team asked when the overexposure issue first surfaced and when it continues to happen."

how

"'How' addresses the extent of the problem. How big is it? By analyzing this aspect, you're able to get a frame on the urgency and significance of the problem."

Notice that all four deviation questions were initially posed in the positive sense, that is, what the problem is rather than what it is not. The next step is to ask each question in the negative sense. That's how you establish the deviation in performance you're seeking to understand and generate more ideas about the problem at the same time.

See each question in order, to get Grace's insight into completing this aspect of a deviation analysis.

What is the problem not?

"You've determined what you think the problem is. Now ask yourself what the problem is not. In my case, the problem was not the color saturation of the film or the resolution quality."

Where isn't the problem happening?

"Where isn't the problem happening? By identifying the location in which the problem doesn't appear, you may discover hidden reasons for the deviation. In our case, the overexposure problem wasn't happening in our premium camera film line."

When doesn't the problem take place?

"When doesn't the problem take place? A few team members noted that our product didn't overexpose when a certain film developing machine was used. This really altered their frame on the problem."

Why isn't the problem bigger?

"Ask yourself how big the problem could be. Why isn't the problem bigger? This question gives you a better feel for the real scope of the issue than if you simply asked the question in the positive sense."

Question

Practice what you've learned so far. Select valid examples of deviation questions.

Options:

1. Why is the problem so costly?
2. What is the problem?
3. Where doesn't the problem take place?
4. How big could the problem be?
5. How does the problem affect others?

Answers:

What is the problem, where doesn't it take place, and how big could it be are all valid deviation questions. The other two questions don't really address deviation.

Option 1: Incorrect. This question does not apply; it does not address deviation, which asks what, where, when, and how.

Option 2: Correct. Answering this question will give helpful information in determining the amount of deviation.

Option 3: Correct. After asking the deviation questions in the positive form, ask them in the negative form. The answers to these questions establish the deviation.

Option 4: Correct. Deviation questions are designed to facilitate a deviation analysis and can be posed both positively and negatively.

Option 5: Incorrect. This is not a good example of a deviation question. Its answer will not clarify how far the problem currently is from the desired goal.

As you saw in the previous question, you need to pose the four questions in a positive and a negative sense to better frame a performance deviation. And when performing this framing technique in a group, make sure team members carry out this procedure anonymously.

Once the initial analysis is complete, you can move on to the second component of a group deviation analysis: **comparing and analyzing the initial results.**

Grace met with her team members, Amelia and Barry, to compare and analyze their initial deviation analysis results.

Grace: So we have some differences of opinion on a couple of deviation questions, huh? That's fine. In fact, it's to be expected. First, let's discuss our frame on when the problem is and isn't taking place.

Amelia: Well, Barry's notion that the overexposure only happens when pictures are taken outdoors really gave me a new perspective.

Grace: Right. That really narrowed our focus, Amelia.

Barry: Several heads are better than one, that's for sure. I hadn't considered Amelia's vantage on the "how" question. She pointed out we have more of this film on the production line than I thought. This problem's much bigger than I had anticipated.

Amelia: Now that we know that, Barry, we can take appropriate measures. I think we're ready to start proposing solutions.

Grace: Not so fast. We haven't discussed the other deviation questions we agree on. Plus, we need to restate our overall problem frame. Let's not cut this procedure short. I'd rather get a solid frame in place before we generate solutions.

Barry: Grace, you're such a taskmaster.

Grace: Hey, you can bet that's one thing I'll never deviate from.

Grace and her team members were well on their way to effectively framing the problem. Notice how Grace prohibited team members from thinking about solutions to the problem. An accurate problem frame is important enough to justify its own dedicated discussion.

See Disagree and double check to discover Grace's remarks on this stage of a group deviation analysis.

Question

Practice what you've learned about the second half of a group deviation analysis. Identify valid strategies for comparing and analyzing the initial deviation analysis results.

Options:

1. Compare the answers of the initial deviation questions, and investigate differences of opinion as well as agreement.

2. Engineer solutions to the problem that address the parameters of the enhanced problem frame.

3. If there is complete agreement on the initial deviation analyses, re-examine the existing problem frame.

4. Concentrate more on the responses to the "what" questions than on the other three.

Answers:

In fact, you should compare the differing and uniform opinions and revisit the existing problem frame if there is complete agreement on the initial deviation questions. Don't design solutions and treat all questions equally.

Option 1: Correct. There should be both agreement and disagreement between answers if careful thought was involved. Both need to be discussed.

Option 2: Incorrect. This discussion needs to stay focused on framing the problem. Solutions should not be discussed yet.

Option 3: Correct. Complete agreement among the group signifies either conformity or lazy thinking. In this case, the initial answers should be re-checked.

Option 4: Incorrect. All of the deviation questions carry the same amount of weight and should be equally considered.

In the previous question, you noted effective ways to compare and analyze the initial results. So how do you determine if a team has effectively performed.

The problem-redefinition technique

J.C. wore a suit to a party in which every other guy was dressed in a tux. J.C. immediately felt out of place. That was before a person wearing shorts and a T-shirt showed up.

J.C.'s party problem had just been redefined and reframed. In this topic, you'll learn how to more effectively frame a problem by using the components of the problem-redefinition technique:

- turning the problem upside down,
- enlarging your picture of the problem,
- using the "why" strategy.

Follow along as Michael and Ashley used the first component of the problem-redefinition technique, turning the problem upside down.

Michael: Our new electric cars are perfect except for one thing: They don't go fast enough for highway travel.

Ashley: I hear you, Michael. How about redefining the problem by really turning it on its head? Imagine that the real problem is that our cars are too fast. Their speed is scaring people.

Michael: Great idea, Ashley. In that case, we'd have to convince customers to ignore the extra power and step off the gas.

Ashley: So let's take that idea and apply it to our existing problem. Maybe we should frame the problem as convincing customers that slower travel is better travel. It's more relaxing.

Michael: In other words, we frame our speed problem as a marketing dilemma: how to convince customers they need an around-town car and not an all-purpose vehicle.

Ashley: And another thing. If our electric cars were too fast, we'd need additional "fast" lanes for that kind of traffic.

Michael: We could also frame our real problem as a need to talk state governments into building extra lanes for slower, environmentally friendly transportation.

Ashley: After this exercise, my frame's really changed, Michael. The problem may be changing consumer and governmental sentiments rather than altering our existing product.

Notice how Michael and Ashley really turned the inadequate speed problem upside down and didn't just change or tweak some aspect of it. They thought about the electric car as being too fast instead of too slow. This process forced them to think about the problem in new ways.

The second component of the problem-redefinition technique is to enlarge your picture of the problem. You do this by restating the problem in a larger context.

It's tempting to narrow a problem down and shrink it, but sometimes a business problem needs to be enlarged.

For example, if you fail to solve a problem at a departmental level, perhaps it's time to look to the divisional or overall customer pictures. Problem-solving action taken at the wrong level is worse than no action at all because it can easily lead to lost time and frustration.

See my problem and enlarged focus to find out more from Gillian, an unsatisfied employee.

My problem

"I've been unhappy at my marketing job for a while now. I just don't find it fulfilling anymore. My problem is whether or not to change jobs. Before doing anything, I wanted to frame my situation by setting it within a bigger picture."

Enlarged focus

"Having a satisfying life inside and outside work became my enlarged focus. I pictured my ideal life. What activities would bring me happiness? After prioritizing my desires, I realized I could attain them in this job; I'd just have to restructure my time."

Gillian's original frame was redefined from possibly changing jobs to reprioritizing and rearranging her time within her existing position. By enlarging her picture, she actually narrowed her focus.

Question

Practice what you've learned so far. Which of the statements are true of the first two components of a problem- redefinition technique?

You need to:

Options:

1. completely turn the business problem upside down.

2. think about the problem in a more narrow manner.
3. focus on the consequences of the business problem.
4. enlarge your perspective instead of shrinking it.

Answer:

In fact, you turn the problem completely upside down and don't just slightly alter it. Enlarge your picture instead of shrinking and narrowing it. In the problem-redefinition technique, you reframe a problem; you don't study potential consequences.

CHAPTER THREE

Generating Alternatives

Getting into the Flow

Whitewater rafting can be an exciting experience. A key to a great ride is being in the current, catching the best flows. Not only do you go faster, you have more fun too.

As with rafting, a key to generating alternative solutions to problems is "getting into the flow." In this case, the flow refers to a creative mind-set that supports generating the alternatives. Benefits of getting into the flow include:

- diminishing your fear of failing to solve the problem,
- enhancing your ability to generate alternatives,
- increasing your enthusiasm for solving problems.

"Success is a state of mind. If you want success, start thinking of yourself as a success." --Dr. Joyce Brothers

Dr. Brothers' advice applies to more than just success. Achieving the right mind-set is also critical for generating alternative solutions to problems. If you have an ineffective mind-set, you won't find alternatives.

The first principle of productive brainstorming is generating many ideas. A common method of crop planting is to "overseed" a field. The reason for this is that some seeds will sprout and others won't. Brainstorming is similar--some ideas will work and some won't.

The more ideas you can generate, the more likely it is that some will take hold and grow into viable solutions. As you brainstorm, either in a team or on your own, do your best to generate as many ideas as possible.

Getting into a creative mind-set

Whitewater rafting can be an exciting experience. A key to a great ride is being in the current, catching the best flows. Not only do you go faster, you have more fun too.

As with rafting, a key to generating alternative solutions to problems is "getting into the flow." In this case, the flow refers to a creative mind-set that supports generating the alternatives. Benefits of getting into the flow include:

- diminishing your fear of failing to solve the problem,
- enhancing your ability to generate alternatives,
- increasing your enthusiasm for solving problems.

Have you ever been trapped by the fear of failing to solve a problem or to find alternative solutions? Most of us have felt trapped at one time or another. One of the most important benefits of getting into the flow is that you diminish your fear of failure and release the pressure of the "trap." By getting into the right mind-set, you'll be better able to create alternatives for solving your problem.

Once you've diminished or stopped the fear, you can move on to generating ideas and gaining enthusiasm for solving the problem. Select each engineer for information about the benefits of getting into the flow.

Engineer 1

"It's easier for me to generate alternatives when I'm in the right mind-set. The ideas just seem to flow. When I'm tense or afraid, I can't think of anything."

Engineer 2

"My enthusiasm for solving problems increases when I'm in the right mind-set. I become more optimistic, and as a result, I start seeing new alternatives."

Question

Getting into the right mind-set for creating alternative solutions to problems can be the catalyst for actually solving the problems. Identify benefits of getting into a creative mind-set before generating alternative solutions to problems.

Options:

1. lowers your fear of failing to solve the problems
2. ensures that you will generate alternatives
3. increases your ability to generate alternatives
4. solidifies your chances for success
5. increases your enthusiasm for solving the problem

Answer:

Actually, getting into the right mind-set can help you in all the ways mentioned except ensuring you'll generate alternatives or solidifying your chances for success.

Option 1: This is a correct choice. Once you've gotten into the flow of generating alternatives, your fear of not solving the problem will diminish, further enhancing the creative mind-set needed for success.

Option 2: This is not a benefit of getting into a creative mind set. Getting into a flow of generating alternatives will lower your fear of failing to solve the problem, but there are never guarantees.

Option 3: This is a correct choice. As you get into a creative mind set, you will be better able to generate alternatives that bring you closer to solving the problem.

Option 4: This choice is incorrect. While your chances for success greatly increase as you get into a creative mind-set, there are no solid guarantees.

Option 5: This is a correct choice. A creative mind-set will allow you to begin generating alternatives, which then increases your enthusiasm.

In this lesson, you'll explore two ways of getting into the flow:

- achieving the right mind-set,
- brainstorming.

Attitudes for achieving an effective state

"Success is a state of mind. If you want success, start thinking of yourself as a success." --Dr. Joyce Brothers

Dr. Brothers' advice applies to more than just success. Achieving the right mind-set is also critical for generating alternative solutions to problems. If you have an ineffective mind-set, you won't find alternatives.

See each mind-set type for more information.

Closed

A poor mind-set is like a library that's locked. All the ideas and information inside are inaccessible, with no way of being applied.

Open

An effective mind-set is like an open, busy library, with almost limitless information and ideas that can be applied to problem solving.

Having an effective state of mind is crucial for getting into a productive flow for generating alternatives. Achieving the right mind-set starts by being:

- optimistic,
- open-minded,
- daring.

Being optimistic is the foundation for a productive mind-set. When you're optimistic, you look forward to the future with a positive view--you expect good things to happen. Champion athletes are masters at being optimistic. They find themselves as winning, not losing. The key is choosing your outlook. You're the one who paints a picture of the future as good or bad. Choose a positive, can-do outlook as you get ready to generate alternative solutions to your problems.

Once you're feeling optimistic about generating solutions, it's your open-mindedness and daring that help you to actually create the solutions. Select each concept for more information.

Open-minded

Open-mindedness is the opposite of judgment. By not judging, you can see and hear new ideas. The ideas can come from your insight, as well as insight from others.

Daring

Being daring is what you do with your open-mindedness. You think and act "outside the box." It's through your daring that radical new solutions emerge.

The Wright brothers were successful partly because of their open-mindedness and daring. Their open-mindedness allowed them to see new ideas, such as using motors and lightweight materials to create an airplane.

Thinking "outside the box" allowed them to actually design and build their airplane. Combining optimism, open-mindedness, and daring forms a powerful mind-set for generating solutions to problems.

How did you see yourself? Is it difficult for you to be optimistic, open-minded, or daring?

Question

Achieving the right mind-set will have a big effect on your ability to create solutions. Select attitudes for achieving an effective state of mind for the generation of alternatives.

Options:

1. avoiding pessimism
2. being intolerant
3. taking risks
4. discounting radical ideas

Answer:

Actually, being intolerant and discounting ideas will limit your ability to think of options and new insights.

Option 1: This is a correct choice. When you look forward to the future with a positive view, you are establishing a foundation for a productive mind-set.

Option 2: This choice is incorrect. Intolerance will not foster a productive mind-set because it is limiting. In fact, it is more likely to hinder it. You need to look forward to the future with a positive view.

Option 3: This is a correct choice. Taking risks will enhance your ability to generate creative solutions. While risks may not always be successful, they are where the most creative solutions spring from.

Option 4: This choice is incorrect because radical ideas are where the most creative solutions tend to originate. Discounting them will have the opposite effect.

Remember to get into the right mind-set before trying to generate alternative solutions to problems. Being optimistic, open-minded, and daring will carry you a long way toward your goals.

Productive brainstorming

Question

Take a minute to think about this question: How many uses are there for an ordinary lead pencil?

Options:

1. less than ten
2. ten to 100
3. 100 to 5,000
4. 5,000 to 1 million
5. limitless

Answer:

The number of possible uses is almost endless. For every person you ask, you'll probably get another idea. The best way to uncover those ideas is through brainstorming.

Brainstorming, which is the generation of ideas, is key to finding alternatives for your problems. There are some simple principles behind productive brainstorming.

- generating many ideas,

- withholding judgment on ideas,
- exploring all the ideas.

The first principle of productive brainstorming is generating many ideas. A common method of crop planting is to "overseed" a field. The reason for this is that some seeds will sprout and others won't. Brainstorming is similar--some ideas will work and some won't.

The more ideas you can generate, the more likely it is that some will take hold and grow into viable solutions. As you brainstorm, either in a team or on your own, do your best to generate as many ideas as possible.

Tina, a production specialist for a producer of promotional items, needed to resolve a production line glitch. She set up a brainstorming meeting with Sue, another specialist, and two production line workers. After discussing the problem, they started to generate ideas. Tina encouraged them to generate as many ideas as possible and told them that she had a reward for the whole group if they could come up with 20 or more ideas for resolving the problem.

The second principle of productive brainstorming is withholding judgment on ideas. Judgment is the quickest way to kill a brainstorming session. It not only stops the flow of ideas, but it can also leave participants feeling closed or angry. Make sure you record everyone's ideas as you go, and help others to withhold judgment until the brainstorming process is complete.

After Tina and her team had been brainstorming for a few minutes, Sue started to criticize one of the ideas. Tina held up her "no judgment" sign, which brought a laugh from everyone. She reminded them that all ideas, no matter how "silly," were important.

The third principle of good brainstorming is exploring all the ideas. Have you ever gone on a walk and explored all the branching pathways, finding an unexpected view or place? It's important to do the same when brainstorming.

See each idea for more information.

Triggering ideas

If someone's idea triggers an idea of yours, then share it. Your idea could lead down a branch that provides the eventual solution. All ideas are valuable.

Follow all branches

When brainstorming, go down all the paths and follow all the branches that come out of an idea. Keep going with idea after idea until you run out of solutions on the branch you're on.

Tina and her team continued brainstorming for more than one hour. They were particularly successful with an idea for changing production flow. Sue started it, and others branched on. They had 38 items on the list by the time they stopped. Tina's reward of lunch, paid for by the company, was well-received.

Tina did a good job of keeping her group on track. As she walked back to her office with Sue, they discussed how they'd implement the solution the team had chosen.

Question

Tina had a successful brainstorming session. Select principles of productive brainstorming that Tina used.

Options:

1. Tina and her team created more than 30 items.
2. Tina talked with Sue about implementation.
3. Tina asked Sue to hold her criticism until later.
4. Tina's team expanded on Sue's idea.
5. Tina rewarded her team.

Answer:

Although it was beneficial for Tina to talk with Sue and reward her team, neither action demonstrated a principle of productive brainstorming.

Option 1: This choice is correct. Successful brainstorming requires that many ideas be generated without judgment. Tina was clearly able to get her team to generate lots of ideas.

Option 2: This choice is incorrect. A brainstorming session is not the time to be thinking about implementation. Ideas must be generated without judgment, particularly judgment relating to implementation.

Option 3: This choice is correct. In successful brainstorming, ideas must be generated without judgment. By having Sue hold her criticism, Tina is ensuring the free flow of ideas.

Option 4: This is a correct choice. By exploring any ideas that may flow from Sue's idea, Tina's team may be able to hit upon unexpected alternatives. This is a key element of successful brainstorming.

Option 5: This choice is incorrect. While rewards may be beneficial for a successful session, they have no real bearing on the creative process or successful brainstorming.

As you lead or participate in brainstorming sessions, remember to help others generate lots of ideas, refrain from judgment, and explore all the branching ideas. Your commitment to productive brainstorming will pay off.

Taking Rational Approaches

There are many approaches to solving problems. Some are very complex, and though the solutions may be imaginative, they may also be too complicated and costly. Rational approaches tend to be simpler and more straightforward.

Imagine you're getting ready to buy a new computer. You've done all the research and have come up with five different models that appeal to you. How would you go about making your choice?

If you're like many people, you'll take a look at the pros and cons for each system before deciding. Looking at the pros and cons for alternative solutions is also a very rational way of choosing the right approach for solving a problem.

"Everything starts with the customer." --Louis V. Gerstner, Jr., former chairman and CEO of IBM

Gerstner chose a customer focus, including a focus on problems. By seeing from a customer's viewpoint, you can generate a greater number of problem-solving alternatives, and they're likely to be more applicable as well. You can think like your customers by:

- examining best practices for your industry,
- monitoring industry chat boards and forums,
- surveying your customers.

Using rational approaches to problem solving

What's the quickest way of getting from one point to another? It's a straight line. In problem solving, taking a rational approach is like traveling in a straight line--it's the quickest way to a solution.

Question

A rational approach is often the quickest and easiest way to generate problem-solving alternatives. Based on your knowledge, what is the definition of rational?

Options:

1. consistent with or based on reason
2. stemming from direct, immediate action

Answer:

Actually, rational approaches are based on reason and logic.

Option 1: Correct. Following a flow of thoughts based on reason reflects a rational approach.

Option 2: Incorrect. A rational approach does not necessarily rely on action. It follows a flow of thoughts based on reason.

There are many approaches to solving problems. Some are very complex, and though the solutions may be imaginative, they may also be too complicated and costly. Rational approaches tend to be simpler and more straightforward.

See each approach for more information.

Quick

Choosing a rational approach is often the quickest way to get alternatives for solving problems.

Dependable

Choosing a rational approach is usually a dependable way of developing alternatives for solving problems.

Question

Rational approaches to problem solving are often the best approach for you to take. From your experience, what do you think are benefits of using rational approaches to generating alternatives for solving problems?

Options:

1. You're more likely to have shortened time frames for generating solutions.
2. Solutions tend to be more applicable.
3. It's easy to help others learn rational approaches.
4. They ensure you'll be successful.

Answer:

Actually, rational approaches can be all of the points mentioned, except ensuring that you'll be successful.

Option 1: Correct. Taking a rational approach is typically the quickest route to a solution.

Option 2: Correct. Relying on reason is more likely to bring you to a solution that directly addresses your problem.

Option 3: This is a correct option. A rational approach is much easier to show others than more complicated methods.

Option 4: This choice is incorrect. While taking a rational approach increases your chances of success, it does not ensure success. There are no guarantees.

In this lesson, you'll explore two rational approaches to generating alternatives in problem solving:

- the BEST model,
- thinking like your customer.

The BEST model for generating alternatives

Imagine you're getting ready to buy a new computer. You've done all the research and have come up with five different models that appeal to you. How would you go about making your choice?

If you're like many people, you'll take a look at the pros and cons for each system before deciding. Looking at the pros and cons for alternative solutions is also a very rational way of choosing the right approach for solving a problem.

Pros and cons are at the center of the BEST model for generating alternatives for problems. BEST stands for brainstorming, evaluating, simplifying, and targeting. There are four steps.

- brainstorming alternative solutions for the problem,
- evaluating the alternative solutions by listing pros and cons,

- simplifying the list of cons by reducing and defusing them,
- targeting a solution for actual implementation.

The first step in the BEST model is brainstorming alternative solutions for the problem. The more alternatives that you or your team can generate, the better. If you're working by yourself, it may be helpful to get others involved in the brainstorming meeting. Two (or more) heads usually are better than one, especially for creative processes.

Katie is the development director for an Internet-based company that creates online multiplayer games. She's meeting with her implementation team about solving a problem: The company is losing money on too many of its online fantasy games.

Katie started the meeting with a brainstorming session. The team identified a range of alternatives, including expanding marketing, raising user fees, dropping games, and making operations more efficient. The list was a good start.

The second step in the BEST model is evaluating alternative solutions for the problem, which is accomplished by listing the pros and cons for each solution. Select each step element for more information.

Pros

List the pros for each alternative. The pros include any benefits, advantages, pluses, or merits for the given alternative.

Cons

List the cons for each alternative. The cons include any negatives, minuses, disadvantages, or objections for the given alternative.

Katie and her team then did a detailed evaluation of the alternatives, listing the pros and cons for each one. For example, a con of expanding marketing and making operations more efficient was the need to spend money upfront. A pro for both was higher profitability further down the line. A pro of raising user fees was more income per user, while a con was expected decreases in user levels. Dropping unpopular games had numerous pros and few cons. The team members were pleased with their efforts by the end of the evaluation step.

The third step in the BEST model is simplifying the list of cons. You can simplify the list by reducing and defusing the cons.

See each element for more information.

Reduce

Reduce the cons on your list by merging them or eliminating duplicates. Merging allows you to combine similar cons into one. Eliminating duplicates or cons that aren't true is another way of reducing the cons.

Defuse

Defusing cons is done by brainstorming ways to eliminate the cons or change them into pros. In either case, defusing the cons removes them from consideration.

Katie and her team spent some time simplifying the cons. For example, the con of spending upfront money was defused because the team saw a way of using funds from another project on the marketing and efficiency items.

They also combined the cons on two of the listed items into one. By the end of the simplification process, they had whittled the cons lists down to just a few that looked unchangeable.

The fourth step in the BEST model is targeting a solution. Targeting is the process of zeroing in on an optimum solution by looking at the pros and unchangeable cons for each alternative and then choosing one or more alternatives for implementation. Targeting may require a lot of thinking and some frank discussion about consequences. Regardless, the idea is to get to the best alternative, or combination of alternatives, for solving the problem.

The targeting step led to some heated discussion among Katie's team members. In the end, they decided to expand marketing and make operations more efficient, as well as drop some unpopular games. They also decided not to raise user fees. Over the next year, the company became quite profitable.

Question

Katie successfully led her team through the BEST model for generating alternatives. How did she do it? Correctly sequence the steps.

Options:

A. Katie and her team thought that expanding marketing was one way to solve their problem.

B. The team decided that raising user fees could increase income streams.

C. The team realized that the con of spending money upfront wasn't a factor because other funds could be used.

D. The team chose to make operations more efficient, along with a combination of other alternatives.

Answer:

Learning the steps in the BEST model is fundamental to using it as a rational approach for generating alternatives for problems.

Correct answer(s):

Katie and her team thought that expanding marketing was one way to solve their problem. is ranked the first step. The first step of the BEST model is to come up with ideas using brainstorming. This must happen first because you have to have the ideas before you can do anything with them. Katie's team came up with expanding marketing.

The team decided that raising user fees could increase income streams. is ranked the second step. The second step of the BEST model is evaluating the alternatives by listing pros and cons. This happens second to lay the foundation for reducing the options. Katie's team listed increased income as a pro for raising user fees.

The team realized that the con of spending money upfront wasn't a factor because other funds could be used. is ranked the third step. The third step of the BEST model is simplifying the list of cons. This further narrows the field of ideas before actually selecting one. Katie's team eliminated a con by deciding that it could be compensated for.

The team chose to make operations more efficient, along with a combination of other alternatives. is ranked the fourth step. The final step of the BEST model is actually selecting the best alternatives. Once the cons have been simplified, you can select the most appropriate ideas.

Understanding the BEST model is necessary before you can use it. Once you've applied it, how do you know you did it correctly? By asking yourself some questions, you can analyze how well you did at applying the BEST model. If you can say "yes" to all the BEST questions, then you probably have the "best" alternative for your problem.

See each element of the BEST model for more information.

Brainstorming

Did you go through a brainstorming process to create alternatives? If you just moved forward with some of the ideas you already had, then you didn't complete this step correctly.

Evaluating

Did you list the pros and cons for all the alternatives on your list? Just looking at pros or cons won't allow you to choose the best alternatives. You need both sides of all the options.

Simplifying

Did you simplify the cons for all the alternatives? And did you both reduce and defuse the cons? Remember, reducing means merging or eliminating duplicate cons. And defusing means brainstorming ways to eliminate the cons or change them into pros.

Targeting

Did you actually target one or more desired solutions? Did you look at the pros and unchangeable cons for each alternative before making your choice?

When the meeting was over, Katie took a few minutes to analyze how well she did with the BEST model. She quickly realized she had been successful.

Sandra and Pete were successful because they walked through all the steps for the BEST model--a very rational approach.

Use the BEST model when generating alternatives for solving your problems. Teach your colleagues about the BEST model too, so that you have a common set of guidelines to work with.

The customer's viewpoint

"Everything starts with the customer." --Louis V. Gerstner, Jr., former chairman and CEO of IBM

Gerstner chose a customer focus, including a focus on problems. By seeing from a customer's viewpoint, you can generate a greater number of problem-solving alternatives, and they're likely to be more applicable as well. You can think like your customers by:

- examining best practices for your industry,
- monitoring industry chat boards and forums,
- surveying your customers.

Question

Thinking like your customers is a logical and rational way of creating alternatives for solving customer problems. Do you have a clear picture of how your customers think about your company?

Options:

1. None
2. Little

3. Some
4. A lot
5. Total

Answer:

It's important to be customer-centric when solving customer problems. If you can't think of the situation from their viewpoint, you'll miss what they're seeing and miss possible alternatives.

One way of learning how to think like your customer is examining best practices for your industry. Best practices are the ways that companies in your field achieve success. Knowing best practices will help you know what customers might expect, and therefore how they might think.

See each information source for more information.

Industry magazines

Industry magazines and articles are a good source of best practices. Keep current by reading as many sources as possible.

Web sites

Web sites for your industry, as well as your competitors' Web sites, can provide information on best practices. Look for customer feedback and white paper sections.

Jed worked for a national construction company. The company's market niche was building facilities for high-technology manufacturing companies. Jed was constantly reading industry magazines to find success stories, as well as to find what didn't work. He also spent time every week reviewing his competitors' Web sites. He found a white paper on one site that outlined practices to avoid for a company to be successful. Fortunately, his company was already doing everything on the list.

Another way of learning how to think like your customer is monitoring industry chat boards and forums. Online chat boards and forums often contain valuable feedback about companies and how they treat their customers. Reviewing the chats and forums can lead to insights that may be missed in normal business operations.

Jed discovered his company was a subject on one of the online forums for his industry. It was a customer giving some negative feedback. It was bad press, but Jed was able to get the information to the right person and the issue was resolved. The customer placed a positive posting online the next week.

One of the most accurate ways of thinking like your customer is by surveying your customers. A good survey can provide you with a wealth of information about your company, and all of it is from your customer's viewpoint.

See each information source for more information.

Live surveys

Live surveys allow you to probe for information and listen to voice tones for hidden clues.

Mail surveys

Surveys by mail or e-mail give customers time to think about your company and how they really feel. These surveys can also be longer than face-to-face surveys.

Jed used both live and e-mail surveys to find out more about how his customers saw his company. The information was quite valuable as Jed designed ways to improve customer support.

Question

Jed was successful at thinking like his customers because he took the time to really understand their viewpoint.

Identify ways to think of a company from the customer's viewpoint.

Options:

1. Use e-mail or printed surveys to get customers' views.
2. Review changes in sales data to find out who is buying or not.
3. Review competitors' Web sites and online forums or chats.
4. Read industry-focused magazines and articles.

Answer:

Actually, learning how to think of your company from your customer's viewpoint will give you important options for generating alternatives for problems.

Option 1: This choice is correct. Printed or e-mailed surveys give customers time to think and formulate responses so that you can get their considered perspectives.

Option 2: This is incorrect. Sales data may be a valid research tool for other things, but it does not give you perspective on how your customers think.

Option 3: This is a correct choice. Competitor Web sites and forums can often contain valuable feedback about companies and how they treat their customers, leading to insights that might not otherwise be available.

Option 4: This choice is correct. Industry magazines and articles are an excellent source for best practices, which can be a gauge of customer expectations.

Thinking like the customer is essential for solving customer-related problems. A customer viewpoint will also give you insights when generating alternatives for solving other problems you may encounter at your company.

Using Creative Approaches

"Whatever creativity is, it is in part a solution to a problem." --Brian Aldiss, science fiction writer When it comes to business, there's a huge difference between mere survival and true excellence.

What separates the two? It's usually the degree to which the person or organization uses creative approaches to solving business problems.

But with the frenetic pace of today's world of commerce, who can afford the time required to become a creative problem solver? You can, and should. There are many benefits of using creative problem- solving techniques. And the techniques themselves don't require any more time than the obsolete.

Scientist F.A. Kekule had difficulty imagining the chemical structure of carbon atoms. One night he dreamed of a snake swallowing its tail. Kekule brilliantly used that analogy to envision the linked composition of a benzene ring.

Luckily, you don't have to wait for ideas to come to you in your sleep. You can use analogies (while fully awake) to generate alternative solutions to your business problems. In this topic, you'll learn how to use analogies as problem-solving tools by:

- listing several related analogies,
- listing the analogies' associated activities,
- using the analogies list to generate alternative solutions to the original problem.

Amanda knew there were two ways into work: the direct route and the scenic route.

For Amanda, the scenic way took her far out of her normal routine. Following this unconventional route allowed her to find unexpected aspects of the city. Similarly, whenever she was stuck on a problem at work, getting off the beaten path inspired new ideas.

Then there were days when she just needed to accomplish her business goals. Amanda opted for the direct route to work on those occasions. After all, practicality had its benefits as well.

Mind-maps actually mimic the layout of the brain. Brain cells have a central body, or nucleus, from which branches radiate. These branches carry information emitted by that nucleus to other parts of the brain. Researchers believe the more branches your brain contains, the more effective your thinking.

Creative approaches

"Whatever creativity is, it is in part a solution to a problem." --Brian Aldiss, science fiction writer When it comes to business, there's a huge difference between mere survival and true excellence.

What separates the two? It's usually the degree to which the person or organization uses creative approaches to solving business problems.

But with the frenetic pace of today's world of commerce, who can afford the time required to become a creative problem solver? You can, and should. There are many benefits of using creative problem- solving techniques. And the techniques themselves don't require any more time than the obsolete, thread-worn strategies that have failed so many times in the past.

You'll discover some of the more prevalent benefits of using creative approaches to problem solving.

See each benefit to learn more.

Increased vigor

Few things invigorate a problem solver more than working with innovative ideas. The enjoyment you gain from discovering new problem-solving vistas by using creative approaches keeps you inspired and motivated.

Enhanced alternative solutions

The creative approaches to problem solving described in this lesson lead directly to enhanced and increased alternative solutions. Putting these techniques to work, you'll be more assured and confident that you're really generating dynamic options and ideas.

Enhanced reputation

You'll enhance your reputation as a creative, "out-of-the-box" thinker by taking the creative approach to problem solving. Especially today, that's something worth being known for.

Question

You'll find creative problem solving to be a very fulfilling activity. What are the benefits of using creative approaches to generating alternatives?

Options:

1. You'll be able to enhance your reputation as a creative thinker.
2. You'll be invigorated by investigating original, innovative ideas.
3. You'll be able to better communicate the problem to others.
4. You'll be able to design powerful alternatives more confidently.

Answer:

In fact, you're likely to be known as an "out-of-the-box" thinker, be invigorated from exploring innovative ideas, and confidently generate dynamic alternatives.

Communicating with others about a problem is not a benefit of this approach.

Option 1: This is a correct answer. Taking the creative approach to problem solving will enhance your reputation as a problem solver.

Option 2: This is a correct choice. Working with innovative ideas invigorates creative problem solvers. Using creative approaches will inspire you.

Option 3: This option is incorrect. Using creative approaches has no bearing on your ability to communicate problems to others. That has more to do with your interpersonal communication skills.

Option 4: This is a benefit of using creative approaches. You will be more confident in your solutions as you use creative techniques to generate innovative alternatives.

Set yourself apart. Use the creative strategies presented in this lesson and you'll notice a world of problem-solving difference. You're about to learn how to use several creative approaches to problem solving:

- analogies,
- idea nets,
- mind-mapping.

The effective use of analogies

Scientist F.A. Kekule had difficulty imagining the chemical structure of carbon atoms. One night he dreamed of a snake swallowing its tail. Kekule brilliantly used that analogy to envision the linked composition of a benzene ring.

Luckily, you don't have to wait for ideas to come to you in your sleep. You can use analogies (while fully awake) to generate alternative solutions to your business problems. In this topic, you'll learn how to use analogies as problem-solving tools by:

- listing several related analogies,
- listing the analogies' associated activities,
- using the analogies list to generate alternative solutions to the original problem.

So what are analogies? They're essentially statements about how an object, person, situation, or action is similar to another in process and relationship. Analogies can lead to new perspectives on and ideas about a business problem.

The first step in using analogies to generate alternative solutions is to list several analogies related to your business problem. Generate a large number of alternatives--it's important to use more than just one or two.

Louise managed the largest department store in a major mall. She looked for ways to increase the customer foot traffic in her store by using analogies to produce alternatives.

See each analogy to discover how she took the first step in using this technique.

Traffic

"I thought about analogies that related to my traffic problem. That relationship could be based on similar concepts or actions. Take fishing, for example."

Fishing

"It related to my customer flow problem because fishing entails luring and enticing the catch to join you in your boat"

The fishing analogy struck an immediate chord with Louise. But she knew not to stop there. She listed three other related analogies, including highway traffic management, tug-of-war contests, and gold mining. She even noted a few other related analogies she could use if her original four failed to generate the desired number of alternatives.

Analogies in hand, Louise was ready to tackle the second step, listing the analogies' associated activities.

Each analogy you list will be composed of various concepts or actions. In this step, you break down the analogies into their more specific, often step-by-step components.

See each activity to find out more about what Louise listed for her fishing analogy.

Choosing the bait

"When thinking about the activities associated with fishing, the notion of selecting the right bait jumped out at me right away."

Sizing the hook

"Another activity that came to mind involved making sure the hook is the right size."

Picking your spot

"And certainly, you have to fish the right spots. No use dragging up old boots from a lifeless lake."

Casting the line

"I also realized it's important to cast and present the bait in a way that draws the attention of the fish and lures it to bite."

Reeling in the fish

"Once you hook the fish, you need to properly reel in and net it."

Releasing the fish

"Since I practice catch-and-release, I make sure I handle the fish gingerly. When I deposit it back into the water, I know there's a chance I'll see it again."

Louise made sure she elaborated on each of her four analogies before taking the next step: using the analogies list to generate alternative solutions to the original problem.

Louise's colleague, Charlie, wanted to learn how to use analogies to generate solutions. They discussed the third step of this technique.

Charlie: You've explained the first two steps of using analogies well, Louise. What comes next?

Louise: Time to put the analogies to work, Charlie. Take one analogy at a time and think about connections between its associated activities and aspects of our customer traffic issue.

Charlie: In other words, you look for similarities between the associated activities of the analogy and the problem itself.

Louise: Exactly. Let's do that with my fishing analogy.

Charlie: OK--one of the activities associated with fishing is using the right bait. That makes me think of the need to sell the kinds of products that will attract a customer's attention.

Louise: There's an idea. We should talk to merchandising about updating our product lines.

Charlie: And as far as choosing the right fishing spot goes, I translate that into ensuring our store is located in a heavily trafficked spot.

Louise: Hmm. I never thought of it that way. Instead of looking for ways to get customers into our existing store, maybe we should simply relocate. Our little chat is going quite nicely, Charlie.

Louise and Charlie gained even more momentum as they used the rest of the analogy list to generate alternative solutions. They wound up with a wealth of options to choose from.

The end of their traffic jam lay just ahead.

As you noticed, it's important to effectively complete each step of the analogy technique before proceeding to the next. In this way, you'll generate the largest number of creative alternative solutions to whatever business problem you aim to solve.

So how do you know if you, or someone else, effectively used analogies to generate alternative solutions? In order to perform that analysis, you must ask several questions.

It's helpful to keep these questions in mind as you proceed from step to step in the analogy technique. That way, you won't have to backtrack and recover from previous inefficiencies.

See each aspect to discover the questions you should ask to gauge the effective use of the solution-generating analogies.

Number of analogies

Ask yourself whether more than one or two analogies were listed. Did you, or another person, note only one favored analogy and not expand the horizons?

Elaboration of analogies

In order to generate an adequate number of alternatives, you need to elaborate on each of the analogies you initially list. Was that task fully accomplished?

Result of using analogies

Were new ideas and insights generated after using the analogy technique? It's almost impossible not to discover at least a handful of novel solutions with this technique. If no alternatives were generated, it's a signal that a step was mishandled.

Case Study: Question 1 of 2

Scenario:

For your convenience, the case study is repeated with each question.

Practice what you've learned in this topic. Brian, a sales manager for a large frozen food manufacturer, pondered how to convince supermarkets to carry more of his products. Brian used analogies to generate viable alternatives.

Answer the following questions in order.

Question:

Was Brian effective at using analogies to generate alternatives for his sales problem?

Options:

1. Brian was effective because he effectively elaborated on the driving analogy's associated activities and generated several new options.
2. Brian was ineffective in that he used valid analogies to his sales problem but elaborated on and generated ideas to only the driving analogy.
3. Brian was effective in that he was able to choose from a number of analogies and design viable solutions to his food sales problem.
4. Brian was ineffective because he listed too many associated activities of the driving analogy and didn't eliminate unrealistic alternatives.

Answer:

In fact, Brian was ineffective because he didn't elaborate on and generate ideas for any analogies other than the driving example. He used the driving analogy well, but failed to fully carry out the second step.

Option 1: This option is incorrect. In order to generate an adequate number of alternatives, you need to elaborate on each of the analogies you initially list. Brian only elaborated one, so he probably missed several viable alternatives.

Option 2: This is the correct answer. Since Brian only elaborated on one of his analogies, he probably missed several approaches to his problem. In order to generate sufficient alternatives, you need to elaborate on each of the analogies you initially list.

Option 3: This option is incorrect. While Brian did come up with several analogies, he only elaborated on one. In order to generate an adequate number of alternatives, you need to elaborate on each of the analogies you initially list.

Option 4: This option is incorrect. Brian was ineffective, but not because he had too many alternatives. He was ineffective because he only elaborated on one of his analogies. To generate sufficient alternatives, you should elaborate on several.

Case Study: Question 2 of 2

What questions did you ask in order to analyze Brian's effectiveness at using analogies to generate alternatives for his sales problem?

Options:

1. Did Brian examine more than one or two analogies to his frozen food sales problem?
2. Did Brian elaborate on the associated activities for each analogy to his sales problem?
3. Did Brian come up with any new alternative ideas about increasing his frozen food sales?
4. Did Brian consider that supermarkets are already overstocked with frozen food items?

Answer:

In fact, you should have asked whether Brian listed more than a couple of analogies and elaborated on the associated activities of each. Also, did Brian generate new ideas? The other question doesn't pertain to the use of analogies.

Option 1: This option is correct. You need to generate more than one or two analogies in order to formulate a sufficient number of alternatives. Brian did list several.

Option 2: This option is correct. In order to generate an adequate number of alternatives, you need to elaborate on each of the analogies you initially list. This was Brian's mistake; he only elaborated on one.

Option 3: This option is correct. You will discover several useful alternatives using this technique. Brian only formulated one because he only elaborated on one analogy.

Option 4: This option is incorrect because this is not a question that pertains to Brian's effective use of the Analogy technique.

Had Brian fully elaborated on all the analogies he listed, he would have devised many more alternative solutions. Learn from Brian's mistake. Take the analogy technique all the way to the bank and don't leave any accounts unsettled.

Analogies are a lot like airplanes. They lift you from the grounds of problem-solving stagnation and deposit you in your ideal location: success. In this topic, you learned how to follow the steps in using analogies to effectively generate solutions to your business problems.

- listing several related analogies,
- listing the analogies' associated activities,
- using the analogies list to generate alternative solutions to the original problem.

Idea nets

Amanda knew there were two ways into work: the direct route and the scenic route.

For Amanda, the scenic way took her far out of her normal routine. Following this unconventional route allowed her to find unexpected aspects of the city. Similarly, whenever she was stuck on a problem at work, getting off the beaten path inspired new ideas.

Then there were days when she just needed to accomplish her business goals. Amanda opted for the direct route to work on those occasions. After all, practicality had its benefits as well.

In this topic, you'll learn to take both paths in designing solutions to a business problem--the unconventional route and the practical route. You'll discover how to apply the steps of idea nets, a dynamic alternative-generating technique.

- casting your idea net,
- hauling in your idea net,

- analyzing and refining your catch of ideas.

Question

When you hear the term "unconventional" applied to business solutions, what does that mean to you? Select the statements that represent qualities of unconventional solutions.

Options:

1. Unconventional solutions are devised only by incredibly creative and talented thinkers.
2. Unconventional solutions require huge amounts of time and effort to be generated.
3. Unconventional solutions arc unnccessary in today's frenzied, bottom-line business world.
4. Unconventional solutions should be a crucial aspect of your everyday business life.
5. Unconventional solutions don't always work, but they often generate other viable ideas in turn.

Answer:

In fact, even impractical unconventional solutions can inspire other ideas. Pursue them for every problem because they don't require huge amounts of time. And you certainly don't have to be an artist or genius to generate them.

Option 1: This option is not correct. Most people can derive unconventional solutions. This topic will show you one way of doing it.

Option 2: This option is not correct. It can be done with reasonable effort and in a practical amount of time.

Option 3: This is not correct. On the contrary, it is today's frenzied, bottom-line business world that requires unconventional solutions.

Option 4: This is correct. Unconventional solutions will be an asset in your everyday business life.

Option 5: This option is correct. While they might not always work, unconventional solutions tend to multiply.

The first step to use idea nets to generate alternative solutions for a business problem, casting your idea net, involves unconventional, or divergent, thinking. Jonah managed a crew that installed sprinklers in office buildings. The better physical condition his workers were in, the more productive they were. Jonah wanted to devise strategies to motivate his employees to stay in shape.

See each piece of advice to find out how Jonah cast his idea net.

Wacky ideas

"I think of really wacky ideas during this step. For example, I thought about paying employees $5 for each push-up they did. I also considered locking the doors at lunch and forcing them to eat a meal of raw veggies and tree bark."

Create more ideas

"The best fishermen net a large quantity of fish. It's the same with problem solvers. I don't stop after devising one or two unconventional ideas. In this case, I added a few more, like having mandatory swimsuit days. Now that would motivate them."

Never judge

"While casting my net, I never judge or evaluate my potential solutions. That just halts the creative gears."

Piggyback on ideas

"Piggybacking on ideas works well too. The swimsuit idea triggered other alternatives for me. For example, I thought about building a moat around the office so people would have to get a workout swimming to their cars."

Jonah did a great job of imagining wacky solutions. He received great satisfaction performing this aspect of idea netting. He didn't spoil the party by censoring himself or limiting his imagination.

Parties eventually end, however. Jonah knew some cleaning up was in order. So he took the next step and hauled in his idea net.

When you haul in your idea net, you reign in your unconventional ideas, realistically narrowing them down to more feasible alternatives. Check each comment to find out how Jonah hauled in his idea net.

Money-for-push-ups

"I brought my money-for-push-ups scheme back down to earth. A great fitness center abuts our building. How about arranging reduced bulk-rate memberships?"

Fitness center

"The gym has a huge pool. We could throw a party and invite local health food stores to bring samples. We could even hold a seminar or two"

Jonah's solutions became quite realistic and feasible after this step. Notice he also clustered his ideas by combining the swimsuit and health food solutions. Cluster your ideas and your haul of business options will grow and grow.

Question

Now, practice what you've learned so far. Match the first two steps in using idea nets to one or more of the appropriate statements.

Options:

A. casting your idea net

B. hauling in your idea net

Targets:

1. Aim for quantity.
2. Be realistic.
3. Don't judge yourself.
4. Evaluate your options.

Answer:

Actually, you cast your idea net by listing a large number of uncensored and unconventional solutions. Haul in your idea net by evaluating and realistically narrowing down those solutions to produce feasible alternatives.

Aiming for quantity represents casting your idea net. Much like brainstorming, casting your net requires a lot of ideas.

Being realistic represents hauling in your idea net. In this step, you rein in your unconventional ideas.

Not judging is part of casting your idea net. Judging will come later.

Evaluating your options is part of hauling in your idea net. This is where you're looking to pull the big fish from your catch of ideas.

How'd you do on the previous exercise? Think about the first two idea steps this way: When fishing, you try to get as many bites as possible. But eventually, bringing in a live fish constitutes your goal.

Once you've reeled in some feasible solutions, it's time to take the last idea net step: analyzing and refining your catch of ideas.

What kind of fish do you have on the line? It's hard to tell until you pull it from the water and analyze it. In this idea net stage, you take a closer look at your feasible solutions and think harder about them.

See each action to find out how Jonah performed the final step of idea netting.

Revising

"I made a few alterations after hauling in my idea net. Swimming and listening to lectures don't really mix. I decided to do both, but at different times."

Refining

"And as far as the health food lectures go, I thought it might be better to have our own employees deliver them. That's probably a more effective and refined way to motivate everyone."

Considering viability

"I also considered the long-term viability of my solutions. After all, quick fixes to health don't cut it. I decided to research fitness and nutrition programs that promote long-lived habits. The lecture contents now had some real focus."

After you've revised and refined your catch of ideas, examining the long-term viability of each, you're ready to tackle your problem. That is, unless you haven't completed the idea net process on all your initial unconventional solutions.

Remember to be thorough and repeat the idea net hauling and revising portions on each unorthodox alternative. As the saying goes, "When it rains, it pours." And in this case, a full idea net translates into a true flood of powerful solutions.

As you noted in the role play, using idea nets effectively requires you to shape your ideas along the way. Try this technique on your next problem. You'll break your business solutions out of their obsolete molds.

Idea nets combine the best of both problem-solving worlds--creativity and practicality. In this topic, you learned to use idea nets to generate alternatives for a given business problem by:

- casting your idea net,
- hauling in your idea net,
- analyzing and refining your catch of ideas.

Steps to make an effective mind-map

After walking through a German science museum's giant brain exhibit, many visitors remark that the sheer complexity of this organ is a difficult concept to get their minds around.

Question

The museum's giant brain is so large that visitors receive a map of its layout before they enter. As a problem solver, you too can visualize your own thinking by drawing a mind-map. Mind-maps are visual representations of your thought processes and tools for generating alternative solutions to business problems.

What about you? Do you find information that's presented visually easier to learn and think about?

Options:

1. Never
2. Rarely
3. Sometimes
4. Often

5. Always

Answer:

Option 1: Some people are more visually oriented than others. Most problem solvers, however, find that picturing a business problem often leads to unforeseen solutions.

Option 2: Some people are more visually oriented than others. Most problem solvers, however, find that picturing a business problem often leads to unforeseen solutions.

Option 3: Some people are more visually oriented than others. Most problem solvers, however, find that picturing a business problem often leads to unforeseen solutions.

Option 4: Some people are more visually oriented than others. Most problem solvers, however, find that picturing a business problem often leads to unforeseen solutions.

Option 5: Some people are more visually oriented than others. Most problem solvers, however, find that picturing a business problem often leads to unforeseen solutions.

You're about to learn why mind-mapping, a technique developed in the late 1970s by Tony Buzan, has gained such worldwide popularity. In this topic, you'll learn how to follow the steps in constructing an effective mind-map.

- Circle the problem description.
- Brainstorm at least five "facet branches."
- Brainstorm the "subissue twigs."
- Analyze the finished mind-map.

Mind-maps actually mimic the layout of the brain. Brain cells have a central body, or nucleus, from which branches radiate. These branches carry information emitted by that nucleus to other parts of the brain. Researchers believe the more branches your brain contains, the more effective your thinking.

The first step in constructing a mind-map is to circle the problem description in the middle of a sheet of paper. For example a "New Toy Launch" is a business problem faced by Reginald, a new products manager at a large toy company.

Reginald constructed a mind-map to aid him in thinking about and generating alternative solutions for boosting the sales of his company's new line of preschool toys. After circling the problem description, he took the next step and brainstormed at least five "facet branches."

See each facet branch to discover how Reginald proceeded.

First facets

"I placed the major problem considerations along the facet branches. In this case, I put "price" along one of the branches and "product" along another."

Other facets

"Then I drew a few more branches. Distribution, promotion, industry trends, and the overall economy comprised the other facet branches"

Next, Reginald took the third step in constructing his mind-map and brainstormed the "subissue twigs." The subissue twigs contained ideas that were more specific breakdowns of the corresponding major facets.

See each element, in order, to get Reginald's insight into this step.

Promotion facet branch

"Notice along the promotion facet branch I listed movie tie-ins, free samples, and mascot tours. These were just some more concrete ideas I had about how to promote our new line of toys."

Subissue twigs

"There's really no end to the number of subissue twigs you can add. Typically, the more branches you add, the more specific your potential solutions will be."

Large quantity of ideas

"What you have here represents just a portion of my mind-map to this point. I continued to add subissue twigs along all the facet branches. I really focus more on generating a large quantity of ideas, rather than on quality."

After diagramming the subissue twigs, Reginald ended up with a huge, sprawling mind-map. Next, he took the last and most important step of analyzing the finished mind-map.

See each element to learn Reginald's tips for completing this crucial stage of mind-mapping.

Recurring themes

"After I finished drawing my map, I noticed that "cost efficiency" and "bright colors" appeared on several branches. I highlighted those instances with a colored marker. That gave me an instant visual cue to think more deeply about these ideas."

Underdeveloped branches

"The branch detailing industry trends didn't contain many subissue twigs. I knew there were lots of ideas to be found under this heading. So I made a special effort to do further research. My analysis paid off. I generated all kinds of alternative solutions based on the trends."

Novel ideas

"I also scanned the final map looking for really novel ideas. I circled several I found along the promotions branch that I could "springboard" from and develop even more innovative alternatives."

Now that you've seen how Reginald constructed his mind-map, take a moment to build your own. It will start you thinking of solutions for increasing your effectiveness at work. When you've completed your map, move on to the next page.

Question

It's time to practice what you've learned. Mind-maps show you where you are and where you may want to go. Identify the steps to make an effective mind-map.

Options:

1. Circle the one best solution to your business problem.
2. Brainstorm a minimum of five facet branches.
3. Think of ideas that will form the subissue twigs.
4. Analyze the mind-map and note recurring themes.

Answer:

Actually, brainstorming at least five facet branches, filling in the subissue twigs, and analyzing the finished mind-map are all valid steps. On the other hand, you circle the problem description, not a problem solution.

Option 1: This option is incorrect. With a mind map, you are not yet looking for the one best solution. You are generating related ideas. You circle the central problem initially, not a solution.

Option 2: This option is correct. In brainstorming facet branches, you want to include all of the major problem considerations relating to the central problem.

Option 3: This option is correct. From each facet branch, you want to draw the subissues that are ideas representing a more specific breakdown of the facets.

Option 4: This is correct. Once you have the mind map drawn, you will look for visual patterns, recurring themes, novel ideas, and underdeveloped branches, which may indicate areas for further research.

Success in this new millennium will belong to those problem solvers who combine clear thinking with studied innovation. Follow the steps detailed in the previous exercise, and your resulting mind-maps will help steer you through your problem-solving future.

In this topic, you learned how to follow the steps in constructing an effective mind-map: circling the problem description, brainstorming at least five facet branches, brainstorming the subissue twigs, and analyzing your finished mind-map.

Getting Out of a Rut

In most Tarzan movies, you could count on one or two hapless explorers to fall into a pit of quicksand. No one ever died, of course. At the last minute, Tarzan or one of his friendly apes always came to the rescue.

Today's business world mirrors Tarzan's jungle in that pitfalls and hazards seem to await the problem solver at every turn.

See things as you would have them be instead of as they are." --Robert Collier

The Collier quote highlights what almost every professional athlete has in common with Albert Einstein. Each of them spent many hours visualizing his success before it actually materialized. Nikola Tesla, another scientist, visualized his inventions piece by piece before he built them. In support of using creative visualization to overcome obstacles, recent medical studies have shown a great deal of problem-solving activity actually takes place at a subconscious level.

This topic will provide you with the tools needed to tap into those hidden problem-solving reserves. You'll learn how to use the components of creative visualization: isolation, relaxation, visualization, and repetition.

It's a good thing rumble strips line most highways today. The jarring noise you hear after veering onto the shoulder signals you to get back on track.

Author Andrew Denton wrote, "Pressure and stress is the common cold of the psyche." In this topic, you'll find out there is indeed a cure for the common cold. You'll learn to overcome the distress of ineffective problem solving by:

- using the big picture technique,
- making a thanksgiving list,
- expressing your feelings.

Moving past roadblocks

In most Tarzan movies, you could count on one or two hapless explorers to fall into a pit of quicksand. No one ever died, of course. At the last minute, Tarzan or one of his friendly apes always came to the rescue.

Today's business world mirrors Tarzan's jungle in that pitfalls and hazards seem to await the problem solver at every turn.

Joel, a bond trader, had trouble moving past his initial stress and lack of inspiration and on to trading success. He then took direct measures to remove those roadblocks. Select each comment to receive Joel's insight.

Confidence

"The strategies I used to eliminate obstacles really worked. Once I overcame a few initial failures, I was much more confident in my ability to bounce back."

More time, less stress

"Those strategies were especially valuable because they gave me more time to focus on other business matters. I even noticed less stress in my personal life."

Question

Once you remove problem-solving roadblocks, you're well on your way to success. Choose the statements that reflect the values of using dynamic strategies to successfully move past roadblocks.

Options:

1. You'll find your personal life will probably be less stressful.
2. You'll be more confident in your ability to recover from setbacks.
3. You'll have more time to concentrate on other business issues.
4. You'll find that many important business problems will seem to solve themselves.

Answer:

Actually, you'll have a less stressful personal life, be more confident in your "bounce-back" ability, and have more time to focus on other business issues. On the other hand, business problems usually require work on your behalf to solve them.

Option 1: Correct. Successfully overcoming problem-solving roadblocks at work will build your confidence, and that confidence can spill over into your personal life, reducing stress overall.

Option 2: Correct. The confidence you develop after overcoming the first few problem-solving roadblocks will make you better able to deal with setbacks that arise in the future.

Option 3: Correct. If you are not spending large amounts of time struggling with problem-solving roadblocks because of your new-found ability to deal with them, you'll have more time to focus on other business issues.

Option 4: This option is incorrect. Business problems rarely solve themselves, and it is a mistake to wait for that to happen. It is your ability to apply effective problem-solving techniques that will solve the business problems.

Olympic hurdlers will tell you success boils down to one thing: technique. In this lesson, you'll learn effective strategies for leaping past roadblocks:

- using creative visualization,
- handling problem overload.
-

Creative visualization

"See things as you would have them be instead of as they are." --Robert Collier

The Collier quote highlights what almost every professional athlete has in common with Albert Einstein. Each of them spent many hours visualizing his success before it actually materialized. Nikola Tesla, another scientist, visualized his inventions piece by piece before he built them. In support of using creative visualization to overcome obstacles, recent medical studies have shown a great deal of problem-solving activity actually takes place at a subconscious level.

This topic will provide you with the tools needed to tap into those hidden problem-solving reserves. You'll learn how to use the components of creative visualization: isolation, relaxation, visualization, and repetition.

You should use creative visualization not only when your problem-solving efforts become stymied, but even when you're experiencing success. The first component of creative visualization is isolation. Retreat to a peaceful setting in which you can:

- eliminate all external noise,
- eliminate any visual distractions,
- habitually return to and associate with positive emotions.

After you've isolated yourself from distractions, you're ready to let go of any stress you've built up while generating alternative solutions to a business problem. It's time for conscious relaxation.

See each piece of advice to get tips on relaxation from Marianne, a marketing manager for a large parcel shipping company.

Get comfortable

"After retreating to my office, I start the process of relaxing by sitting down in my chair. Sometimes I even sit on the floor."

Quiet your mind

"Next, I close my eyes and just sit motionless for a few minutes. My mind is usually racing with thoughts and ideas at first. I take those "hamsters off the wheel" by simply listening to the silence and cutting those thoughts short as soon as they surface. It takes practice, but don't give up."

Relax your body

"Once my mind's calm, I relax my body by slowly counting down from one to ten. On each count, I exhale and imagine the tension in my body flooding out my lungs and disappearing into the air. It sometimes takes a few minutes to completely relax, but somehow I know when I've arrived."

Now totally quiet and relaxed, Marianne is ready to practice the third component of this technique, visualization. Visualization is an active process. It entails forming and rehearsing mental images of your problem in a resolved state. In other words, you don't allow your mind to simply wander at will.

See each comment to find out more from Marianne.

Problems resolved

"When visualizing my business problems in a resolved state, I imagine how it would feel to have my obstacles removed and what that would actually look like. Don't focus on potential solutions or obstacles--only on the achieved solution."

Example: Running meetings

"For example, I have a problem running meetings in an authoritative way. So I picture myself being confident and decisive in that setting. I do this over and over until it genuinely feels real. It's almost the same as actually doing it."

Example: Shipping problem

"We recently had a shipping delay problem. Instead of reaching for knee-jerk solutions, I visualized our operations running with complete efficiency. I pictured what that outcome would look like, and a unique solution became apparent."

Generates solutions

"This visualization process is a great way to blow off steam. But I've also found that concentrating on feelings of success often spontaneously generates once-hidden solutions. I like to call that an "a-ha" experience."

Marianne knew if she couldn't picture productive problem-solving outcomes, they would probably continue to elude her. In the same way actors rehearse their roles, Marianne's practicing of success made it that much easier to obtain.

Lastly, Marianne realized the key to getting the most from creative visualization lay in making this technique habitual: that success resulted from repetition. Just as miners repeatedly dig past the surface for the ore that lies beneath, your subconscious mind doesn't surrender its riches unless you continually access them. And once you've excavated that initial shaft, it becomes easier and easier to bring up the goods.

Question

Practice what you've learned. How do you want your future to look? Identify the components of creative visualization.

Options:

1. mentally picturing a successful outcome
2. removing yourself from distractions
3. relaxing both your body and your mind
4. performing the process only once
5. imagining why solutions aren't available
6. letting your mind wander without focus

Answer:

In fact, the correct answers include isolation, relaxation, and visualization. On the other hand, you should repeat the process numerous times, avoid thinking about potential solutions, and not simply let your mind wander.

Option 1: This option is correct. Picturing what a successful outcome looks like is the third step of creative visualization. This is where you don't focus on potential solutions or Option 3: Option 2: This is a correct choice. Relaxing your body and mind is the second step of creative visualization. Once you've isolated yourself, you get comfortable, quiet your mind, and relax your body.

Option 3: This is a correct choice. Relaxing your body and mind is the second step of creative visualization. Once you've isolated yourself, you get comfortable, quiet your mind, and relax your body.

Option 4: This choice is incorrect. In fact, repetition is an important aspect of successful creative visualization. Making the process habitual offers the best chance of creative solutions.

Option 5: This choice is incorrect. Imagining why solutions aren't available is counterproductive. During the visualization stage of creative visualization, you will focus only on the achieved solution.

Option 6: This choice is incorrect. Letting your mind wander will not help you find a creative solution. When you are relaxing, you must empty your mind of the typical idle chatter of thoughts.

After effectively using the components of creative visualization tested in the previous question, the entire process becomes second nature. Plus, the benefits of creative visualization multiply exponentially with its continued use.

In this topic, you learned how to use the components of creative visualization: isolation, relaxation, visualization, and repetition.

Overcoming the distress of ineffective problem solving

It's a good thing rumble strips line most highways today. The jarring noise you hear after veering onto the shoulder signals you to get back on track.

Author Andrew Denton wrote, "Pressure and stress is the common cold of the psyche." In this topic, you'll find out there is indeed a cure for the common cold. You'll learn to overcome the distress of ineffective problem solving by:

- using the big picture technique,
- making a thanksgiving list,
- expressing your feelings.

The first strategy for overcoming the distress of ineffective problem solving is using the big picture technique. This strategy entails purposely shifting your perspective. Rather than focusing inward on your own distress, turn your attention outward, to others, and enlarge your perception of the circumstances.

Select each social comparison element to get tips from Claude, a psychologist, on using the big picture technique.

Downward social comparison

"When your distress over ineffective problem solving mounts, it's helpful to consider the plights of others even more stressed than you. Your aim isn't to evoke pity, but rather to realize that your business problems aren't as severe as they could be."

Example of downward social comparison

"Pick up a newspaper on any given day. The front section will likely be filled with stories about people experiencing huge setbacks and losses of one sort or another. It usually takes only a cursory reading to put my less serious concerns in a more realistic and favorable light."

Upward social comparison

"On the other hand, I like to recall others who have achieved great personal or business success. Rather than feeling jealous over their status, I feel inspired to duplicate their success."

Example of upward social comparison

"The superintendent in my building arrived in this country with big dreams and empty pockets. He worked much harder than I ever could have to ensure his family was happy and secure. I look to him when I'm overloaded by problems, and I experience a real spark of motivation."

Take your hands from the keyboard for a moment and take out a sheet of paper. Make a note of and briefly describe five aspects of your life you're immensely thankful for. Afterward, proceed to the next page.

Did you identify five things you're thankful for? Congratulations on already using the second strategy for overcoming the distress of ineffective problem solving, making a thanksgiving list. This strategy may seem a bit corny to some, but it's actually a great way to re-envision your problems. For most people, dwelling on negative, stressful aspects of work and life comes easily. Sadly, so does forgetting about the positive things. Thanksgiving lists give you a boost by redirecting your attention to the more important issues.

So important is sharing your feelings with friends or colleagues that it qualifies as the third and perhaps most effective strategy to overcome the distress of ineffective problem solving.

Your goal is not to start a mutual gripe session, but to express your real feelings and the reasons behind them to another person. This practice relieves your stress and builds stronger ties between you and your confidant.

Question

Just as you proactively attack business problems, take active measures to combat the stress that results from those problems. Select correct descriptions of strategies for overcoming the distress of ineffective problem solving.

Options:

1. The big picture technique entails examining problems within a larger perspective.
2. A thanksgiving list entails listing reasons you're fortunate.
3. When you express your feelings to others, you unburden pent-up emotions.
4. The big picture technique lets you think how alternative solutions may work in the long term.

Answer:

In fact, the big picture technique involves gaining an expanded perspective; a thanksgiving list highlights reasons you're fortunate; and expressing your feelings lets you rid yourself of pent-up emotions.

Option 1: Correct. The big picture technique will help to combat stress by using both downward (thinking of those worse off) and upward (thinking of those better off) social comparisons to enlarge your perception of the circumstances.

Option 2: Correct. While this may seem corny, a thanksgiving list is a good way to re-envision your problems. A thanksgiving list will give you a boost by redirecting your attention to the more important issues.

Option 3: This is a correct choice. Expressing your feeling to a confidant is possibly the most effective strategy to overcome the stress associated with ineffective problem solving. It relieves your stress and builds stronger ties.

Option 4: This choice is incorrect because the big picture technique pertains to looking at your situation relative to other more and less fortunate people, not alternative solutions.

When you use the strategies tested on the previous page, you gain a new perspective on your business problems. That shift in perspective not only negates some of the distress you experience from ineffectively solving problems, but also gives you a motivational shot in the arm. And sometimes that's all you need to overcome the problem-solving roadblocks in your path.

In this topic, you learned how to use strategies to overcome the distress of ineffective problem solving: using the big picture technique, making a thanksgiving list, and expressing your feelings to a friend or colleague.

Generating alternative solutions, as you learned, represents one of the more rewarding, and demanding, problem-solving challenges you face. This course equipped you with dynamic strategies to successfully meet that challenge. You discovered techniques for:

- getting into the flow,
- taking rational approaches,
- using creative approaches,
- getting out of a problem-solving rut.

CHAPTER FOUR

Making Decisions Dynamically

Decision Making is Hard Work

To sail his fishing boat safely into harbor, Jason had to consider many factors--wind, hidden reefs, tidal currents--all the while maintaining his balance on the deck. With any luck, Jason brought his "sea legs" on the outing.

After you generate solutions to a business problem, it's time to haul in the net and get your catch to shore. In business, you too have to earn your "decision-making legs."

As with sailing, many factors influence the decision or decisions you eventually make, such as timing, focus, and mind-set. This lesson will help you understand those factors and effectively prepare you for the decision implementation stage.

If you violated one of your elementary school's principles, you probably were summoned to the principal's office.

Violate a principle of decision making, and you'll probably end up in your supervisor's office having to explain the decision you made. In this topic, you'll learn how to avoid that unpleasant trip by practicing principles of sound decision making:

- focusing on the future,
- examining the timing,
- considering linked decisions.

On Oscar night, reporters rate the celebrities according to best- and worst-dressed. The ones who garner the most style points usually receive the most publicity.

You'll grab the decision-making headlines if you use the most effective style to make business choices. In this topic, you'll learn about various decision-making styles and how to adopt the most effective one. You'll explore:

- the reflexive style,
- the emotional style,
- the analytical style,
- the comprehensive style.

Factors that influence decision making

To sail his fishing boat safely into harbor, Jason had to consider many factors--wind, hidden reefs, tidal currents--all the while maintaining his balance on the deck. With any luck, Jason brought his "sea legs" on the outing.

After you generate solutions to a business problem, it's time to haul in the net and get your catch to shore. In business, you too have to earn your "decision-making legs."

As with sailing, many factors influence the decision or decisions you eventually make, such as timing, focus, and mind-set. This lesson will help you understand those factors and effectively prepare you for the decision implementation stage.

Understanding and mastering the various factors that influence decision making is both valuable and crucial.

Question

A single decision results from a host of problem-solving variables. Which of these statements reflect the value of understanding the factors that influence decision making?

Options:

1. You'll be more assured that you're reducing unforeseen complications.
2. You'll be able to communicate every decision with authority.
3. You'll gain the confidence of your co-workers more readily.
4. You'll enjoy saving time as a result of effective decision making.

Answers:

In fact, you'll be more assured you're avoiding unforeseen complications, enjoy saving time, and gain the confidence of your colleagues. On the other hand, communication and decision making are separate domains.

Option 1: This is a correct choice. The more that is known about a problem, the less likely it is that important or relevant issues will be overlooked. This makes it easier to come up with a viable and effective solution.

Option 2: This choice is incorrect. Understanding the factors that influence decision making won't affect how you communicate the decision. It actually makes the decision-making process more efficient.

Option 3: Correct. If your co-workers know that your decisions are carefully researched and logically reasoned, they're much more likely to accept your conclusions.

Option 4: This is a correct choice. Decisions that result from a good understanding of the decision-making process will stick. They won't have to be repeatedly re-visited or re-evaluated--and that will save time.

You're about to focus on the ingredients that comprise skillful decision making. In this lesson, you'll learn to factor the following aspects into your business decisions:

- the mechanics of effective decision making,
- the various decision-making styles.

Sound decision-making principles

If you violated one of your elementary school's principles, you probably were summoned to the principal's office.

Violate a principle of decision making, and you'll probably end up in your supervisor's office having to explain the decision you made. In this topic, you'll learn how to avoid that unpleasant trip by practicing principles of sound decision making:

- focusing on the future,
- examining the timing,
- considering linked decisions.

Question

Think back to a business decision you made in the past that didn't work out as planned. When solving related problems today, do you shape your decision based on that previous mistake?

Options:

1. yes

2. No

Answer:

The answer is yes. It's wise to learn from the past. At the same time, orient your decisions to the future and to the benefits that may accrue from your present-day choice.

Option 1: This is the correct choice. It's very important to learn from experience. When you take the time to analyze where the decision-making process went wrong, you can avoid that pitfall in the future, and make better decisions.

Option 2: Incorrect. Think about it. If you don't learn from past mistakes, you're doomed to repeat them. Learning better decision-making skills is a process in which it's very important to take lessons from your mistakes.

Author Roy W. Williams made an illuminating comment regarding the first principle of sound decision making, focusing on the future: "After you're in a hole, it's no use to continue digging." In other words, you have to base your decisions today on the results desired in the future. If you're mired in the past, the ladder to success will always be out of reach.

For example, "sunk costs" denote funds already spent on certain options. Say you've made poor decisions about a new product. You may feel pressured to stand by your choices because of the money spent. But the initial cost of the campaign shouldn't influence your future decisions to revise your efforts.

Instead, when making choices, consider upcoming cash outlays and the benefits you expect to follow. Your commitment is to future results and not to past mistakes.

The second principle of sound decision making is examining the timing of your decisions. It's often said that timing is everything, and that rule of thumb holds true in decision making.

Lastly, you need to consider decision linkages. Decisions you make at work never affect just you. They ultimately ripple across departments and often to the customer. Ask yourself this simple question before acting on a business solution: "How and where am I adding value to my organization through my decision?"

See each area to discover how Gene thought about the links between one of his decisions and the people around him.

the department

"I toyed with the idea of expanding our operations to international markets. The prospect excited me. But first I had to consider the effect of this decision on my colleagues. What training was necessary? Would we have to increase our staff? Was I adding value to the department?"

other departments

"Branching out so boldly would impact other departments as well. The marketing folks would have to change their promotional approach completely. And the human resources department would need to study up on a host of new and complex regulations."

customers

"Then there's the customer. I questioned whether the move would negatively affect existing customers. What's the value of gaining a new market if it means neglecting an existing one? I decided to take more time and carefully examine all the implications of my proposed decision."

Question

Before you even begin a decision-making effort, know the fundamentals involved in this business activity. From this list, select the descriptions of sound decision-making principles.

Options:

1. Considering decision linkages entails maximizing the value of your decisions.

2. Focusing on the future entails basing your decisions on future benefits.

3. Examining the timing means always trying to beat the competition to market.

4. Considering decision linkages means making multiple choices about the same problem.

Answer:

In fact, you should link your decisions to maximize your companywide value. Focus on the future by examining future benefits. Conversely, effective decision timing may not require being the first to market a product or service.

Option 1: Correct. You should link your decisions to maximize your companywide value. When you know what other functions, people, or departments will be affected, you can make decisions that are best for everybody.

Option 2: This is a correct choice. Focus on the future by contemplating a decision's potential future advantages. This will help you make the best decisions to help your company achieve long-term goals and objectives.

Option 3: Incorrect. Effective decision timing may not require being the first to market a product or service. It's more important to consider decision linkages and focus on the future.

Option 4: This choice is incorrect. Considering decision linkages means maximizing your companywide value. Focus on the future by examining future benefits. It doesn't necessarily involve multiple choices about the same problem.

Luckily, the builders of the Leaning Tower of Pisa installed an impressive foundation before erecting the tower itself. Similarly, when you put the principles you practiced in the previous exercise to work when choosing among business options, you proceed from a solid decision-making foundation.

In this topic, you learned about principles of sound decision making: focusing on the future, examining the timing, and considering decision linkages.

Decision-making styles

On Oscar night, reporters rate the celebrities according to best- and worst-dressed. The ones who garner the most style points usually receive the most publicity.

You'll grab the decision-making headlines if you use the most effective style to make business choices. In this topic, you'll learn about various decision-making styles and how to adopt the most effective one. You'll explore:

- the reflexive style,
- the emotional style,
- the analytical style,
- the comprehensive style.

The first decision-making style is the reflexive style. When you wield the reflexive style, your decision-making weapons are very blunt. That's because you choose among solutions using only reflex and gut instinct, reacting to decisions rather than consciously making them.

Like animals, people with a reflexive style exhibit a flight-or-fight response to decisions. They often adopt the most convenient solution, even though the easy way out is actually the most inefficient route to success.

Using the second decision-making style, the emotional style, may also lead to hasty, inaccurate decisions. People using the emotional style follow their hearts and ignore their heads. When anger, stress, and other internal motivators constitute the primary basis for business decisions, effectiveness usually suffers.

Emotions can't be the unimportant factor that guides important decision making. As you'll learn, relying solely on this or any other one mode of decision-making style restricts your abilities and leashes your effectiveness.

The third decision-making style is the analytical style. This approach opposes the emotional style in that the analytical decision maker, like Mr. Spock from the popular television series "Star Trek," thinks about problems only from a logical, rational standpoint. Because some choices indeed require that you take intuition, emotions, and experience into account, the analytical decision maker limits his horizons by standing only in the cold light of reason.

Lastly, it's your goal as a decision maker to assume the best of all possible styles to solve business problems, the comprehensive style.

See each style, in order, to find out why Carol, a medical research scientist, adopted a comprehensive decision-making style.

Deliberate

"I've found I make the best decisions after carefully considering each and every option. I recently had to decide which scientific protocol to use on a certain experiment at work. I gave myself a period of time to just sit and think about it. As my boss says, only jerks make knee-jerk decisions."

Multifaceted

"Early in my career, I was too rigid in my approach to decision making. I now realize that to be truly effective, I need to draw on my experience and intuition as well as my thinking and feelings. The sum is truly greater than its parts."

Flexible

"At the same time, I realize some decisions require more logic than intuition. I never ignore any decision-making technique, but I remain flexible enough to place more emphasis on one than another when necessary."

Question

When it comes to making decisions, do you have style? Match each decision-making style to one or more descriptions.

Options:

A. the reflexive style

B. the analytical style

C. the emotional style

D. the comprehensive style

Targets:

1. uses experience, knowledge, and an array of other sources

2. reacts instinctively rather than making conscious choices

3. relies strictly on logic and reasoning to make decisions

4. makes a decision based on feelings and motivations

5. employs numerous decision-making techniques

Answers:

In fact, the reflexive style entails reaction rather than action, the emotional style centers on internal motivations, the analytical style relies heavily on logic, and the comprehensive style draws on a host of appropriate techniques and approaches.

The comprehensive style draws on a host of appropriate techniques and approaches. This is the best of all possible styles to solve business problems.

The reflexive style uses these kinds of inner motivations and feelings to make decisions. But keep in mind that this style may cause decision makers to adopt an inefficient route to success.

The analytical style relies heavily on logic, and chooses solutions that are truly sensible. This may limit the decision maker's horizons, since he or she stands only in the cold light of reason.

The emotional style centers on internal motivations. People using this style follow their hearts and ignore their heads, which may also lead to hasty, inaccurate decisions.

The comprehensive style draws on an array of appropriate techniques. This is the best of all possible styles to solve business problems.

As you noticed in the previous exercise, there are big differences among the decision-making styles. Be smart and adopt the comprehensive approach. In this topic, you learned about several decision-making styles:

- the reflexive style,
- the emotional style,
- the analytical style,
- the comprehensive style.

Decision Making in Action

The thought you put into a business decision is a lot like the fuel you put into a car. Unless there's a concrete, engineered method of putting that thought to work, all your potential decision-making energy will simply burn up or evaporate.

However, when you use specific, measured decision-making techniques, you harness your thinking to its fullest extent. And the strategies you're about to learn in this lesson will only add to your fuel efficiency.

Think of a PMI analysis as a type of scale on which you weigh the merits of a potential business decision. Regardless of the direction in which the balance eventually tips, you'll find out whether the decision has the substance necessary to justify its undertaking.

The first step in a PMI analysis is to list the pluses of the potential decision. Pluses are any prospective advantages or gains you expect to receive shortly after implementing the business decision in question.

After you list the pluses, assign each a score between +1 and +5. A score of +1 signifies a negligible advantage, while a score of +5 represents a strong, much-desired benefit.

Imagine this: After turning in your master's thesis on decision making, your professor points out that you repeatedly misspelled "matrix." What do you do?

It's simple: You correct the spelling of that word. You certainly don't rewrite your entire thesis. That solution would be neither easy nor effective.

Prioritizing business decisions works in much the same way. You place more emphasis on solutions that are both easy and effective. In this topic, you'll learn how to perform the steps in using an ease-and-effect matrix to prioritize potential business solutions:

- rating solutions according to "ease" of implementation,
- rating solutions according to "effect" of implementation.

Some people insist that money makes the world go around. Whether you agree or disagree, don't make business decisions without adding it all up. In this topic, you learned how to perform steps of a return-on-investment measure to evaluate the financial prospects of a given business decision.

Those steps were: establishing revenue projections, specifying anticipated expenditures, and calculating the resulting net cash flow.

To make sound decisions, you need to be devilishly sly. In this topic, you'll learn how to use the devil's advocacy technique to evaluate a proposed business decision. The steps of this technique are:

- listing the evidence opposing your business decision,
- explaining both sides of the argument to a colleague and getting his or her input.

Using decision-making techniques

"My basic principle is that you don't make decisions because they are easy; you don't make them because they are cheap; you don't make them because they are popular; you make them because they're right." --Theodore Hesburgh

Question

Hesburgh, president emeritus of the University of Notre Dame, sheds light on the appropriate motivation behind all decisions, business, and otherwise. But how do you arrive at a "right" decision?

How about you? Are your business decisions the result of extensive thought? Or do you feel that, given enough alternatives, the right decision becomes naturally apparent?

Options:

1. They're naturally apparent.
2. Most of them are apparent.
3. I'm neutral.

4. Most of them require thought.
5. They require thought.

Answers:

Option 1: Unless circumstances force your back to the wall, most business decisions call for elaborate thought. Thought alone, however, isn't sufficient. You must structure your thinking using deliberate decision-making techniques.

Option 2: Unless circumstances force your back to the wall, most business decisions call for elaborate thought. Thought alone, however, isn't sufficient. You must structure your thinking using deliberate decision-making techniques.

Option 3: Unless circumstances force your back to the wall, most business decisions call for elaborate thought. Thought alone, however, isn't sufficient. You must structure your thinking using deliberate decision-making techniques.

Option 4: Unless circumstances force your back to the wall, most business decisions call for elaborate thought. Thought alone, however, isn't sufficient. You must structure your thinking using deliberate decision-making techniques.

Option 5: Unless circumstances force your back to the wall, most business decisions call for elaborate thought. Thought alone, however, isn't sufficient. You must structure your thinking using deliberate decision-making techniques.

The thought you put into a business decision is a lot like the fuel you put into a car. Unless there's a concrete, engineered method of putting that thought to work, all your potential decision-making energy will simply burn up or evaporate.

However, when you use specific, measured decision-making techniques, you harness your thinking to its fullest extent. And the strategies you're about to learn in this lesson will only add to your fuel efficiency.

The benefits of purposely using decision-making techniques multiply with their continued use. For one, these techniques help reduce the uncertainty about success that accompanies any decision implementation.

Question

Toss a coin to determine who buys lunch. Use more comprehensive techniques to make business decisions. Which of these statements reflect a benefit of skillfully using decision-making techniques?

Options:

1. You'll be more assured you're reducing personal decision-making biases.
2. You'll enjoy less uncertainty about success while implementing the decision.
3. You'll be able to better substantiate your rationale behind the decision.
4. You'll be able to choose from a larger number of alternative decisions.

Answer:

In fact, you'll be more assured you're reducing personal biases, enjoy less uncertainty during implementation, and better demonstrate your decision rationale. On the other hand, solution generation took place before making your decision.

Option 1: This is a correct choice. Personal biases can lead to poor business decisions. There are many factors that need to be considered, and the repercussions of a bad decision can be severe.

Option 2: Correct. You don't want to be worrying about whether you made the right decision in the course of implementation. Second-guessing yourself causes delays and undermines the confidence of management and co-workers.

Option 3: Correct. Decision makers have to answer for their results, and a good decision-making process is an excellent way to cover yourself. If you can explain your rationale, you can convince others that you made the right decision.

Option 4: This choice is incorrect. A good decision-making process should actually narrow your choices to a few good ones. If many options seem equally viable, you're probably not using a good technique.

If all your business decisions yielded desired results 100 percent of the time, you probably can exit this course and get back to work. Chances are, though, that your "hit rate" is less than perfect, in which case you can vastly improve your decision-making skills by adopting the proven methodology presented in this lesson.

You're about to learn how to use dynamic techniques to analyze the merits of a single decision, choose among multiple options, make decisions with more than one party, and examine the financial aspect of a decision.

The PMI analysis

Nathan and Sally couldn't decide whether to buy the old house. The home had pluses, minuses, and several "interesting" aspects.

How should they assess their potential decision? One way would be to conduct a PMI analysis, in which you evaluate a decision by weighing its pluses, minuses, and "interesting" aspects. In this topic, you'll learn how to perform the steps of a PMI analysis:

- List the pluses of the decision.
- List the minuses of the decision.
- List the "interesting" aspects of the decision.
- Analyze the results.

Think of a PMI analysis as a type of scale on which you weigh the merits of a potential business decision. Regardless of the direction in which the balance eventually tips, you'll find out whether the decision has the substance necessary to justify its undertaking.

The first step in a PMI analysis is to list the pluses of the potential decision. Pluses are any prospective advantages or gains you expect to receive shortly after implementing the business decision in question.

After you list the pluses, assign each a score between +1 and +5. A score of +1 signifies a negligible advantage, while a score of +5 represents a strong, much-desired benefit.

See the advantages to see how Warren, a product manager for an automobile tire manufacturer, listed the pluses of his company's proposed decision to use a new rubber polymer in its tires.

first to market

"This newly developed polymer, which no other automobile tire maker has capitalized on, extends tire wear by a full 33 percent. By being the first company to market this enhancement, we would capture and maintain significant market share. I gave this big plus a score of +4."

enhanced brand image

"Our company's known for manufacturing budget tires. This market niche is stagnant at best. By introducing a tire of superior quality, our brand image would at least moderately improve. I assigned this advantage of the decision a +2."

synergy with other products

"We could also use this polymer in new products, such as tractor and motorcycle tires. In other words, the polymer would make for a strong entry into markets we don't currently occupy but need to. That's why I assigned this decision plus a score of +3."

fewer returns and repairs

"Because the polymer is more stable and lasting than standard tire rubbers, we'd be seeing fewer of them returned and in need of repair. In this business, that translates to big savings. So in my PMI analysis, that translated to a rating of +4."

Did you notice that Warren scored the pluses of his potential decision using subjective ratings? That's fine. PMI analyses purposely incorporate often-neglected factors such as emotion and intuition into the decision-making mix.

After listing the pluses of his possible decision, Warren took the second step of his PMI analysis and listed the minuses of the decision.

Any potential near-term drawback or liability associated with your proposed business decision represents a minus in your PMI analysis. You score minuses on a scale from a relatively inconsequential -1 to a catastrophic -5.

Select the disadvantages to discover Warren's thinking as it concerned the minuses of the proposed tire polymer decision.

potentially neutral consumer reaction

"It's possible, although unlikely, that consumers will give our new tires the cold shoulder. I viewed total product failure as only a flimsy possibility. That's why I gave that minus a score of -1."

increased employee training

"Of course, we'd have to train our assembly line workers on new manufacturing processes. This could be easily accomplished using Web-based training, though. That's why I assigned this aspect a score of -2. It just wasn't a big deal."

purchase of new machinery

"On the other hand, the new machinery required to manufacture the tires would call for a fairly significant initial investment. This minus received a score of -4 in my PMI analysis."

unreliable polymer supply

"The scarcity of the polymer worried me. The supply fluctuated almost as much as the commodities markets. I found out three new manufacturers had just ramped up their output and projections were looking much better. Still, I assigned this concern a score of -2 just to be safe."

Warren, having listed and scored the pluses and minuses, took the third step of his PMI analysis and listed the "interesting" aspects of the proposed polymer decision. Interesting aspects are the extended implications of taking any business action. They can either be pluses or minuses in your analysis. Think about the long term here, perhaps six months to even a few years past the possible decision implementation.

The ease-and-effect matrix

Imagine this: After turning in your master's thesis on decision making, your professor points out that you repeatedly misspelled "matrix." What do you do?

It's simple: You correct the spelling of that word. You certainly don't rewrite your entire thesis. That solution would be neither easy nor effective.

Prioritizing business decisions works in much the same way. You place more emphasis on solutions that are both easy and effective. In this topic, you'll learn how to perform the steps in using an ease-and-effect matrix to prioritize potential business solutions:

- rating solutions according to "ease" of implementation,
- rating solutions according to "effect" of implementation,
- placing rated solutions in the matrix and prioritizing them.

Sarah was ready to throw in the towel. She had been executing the legal work of a large box manufacturer for a number of years and had not yet been fully compensated. What income Sarah did receive, however, she relied on at this stage in her career. She devised six alternative solutions to her predicament, including discontinuing the relationship altogether. Sarah wondered which decision held the most promise.

She constructed an ease-and-effect matrix in order to prioritize her ideas.

First, Sarah rated each of her potential solutions according to its "ease" of implementation. Sarah knew some of her proposed solutions would take less work to implement than others.

See each step to learn how she started her ease-and-effect matrix.

Solutions evaluated

"I evaluated each of my solutions according to how easy it would be to pull it off. At this stage, I didn't consider the consequences of the decisions. I was only concerned with the amount of effort each decision would take to carry through."

Solutions rated

"I then rated the ease of each idea on a scale from 1 to 3, with 3 being the easiest."

Solution 1

"The first solution to my client problem that came to mind was to simply discontinue the relationship. This would be easy--I'd just notify the box maker by mail. That's why I gave the ease of this particular decision a rating of 3."

Solution 2

"I also considered bartering with the client, who was located downtown. I'd love to be able to park in the client's lot while I'm doing business in that area of the city. That idea would require some negotiation, so I assigned it a rating of 2."

Solution 3

"It would require a great deal of time and work to file a suit against my client. Because the lawsuit idea wouldn't be easy to implement, I gave this potential solution a rating of 1."

Once ease ratings were assigned, Sarah took the next step and used the same scale to rate each idea according to its "effect" if implemented. In this technique, "effect" refers to a solution's overall impact on all business sectors of your company, or in Sarah's case, her legal practice.

Sarah thinking

"The lawsuit idea, which has an ease rating of 1, might harm my ability to attract other clients."

Sarah concerned

"A suit would be expensive. Based on these two factors, the effect of this choice on my practice will be minimized. I give the lawsuit idea a low effect rating of 1."

Sarah continued rating each of her proposed solutions according to its anticipated effect on her legal practice. When you perform this step in constructing an ease-and-effect matrix, remember that potential decisions receive an effect rating of:

- 3 for predominantly advantageous effects,
- 2 for a roughly even number of positive and negative effects,
- 1 for mostly negative effects.
-

The nominal group technique

Libby's architectural firm suffered from flagging sales. As sales manager, she had built the company from the ground up. She wasn't about to let her towering achievement plummet.

Libby knew some tough decisions lay ahead. So she assembled a team of colleagues and used the nominal group technique to select among potential sales solutions. In this topic, you'll follow Libby's progress and learn how a team effectively performs the steps of the nominal group technique:

- anonymously voting on initial favored solutions,
- recording the votes in round-robin fashion,
- clarifying any confusing ideas,
- evaluating the final solutions.

Libby's team included several members who were particularly vocal about their opinions. She wanted to reduce the potentially biasing effect of those colleagues. The nominal group technique was a perfect way to achieve her aim because it limits an individual's input to short explanations and relies on anonymous voting to choose among alternative solutions.

In the meeting, Libby passed around a checklist detailing the potential solutions the team had previously generated. Libby then instructed each member to take the first step in the nominal group technique: Anonymously vote for his initial favored solutions.

Before Libby listed the ideas she favored--expanding into the residential market and developing office complexes instead of stand-alone buildings--she passed out notecards on which team members could write their preferences.

See the steps Libby took to find out more about how she conducted this part of the nominal group technique.

Writing solutions

"I told team members to write down their preferred two or three solutions to our sales crisis."

Voting anonymously

"By keeping the voting anonymous, Melvin and Peggy weren't able to bully the others into adopting only the solutions they favored."

After team members jotted down their votes, Libby took the next step in the nominal group technique and recorded the votes in round-robin fashion.

See each step to discover how Libby regimented this part so she again ensured that all ideas received equal emphasis.

Display the results for all to see.

"I usually bring an overhead projector or dry-erase board to the meeting. It's important that all team members see the voting results as they're recorded. We'll revisit them again after this step."

Start the recording process.

"I'm left-handed. Maybe that explains why I always start by asking the person on my left to announce his or her first preferred solution. In this case, Rose endorsed the possibility of shifting our attention to suburban clients. Growth in our urban area had slowed. I wrote that idea on the overhead."

Write down ideas, not votes.

"After Rose was finished, I asked the person next to her for his vote. When I recorded the idea, I simply wrote down a description of that solution. No tally marks were made. I then moved to the next person, and then the next person, and so on."

Continue the recording process.

"After Rose voted for focusing our sales efforts on suburban areas, other team members who had voted for and written down that idea were not allowed to revote for that solution. Instead, they simply said "pass," and the next member took the floor and announced a new idea."

With the initial votes duly recorded, Libby moved on to the next step of the nominal group technique and instructed group members to clarify any confusing ideas.

See each stage, in order, to get a feel for the strict ground rules Libby enforced while performing this step.

Allow queries

"Our firm primarily designs commercial office spaces. Roy wanted some clarification on the potential solution to expand into the residential market."

Clarify ideas

"Emily had been the first to vote on it. I told her to briefly clarify and explain that proposed solution. In other words, she gave Roy the high-level version of her solution. I didn't allow Emily to elaborate on the minutiae."

Prevent pitches

"I made it completely clear that whenever a member clarified an idea for another, there would be no "selling" involved. This didn't please some members, but persuasion has no place in the nominal group technique."

Allow further clarification

"When the questions died down, I asked if anyone required further clarification on any of the solutions. There was no use continuing to the next stage if everyone wasn't on the same page."

By clarifying any confusing ideas, Libby cleared the way for the next step, in which her team evaluated the final solutions. The nominal group will often list ten or more possible solutions.

Return-on-investment

"If your outgo exceeds your income, then your upkeep will be your downfall." --Bill Earle, business executive

Question

Mr. Earle encapsulated the need to study all potential business decisions under a financial microscope.

How about you? Do you make a practice of examining your business decisions with the financial ramifications in mind?

Options:

1. never
2. seldom
3. sometimes
4. usually
5. always

Answer:

In the movie "Wall Street," one of the characters remarked, "Money doesn't sleep." You should always be awake to the need to consider the financial aspects of your business decisions.

One way to be money-wise is to use a return-on-investment measure to evaluate your business decisions. In this topic, you'll learn that steps of such a measure include:

- establishing revenue projections,
- specifying anticipated expenditures,
- calculating the resulting net cash flow.

Gary, vice president of a computer software company, couldn't decide whether to market a new Internet browser program. He wisely chose to use a return-on-investment measure to investigate the browser's merit. The first step he took was to establish the projected revenues that would result from the action.

See each stage to find out how Gary began his return-on-investment analysis.

Time frame

"As with most other projects, I like to look ten years down the line. How much money did I think the decision to market the browser platform would generate over that length of time? I pored over product analyses as well as industry revenue projections to determine those figures."

Subjectivity

"Naturally, many of these estimates are subjective. That's why I obtained input from the accounting department to help guide me. I quantified as many aspects of the potential revenue stream as I could and let my business intuition guide me the rest of the way."

After establishing the software revenue projections, Gary took the next step in his return-on-investment measure and specified the anticipated expenditures of his potential decision.

These cash outlays will vary from project to project. Gary's estimated expenditures were the development of the product itself, promotional costs, and administrative expenditures.

Gary avoided making the mistake of including "sunk costs" in his expenditure assessment. Sunk costs are funds already spent on certain aspects of a decision, such as existing staff, equipment, and facilities.

Gary's last step in his return-on-investment measure was to calculate the resulting net cash flow. Essentially, the net cash flow represents the profits you expect to gain from adopting your proposed decision.

See the calculation steps, in order, to find out just how attractive Gary's proposed decision turned out to be.

Step 1

"In order to calculate the net cash flow from my potential software project, I first totaled the estimated after-tax revenues over the ten-year forecast."

Step 2

"Then I subtracted the anticipated cash outlays. Keep in mind that the expenditures above don't include any sunk costs."

Final returns

"According to my return on investment measure, I could expect to net $450,000 by the end of the ten years following implementation."

To obtain the net cash flow of his decision, Gary subtracted the anticipated expenditures from his revenue projections.

Gary also expressed the return on investment in the form of a percentage. He divided the net cash flow, $450,000, by the expenditures, $265,000, to get a return of 170 percent over ten years. These kinds of numbers made Gary's decision a lot easier.

Question

Always consider the bottom line when evaluating business decisions. Identify the steps of using a return-on-investment measure to evaluate a potential business decision.

Options:

1. Determine the expected revenue from the decision.
2. Record the anticipated expenditures of the decision.
3. Factor in quantitative risks of undertaking the decision.
4. Tally the resultant net cash flow of the decision.

Answers:

Actually, the steps of a return on investment measure are determining the expected project revenue, recording your anticipated expenditures, and calculating the resulting net cash flow of the project. The other answer is incorrect.

Option 1: Correct. Establishing revenue projections will determine how much money a decision will generate over a length of time. This requires the decision maker to quantify as many aspects of the potential revenue stream as possible.

Option 2: This is a correct choice. It's necessary to subtract anticipated expenditures to calculate net cash flow. These cash outlays, which vary from project to project, may include such costs as development, promotion, and administration.

Option 3: This is an incorrect choice. Quantitative risks are not part of the return-on-investment measure, which includes establishing revenue projections, specifying anticipated expenditures, and calculating the resulting net cash flow.

Option 4: This is a correct choice. The net cash flow represents the profits expected to be gained from adopting a proposed decision. To obtain the net cash flow of a decision, subtract the anticipated expenditures from revenue projections.

Businessman John Howard noted that "You can't fatten the pig on market day." Use the steps covered in the previous exercise and you'll make sure your cash cows fetch a hefty price at market.

Some people insist that money makes the world go around. Whether you agree or disagree, don't make business decisions without adding it all up. In this topic, you learned how to perform steps of a return-on-investment measure to evaluate the financial prospects of a given business decision.

Those steps were: establishing revenue projections, specifying anticipated expenditures, and calculating the resulting net cash flow.

The devil's advocate technique

Why should you not implement your favored, proposed decision? The word "not" in this question may be your best decision-making ally.

Question

Do you agree with this statement?

Before acting on a business decision, it's wise to reconsider all the reasons not to follow through with its implementation.

Options:

1. disagree
2. somewhat disagree
3. neutral
4. somewhat agree
5. agree

Answers:

Option 1: Be decisive after you've committed to a business decision. Beforehand, be smart and review all the evidence for and, more important, against your proposed idea.

Option 2: Be decisive after you've committed to a business decision. Beforehand, be smart and review all the evidence for and, more important, against your proposed idea.

Option 3: Be decisive after you've committed to a business decision. Beforehand, be smart and review all the evidence for and, more important, against your proposed idea.

Option 4: Be decisive after you've committed to a business decision. Beforehand, be smart and review all the evidence for and, more important, against your proposed idea.

Option 5: Be decisive after you've committed to a business decision. Beforehand, be smart and review all the evidence for and, more important, against your proposed idea.

To make sound decisions, you need to be devilishly sly. In this topic, you'll learn how to use the devil's advocacy technique to evaluate a proposed business decision. The steps of this technique are:

- listing the evidence opposing your business decision,
- explaining both sides of the argument to a colleague and getting his or her input.

The devil's advocacy technique received its name from a traditional practice within the Roman Catholic Church. Before a church member was elevated to sainthood, the College of Cardinals appointed an official to investigate and express all the reasons the candidate's canonization should not be approved.

Want to find out just how exalted a present-day potential decision really is? Get started on the right foot. The first step in using the devil's advocacy technique is to list the evidence opposing your business decision.

Gwen made a tentative decision to install solar energy panels on the roof of the office complex she managed. She loved the idea of saving her property management company substantial money by reducing its energy costs.

See each stage to find out how Gwen first assumed the role of devil's advocate.

first-order opposing evidence

"I took the other side of my thinking by listing the reasons I knew the solar panel idea was flawed. For example, the purchase and installation required a sizable upfront investment. Because I knew this evidence against the panels, the initial expense, to be true, I listed it as first-order evidence."

second-order opposing evidence

"As opposed to verifiable facts, I also noted points I didn't know to be true, but that, if substantiated, would argue against the solar panels. My second-order evidence included the future possibility that increasing regional pollution could reduce the panel's generation ability."

In effect, listing both the first- and second-order opposing evidence forced Gwen to conscientiously reconsider the reasons her solar panel idea was less than ideal.

Decision Making with Uneasy Partners

Which option sounds more attractive: butting heads or putting them together?

Make no mistake: The first option results in far more headaches.

It's crucial to talk about your business options in a productive way. By effectively discussing potential business decisions with uneasy or competitive counterparts, you'll reap several benefits, such as:

- avoiding wasted time caused by misunderstandings,
- building better relationships with all business associates,
- enhancing your career success.

Not everyone is your business ally. In fact, the world of commerce has always hinged on the tug of war known as "friendly competition." This doesn't mean you can't reach productive decisions with people you don't completely trust or with business associates and competitors who keep their own priorities topmost in their minds. Stand tradition on its head. Change the rules of the tug-of-war contest, and try pulling in the same direction. Now there's a productive compromise for you.

Compromises and trade-offs don't have to take place between a winner and a loser. In fact, they shouldn't.

Here's a trivia question for you: What line made television star Joan Rivers so famous?

Rivers was best-known for exclaiming, "Can we talk?" No matter what the response from her talk show counterpart, that's exactly what she continued to do.

And that's precisely what you should do when discussing a potential business decision with another person-- even if you don't know that party to be a true ally.

Keep this in mind, though: There's talk, and then there's genuine dialogue. In this topic, you'll discover how to engage in the latter and truly open the doors to productive decision making by:

- inquiring about assumptions,
- generating options instead of ultimatums,
- focusing on common ground and not on positions.

Discussing potential business decisions

Which option sounds more attractive: butting heads or putting them together?

Make no mistake: The first option results in far more headaches.

It's crucial to talk about your business options in a productive way. By effectively discussing potential business decisions with uneasy or competitive counterparts, you'll reap several benefits, such as:

- avoiding wasted time caused by misunderstandings,
- building better relationships with all business associates,
- enhancing your career success.

Question

Some people claim conversation is a lost art. Choose the benefits of effectively discussing potential business decisions with uneasy or competitive parties.

Options:

1. You'll enhance your relationships with business colleagues.

2. You'll cut down on time lost because of misunderstandings.

3. You'll choose your decision-making partners more insightfully.

4. Your career will likely benefit from engaging in effective dialogue.

Answers:

In fact, you'll enhance both your business relationships and your career success. You'll also avoid losing time because of misunderstandings. Choosing your decision-making counterparts takes place before actual discussion.

Option 1: This is a correct choice. Conversation builds trust and respect. Without good communication, it's very difficult to overcome distrust, suspicion, or competitiveness.

Option 2: Correct. Discussing potential business decisions is the best way to make sure that uneasy or competitive parties won't misinterpret or misunderstand your decision. So they are less likely to waste time by acting inappropriately.

Option 3: This is an incorrect choice. Choosing a decision-making partner comes before you actually discuss any business decision, and discussing decisions with existing partners will not help you choose a partner more insightfully.

Option 4: Correct. Effective conversations with decision-making partners will help you work cooperatively, and improve the likelihood that your partnership will succeed. That, in turn, will enhance your reputation.

Lasting decisions require lasting relationships. In this lesson, you'll discover ways to establish both by:

- making compromises and trade-offs,
- engaging in meaningful conversation.

Making compromises and managing trade-offs

Luke chose to let his neighborhood pals have equal access to his prized possession: his sandbox. Luke's parents hailed his offer as a triumphant, break-through decision.

Luke's decision opened the way for all kinds of toy-sharing opportunities. In this topic, you'll learn how to dig your way out of decision-making stagnation by effectively making compromises and managing trade-offs with business associates. You'll do this by using the following strategies:

- aiming for a win-win outcome,
- generating as many options as possible,
- establishing an objective standard.

Not everyone is your business ally. In fact, the world of commerce has always hinged on the tug of war known as "friendly competition." This doesn't mean you can't reach productive decisions with people you don't completely trust or with business associates and competitors who keep their own priorities topmost in their minds. Stand tradition on its head. Change the rules of the tug-of-war contest, and try pulling in the same direction. Now there's a productive compromise for you.

Compromises and trade-offs don't have to take place between a winner and a loser. In fact, they shouldn't.

Stan is a manager of a long-distance telephone service provider.

See each of Stan's statements to find out how he used the first strategy by aiming for a win-win outcome in his discussion with a competitor.

Stan concerned

"Amelia contacted me about the need for our companies to share fiber optic infrastructure. I knew right away this arrangement would be tricky, but feasible."

Stan determined

"I took the initiative. I told her I could picture a scenario in which both our companies came out ahead. I emphasized that we should shoot for that outcome."

Amelia echoed Stan's sentiments word-for-word. Suddenly, the two were decision-making allies rather than mere competitors.

Next, Stan employed the second strategy for making compromises and managing trade-offs by generating as many options as possible.

See each problem and its solution to find out how Stan devised alternatives instead of remaining at loggerheads.

Problem 1

"Amelia mentioned that her company wanted to maintain control over a network crucial to our operation."

Solution 1

"I suggested we consider expanding that network to the point that it could handle both companies' volumes. That would cost much less than putting in separate infrastructures."

Problem 2

"I also knew we controlled the infrastructure in another region Amelia's company wanted to penetrate."

Solution 2

"I presented the option of expanding both networks at the same time. We could even share the cost of staffing the needed engineers. The possibility of teaming together on the purchase of the equipment would translate into lower expenditures for both our organizations."

Stan's thinking encouraged and impressed Amelia. He not only made the eventual decision easier to make but also increased the likelihood they would find innovative ways to enhance the success of both their companies.

After the preceding strategies were used, Stan and Amelia had to iron out some remaining details. So Stan used the final compromise strategy and insisted on using an objective standard on which to base future compromises.

When you make decisions based on objective standards, it means both parties understand the exact terms of agreement. This provides clear-cut measures of responsibility and reduces the potential for future disputes.

See the details to discover how Stan set the bar for his and Amelia's final compromises.

research

"Expanding the network infrastructure would require research on behalf of both companies. I suggested that Amelia and I decide which specific tasks each company would be responsible for, as well as how much time we'd allot for this investigation."

costs

"We also agreed to spell out exactly what expenditures our respective companies would be willing to make. Plus, we each agreed to pay a specified portion of the cost of network upkeep. Without those specific numbers, we had nothing on which to base compromises."

staffing

"Say our team of engineers failed to complete a shared project on time. I suggested my company would pay the engineers from her company who helped finish the project. Of course, her company agreed to do the same. That way, we had a preapproved protocol to fall back on."

By effectively making compromises and trade-offs, Stan and Amelia made an array of mutually beneficial decisions.

Question

As the popular saying goes, "You can't always get what you want." Select effective strategies for making compromises and managing trade-offs.

Options:

1. Make sure you establish and follow an objective standard.
2. Always strive to settle on a decision that benefits both parties.
3. Devise as many options and alternatives as you possibly can.
4. Insist your counterpart express her most- and least-favored ideas.

Answers:

Actually, you should insist on using an objective standard, aim for a win-win outcome, and generate as many options as possible.

Option 1: This is a correct choice. It's important to insist on using an objective standard when compromising, so both parties understand the exact terms of agreement. This reduces the potential for future disputes.

Option 2: This is a correct choice. Win-win solutions build strong partnerships and encourage continuing cooperation. If one side feels taken advantage of, they may look for ways to undermine the agreement.

Option 3: This is a correct choice. The more alternatives and options you can come up with, the more likely it is that you will settle upon an innovative solution that satisfies both parties and satisfactorily resolves the underlying issue.

Option 4: This is an incorrect choice. It is unlikely that potential decision- making partners will express ideas that they deem unsatisfactory, and trying to force them to consider unfavorable solutions will only undermine negotiations.

When you use all three strategies tested in the previous exercise, you're bound to advance your own interests as well as those of your business associates.

And that's what part of advanced decision making is all about.

In this topic, you learned how to make effective business decisions by effectively using strategies to make compromises and manage trade-offs.

You explored these strategies for achieving that goal: aiming for a win-win outcome, generating as many options as possible, and insisting on using an objective standard.

Techniques to conduct a genuine dialogue about a business decision

Here's a trivia question for you: What line made television star Joan Rivers so famous?

Rivers was best-known for exclaiming, "Can we talk?" No matter what the response from her talk show counterpart, that's exactly what she continued to do.

And that's precisely what you should do when discussing a potential business decision with another person-- even if you don't know that party to be a true ally.

Keep this in mind, though: There's talk, and then there's genuine dialogue. In this topic, you'll discover how to engage in the latter and truly open the doors to productive decision making by:

- inquiring about assumptions,
- generating options instead of ultimatums,
- focusing on common ground and not on positions.

Genuine dialogue between two business colleagues happens rarely. It takes place even less frequently among parties that have an infrequent relationship and no established strategic alliance.

Some people liken business conversations to tennis matches. One person lobs a demand over the table, and the opponent fires a preferred idea right back.

On the flip side, truly effective decision makers realize dialogue actually resembles a jazz quartet. The musicians attempt to integrate their polished playing with the musical goals of the entire band.

See each step to find out how Anne used the first technique, inquiring about assumptions, to conduct a genuine dialogue about a business decision with another party.

Assumptions

"All business choices involve assumptions. An assumption is any aspect of a proposed decision assumed to be true. If you don't uncover your counterpart's assumptions and express yours, they remain unverified and potentially harmful."

Inquiring about assumptions

"For example, Robert, a local school superintendent, approached my musical instrument company about forming a strategic alliance. I knew Robert had certain pre-existing ideas about this partnership."

Asking openly

"Rather than assume Robert wanted reduced-rate instruments in exchange for promotion of some kind, I simply asked Robert how he envisioned the formal arrangements of this alliance."

Open-ended inquiry

"Making an open-ended inquiry is the key to uncovering assumptions. I didn't ask him specifically about financial arrangements or other responsibilities. I merely said, 'Tell me about your thinking regarding our potential partnership.'"

Clarifying ideas

"Robert informed me that he hoped we'd be interested in hosting "musical fairs" in his school district. At the fairs, our company would provide instruments for students to demo and, in return, we would receive free ads in yearbooks and newsletters."

Developing mutual benefit

"Robert also told me the details behind several other ideas he had, all of them mutually beneficial. By open-endedly inquiring about his assumptions, I uncovered valuable information and established our relationship on the 'right note.'"

Question

After Robert aired his assumptions regarding the proposed decision, Anne volunteered hers. The basis for genuine dialogue had been established and possible future misunderstandings avoided. Can you identify the key to effectively inquiring about a potential business decision with another party? Which of these choices completes this sentence?

You should inquire about another person's assumptions by:

Options:

1. directing his or her attention to specific items, such as financial terms of agreement.
2. asking for the person's ideas in a nondirective way and allowing him to volunteer information.

Answers:

Actually, if you direct your counterpart's attention to specific matters, it appears to him as if you're making assumptions about his assumptions. An open-ended approach implies respect and produces more fruitful results.

Option 1: This is an incorrect choice. If you jump right to specifics, you may miss important assumptions that color the other party's thinking. This can make it harder to understand his or her position and achieve win-win solutions.

Option 2: Correct. Making an open-ended inquiry is the key to uncovering assumptions. Try to avoid asking specifically about a proposed decision, and merely inquire about the other party's thinking regarding the potential partnership.

Assumptions about the proposed business decision uncovered, Anne used the second technique to further her dialogue with Robert. She generated options instead of ultimatums.

See how Anne built on her and Robert's progress by looking to the future rather than trying to solidify any present concerns.

Anne: Before we get mired in the details of what we've already discussed, Robert, let's think of other ways to make this potential alliance more valuable. For example, we could consider providing guest instructors to conduct periodic workshops. How does that sound?

Robert: Our students would love that, Anne. We could send out workshop flyers to the parents detailing your company's involvement with and commitment to the community.

Anne: Excellent. There's also the option of using our company's vans to transport students to regional band competitions.

Robert: While you're parked at the competitions, it may be possible to distribute brochures about your instruments. You could have representatives there to answer questions and give demonstrations.

Anne: I'm sure we could work out those arrangements, Robert. I've been making notes about our conversation. Let's hammer out the specifics once we've explored all our options.

Robert: I'm with you on that.

Notice how Anne generated options that enabled both sides to achieve more than the obvious possibilities. She expanded the collective pie by offering the first alternative herself. Rather than burden Robert with that responsibility, Anne took the initiative. Robert, as most people do in that situation, responded in kind. Anne established an atmosphere of trust and camaraderie by finding ways between the horns of potential dilemmas.

Their dialogue was proceeding smoothly. To keep it moving in that direction, Anne used the last strategy for effectively discussing the proposed decision. She focused on common ground and not on positions.

Anne wanted to set the decision-making stage by moving forward on the benefits and opportunities she and Robert had discussed.

See each stage to find out how Anne continued their dialogue.

shared interests

"I told Robert I wanted both of us to arrive at a mutually advantageous arrangement. I emphasized our agreement on the band workshop and competition ideas. I then explained we should build on those possibilities before advancing to formal negotiations."

positions

"Initially, I didn't think that my company would be willing to offer deep discounts on the instruments in return for publicity. I kept that notion to myself at this stage. The momentum toward a beneficial solution would have been negated had I forced Robert to take a position as well."

the results

"By emphasizing the need to focus on common ground instead of potential sticking points, I effectively relayed my desires to Robert. He knew I had a specific agenda for our next discussion, but felt it was one that would advance his interests as well."

The bargaining that takes place once concrete issues get narrowed down represents a comparatively narrow aspect of decision making. Anne deftly concentrated on the broader underlying concern of first establishing a relationship and setting mutual goals with her counterpart.

And she did that by conducting a genuine dialogue with Robert. That dialogue formed the foundation of their now-realizable decision-making success.

Do you have a desire to make innovation a habit and break-through results your business norm? If so, master the art of dialogue. Your fellow decision makers will respond in kind. In this topic, you learned how to conduct a genuine dialogue with another party about a business decision by:

- inquiring about assumptions

• generating options instead of ultimatums
• focusing on common ground and not on positions.

Ralph Waldo Emerson wrote, "Once you make a decision, the universe conspires to make it happen." Now that you've completed this course, you know how to make the universe's job much easier by setting only the wisest choices into motion.

In this course, you not only learned about the principles that influence successful decision making, but you discovered concrete techniques to arrive at dynamic choices, both by yourself and with others.

CHAPTER FIVE

Implementation and Evaluation

Planning the Action

Thomas Edison said that success is only 1 percent inspiration. It takes a lot of hard work to put that inspired decision into action. Successful implementation of a decision requires you to plan your actions carefully.

Chess is a game of decision making. Why do you think it takes so long to play? Chess players all want to accomplish the same goal. They want to win.

Before they can act on that goal, they have to think about what they have to work with, weigh the alternatives, and anticipate their opponents' responses.

Implementing a business decision is a lot like playing a chess game. You already know your goal. To reach that goal you have to consider your resources, your alternatives, and your opposition. In this topic, you'll learn these three basic steps in implementing a decision:

1. Form an integration team.
2. Establish timelines and milestones.

3. Create an ongoing communication plan.

No matter how hard you push, some doors just won't open.

But a gentle pull may get the job done.

Pushing with more force doesn't always get you the result you want, whether you're opening doors or implementing business decisions. In this topic, you'll explore a technique for analyzing the forces that drive or restrain an implementation. This technique is called "force-field analysis" and was developed by Kurt Lewin, a pioneer in the study of change. Lewin suggests that change results from the relationship of competing forces.

When people say, "Somebody should do something about that," who are they usually talking about?

Many companies have one person who seems to be able to get things done. But should a company rely on one person to implement a major decision? That's a heavy load for anyone to carry, especially if the decision will affect people throughout the company. Convincing a group of people with differing priorities to work together toward a single goal is time-consuming and difficult. That's why some people compare leading a committee to herding cats. The job seems nearly impossible.

Effective implementation planning

Lisa is a baker. When she decided to open her own shop, she chose a location in an affluent neighborhood. She quickly gained many loyal customers, but after a few months she realized her new business wasn't making a profit.

Question

Lisa decided the rent was too high for the location she had chosen. She soon sold the business.

She was surprised when the new owner turned the bakery into a big success. Do you think Lisa made the wrong decision when she chose the location for her bakery?

Options:

1. Yes. Her poor decision contributed to the failure of the business.
2. No. She made a good decision but failed to implement it properly.

Answer:

Actually, the new owner of the business proved the validity of Lisa's original decision. She simply failed to make careful plans to implement her decision.

Option 1: Incorrect. Because another business owner was able to successfully operate the same kind of business in the same location, we know that the location was a good choice.

Option 2: Correct. The success of the bakery business that followed Lisa's business shows that the decision for the location was a good one. The problem was that Lisa did not follow the steps that were required to implement the decision.

When Lisa chose the location for her business, she weighed the alternatives and made an excellent decision. But that decision alone wasn't enough to make her business a success.

Thomas Edison said that success is only 1 percent inspiration. It takes a lot of hard work to put that inspired decision into action. Successful implementation of a decision requires you to plan your actions carefully.

Gilbert supervises new product development for a software company. He's an expert when it comes to implementing business decisions.

See each of the benefits to find out what Gilbert says he gains by planning the action before he begins implementing an important decision.

Foresight

"Taking the time to plan how I'm going to implement a decision helps me foresee some of the obstacles or objections that can come up later."

Cooperation

"When I take the time to consider what people's objections might be, I can plan how I'll respond. That helps me gain cooperation from people affected by the decision."

Gilbert realizes that the time he puts into planning how he'll implement a decision isn't wasted. It's invested. When he takes time to plan carefully, he's able to implement decisions more quickly and efficiently.

Question

A business decision usually begins a long process of change. Implementing the decision for change requires careful planning. Which of these statements describe benefits of planning the action before the implementation begins?

Options:

1. Decisions are implemented in less time.
2. Implementers gain the cooperation of people affected by the change.
3. Implementers encounter fewer surprises and obstacles.
4. Less time is spent gathering irrelevant opinions from others in the organization.
5. The costs of implementing the decision are more likely to be recovered quickly.

Answer:

Actually, careful planning means decisions will be implemented more quickly with a higher degree of cooperation from people affected by the decision. The implementers also encounter fewer obstacles or surprises.

Option 1: Correct. Spending the time and resources to carefully consider a decision before implementing it saves time later.

Option 2: Correct. Getting the cooperation of the people affected by the decision is facilitated by generating possible objections and their solutions in the planning stage.

Option 3: Correct. Careful planning allows the implementer to foresee possible problems, reducing surprises and obstacles.

Option 4: Incorrect. Time spent gathering the opinions of the other people involved in the decision is time well invested. It will save time and resources later.

Option 5: Incorrect. The time and resources spent in the careful consideration and planning of a decision must be seen as an investment that pays itself back over time, not right away.

Even the finest actors don't step onstage without rehearsing. It's just as important to plan your actions before you begin to implement a decision. In this lesson, you'll learn these important first steps in planning those actions:

- implementation basics,
- force-field analysis,
- grass-roots analysis.

Three basic implementation strategies

Chess is a game of decision making. Why do you think it takes so long to play? Chess players all want to accomplish the same goal. They want to win.

Before they can act on that goal, they have to think about what they have to work with, weigh the alternatives, and anticipate their opponents' responses.

Implementing a business decision is a lot like playing a chess game. You already know your goal. To reach that goal you have to consider your resources, your alternatives, and your opposition. In this topic, you'll learn these three basic steps in implementing a decision:

1. Form an integration team.
2. Establish timelines and milestones.
3. Create an ongoing communication plan.

When you implement a business decision, you have to convince people to do something most people dislike. You have to ask them to accept change.

So the first step in implementing a decision is to recruit partners in your effort. You can accomplish this by recruiting an integration team. You should include representatives from each department affected by the decision.

Byron is a management consultant for an international accounting firm. He helps companies all over the world make dramatic changes to the way they operate.

See each of Byron's comments for his advice about building an integration team.

Comment 1

"When committees make decisions, I recruit from those committees for my integration team. They understand the background behind the decision."

Comment 2

"Sometimes I want to add new perspectives to my integration team. If I recruit new members, I make sure to brief them on the history of the decision."

When changes are announced, the first thing people want to know is "When is this going to happen?" People in charge of an implementation should be prepared to answer this question.

The second step in implementing a decision is creating an implementation calendar. This calendar sets timelines and milestones for the project.

An integration team's effectiveness is often judged by how closely it sticks to the project calendar. When creating project calendars, integration teams should:

- involve the managers of the project or the decision makers,
- set realistic goals for each stage of implementation,

- keep written documentation that is updated regularly,
- plan periodic milestone celebrations to publicize progress toward the goal.

Question:

Think about the teams you've observed that didn't accomplish their goals.

How often was a lack of communication one of the main reasons for the team's failure?

Options:

1. never
2. a few times
3. half the time
4. most of the time
5. every time

Answer:

Option 1: Poor communication is usually the reason teams don't meet their goals. People who have experienced many team failures report that poor communication is a major problem most of the time.

Option 2: Poor communication is usually the reason teams don't meet their goals. People who have experienced many team failures report that poor communication is a major problem most of the time.

Option 3: Poor communication is usually the reason teams don't meet their goals. People who have experienced many team failures report that poor communication is a major problem most of the time.

Option 4: Poor communication is usually the reason teams don't meet their goals. People who have experienced many team failures report that poor communication is a major problem most of the time.

Option 5: Poor communication is usually the reason teams don't meet their goals. People who have experienced many team failures report that poor communication is a major problem most of the time.

The third step in implementing a decision is to decide how the integration team's progress will be reported to the rest of the organization. Byron, the international management consultant, includes four important elements in his communication plans.

See each aspect of Byron's communication plan to learn more about it.

Audience

Every integration team must communicate to at least two different audiences: the members of the team itself and the rest of the organization. There may be subgroups within each of these audiences with special information needs.

Frequency

How often should the group communicate with each audience? Too many updates can overwhelm the audience with details. But not communicating frequently enough creates an air of secrecy. Decide how often the team should report to each audience.

Method

What's the best way to communicate what the team is doing? Major milestones should be communicated in a face-to-face meeting with the audience. This promotes a feeling of openness. Minor milestones may be communicated in memos or by e-mail.

Feedback

Will the audiences be given an opportunity to reply to communication from the integration team? If the audience is large, receiving feedback may be impractical. But allowing feedback when possible lets the audience become a bigger part of the process.

There's also one obstacle integration teams should avoid, according to Byron. Integration teams are responsible for implementing decisions that have already been finalized. They should avoid debating the issues that were part of the decision-making process. For example, if the decision to invest in expensive new equipment has been made, the integration team shouldn't reopen a debate over whether the money should be spent. It should only consider the best source for the purchase.

Question

Melinda leads a process improvement team for a catalog retailer. Her team recommended changes to the way orders are taken on the phone. The company's senior managers approved the changes. Now Melinda has to implement them. Which steps should she take?

Options:

1. recruit an integration team, including only people who are already familiar with the reason for the changes
2. recruit an integration team that includes members from all affected departments
3. create a calendar of timelines and milestones for implementing the changes
4. solicit input from affected departments to estimate the cost of the changes
5. establish an ongoing communication plan to inform the rest of the company about the changes

Answer:

Actually, the three basics of implementing a decision are recruiting an implementation team, setting timelines and milestones, and creating an ongoing communication plan.

Option 1: Incorrect. An integration team should include people from every department that is going to be affected by the change. This will involve people who are not familiar with the reason for the change.

Option 2: Correct. It is difficult for people to change. When you involve people from all the departments that will be affected by the change, it makes it easier for them to accept it.

Option 3: Correct. When people are faced with change, they want to know when it is going to happen. Establishing timelines and milestones will ease the transition.

Option 4: Incorrect. Determining cost is part of the decision making process and has already been done. It is important to not get involved in debating the issues that were part of the decision making process during implementation.

Option 5: Correct. Communicating regularly, personally, and clearly with the rest of the organization during implementation will engender support for the changes.

Melinda's team used the three basic implementation steps. The team planned each move carefully to make sure the implementation worked well for everyone in the company. In this topic, you learned the basics of implementation:

- recruiting an integration team,
- establishing a calendar of timelines and milestones,
- creating an effective communication plan.

•

The force-field analysis

No matter how hard you push, some doors just won't open.

But a gentle pull may get the job done.

Pushing with more force doesn't always get you the result you want, whether you're opening doors or implementing business decisions. In this topic, you'll explore a technique for analyzing the forces that drive or restrain an implementation. This technique is called "force-field analysis" and was developed by Kurt Lewin, a pioneer in the study of change. Lewin suggests that change results from the relationship of competing forces.

Lewin's research shows that many people misunderstand the relationship between the forces that control change.

The easiest ways to implement change are often overlooked.

Why should an integration team use a force-field analysis to implement business decisions? Examining the competing forces that drive and restrain change can help the team evaluate its priorities more clearly. The force-field analysis takes the form of a simple diagram. To create the diagram:

- list the driving forces on half of the diagram,
- list the restraining forces on the opposite half of the diagram,
- assign a strength score or weight to each force.

The first step in creating a force-field analysis is to list the driving forces supporting the implementation.

For example, a computer book publisher recently made an important decision to require its sales representatives to call on small, independent bookstores more frequently. Warren, a senior account representative, led the implementation team.

Warren and his team discussed the driving forces that would make the decision easier to implement. Select each driving force identified by Warren's team to learn more about it.

People's attitudes

"People's attitudes toward a change can be a driving force. Our salespeople felt the company was making a commitment to providing service to our small accounts."

Dollars-and-cents

"Tangible dollars-and-cents benefits are strong driving forces. In this case, we anticipated our sales to small accounts would increase by 60 percent or more."

Warren began diagramming his team's force-field analysis by listing the driving forces down one side of a piece of paper. His diagram is shown below.

Next, the team listed the restraining forces. Restraining forces are influences and attitudes that hinder the implementation of the decision.

Like driving forces, some restraining forces arise from people's attitudes, while others arise from objective facts.

Warren's committee identified each of the following items as restraining forces. Note which items are based on attitudes and which are based on fact.

- The sales representatives fear that the change will reduce the time they can devote to the largest accounts.
- Salespeople currently travel two weeks out of every month. They will resist any increase in travel time.
- Travel costs will increase by 15 percent.

Warren added the restraining forces to the diagram his team was building. The result is shown.

Notice that there are more restraining forces than driving forces. The diagram does not have to contain an equal number of forces on each side. Also, adding a force on one side does not require an opposing force on the other side.

Not all forces in the diagram have the same strength. So the third and last step in creating the force-field diagram is to quantify the strength of each force. To quantify the strengths:

- choose a scale, usually 1 to 5 or 1 to 10,
- assign a weight or strength to each force,
- calculate the totals of the weights on each side.

Assigning weights isn't a scientific process. Just use your best judgment. The completed analysis diagram created by Warren's integration team is shown.

Question

Force-field diagrams can be built quickly and can help integration teams set priorities. Which statements describe the steps in creating a force-field analysis?

Options:

1. Assign a weight to each of the forces.
2. List the driving forces on half of the diagram.
3. Rank the driving and restraining forces according to strength.
4. Calculate how much change is required to make the total weight of driving forces twice the weight of the restraining forces.
5. List the restraining forces on half of the diagram.

Answer:

Actually, to create a force-field analysis, list the driving and restraining forces and assign a weight to each force. Then determine which forces can be altered in your favor.

Option 1: Correct. The third step in creating a force-field diagram is to assign each force a number that indicates its strength or weight.

Option 2: Correct. To build a force-field diagram, the first step is to generate a list of the forces that are moving the change forward.

Option 3: Incorrect. To create a force-field diagram according to Kurt Lewin's model, the driving and restraining forces are assigned a weight rather than a ranking.

Option 4: Incorrect. In the creation of a force-field diagram, each force is assigned a weight. The weights of the driving forces and restraining forces are calculated. Analyzing the data is not part of the creation process.

Option 5: Correct. The second step in the building of a force-field diagram is making the list of the restraining forces on the right side of the diagram.

After integration teams create a force-field diagram, how do they use it? Next, you'll see how an automotive components manufacturer used a force-field analysis while implementing a new method of buying raw materials.

The company made the decision to switch to a just-in-time manufacturing process. The integration team mapped out the driving and restraining forces, then analyzed the results by:

- estimating the probability of a successful implementation,
- examining restraining forces to see which ones can be altered favorably,
- examining driving forces to see which can be altered favorably.

Here's the force-field diagram developed by the company's integration team. It decided to weight each of the forces using a scale from 1 to 10.

Gwen led the integration team. When the force-field analysis was complete, she asked the team to estimate the probability that the proposed changes could be implemented successfully.

See each potential answer to her question to learn how Gwen analyzed the results.

Opposition to change

When the weight of restraining forces is larger or even close to the weight of driving forces, there will be strong opposition to implementing a change.

Smooth change implementation

When the weight of driving forces is much greater than the weight of restraining forces, the implementation will go more smoothly.

Gwen's team found that the restraining forces for change outweighed the driving forces by a small amount. As a result, the integration team agreed that the proposed changes would meet with significant resistance. First, the team examined each of the restraining forces to determine which ones could be altered favorably.

Select each of the arrows in the Restraining Forces column to learn how Gwen's team decided to handle each of these forces.

Supply interruptions -7

The new just-in-time inventory system increases the risk that the company may run out of important raw materials. The team suggested identifying new sources from which the company could purchase these materials before the new system is implemented.

Retraining staff -3

Retraining the purchasing staff is an important part of implementing this decision. The company must accept the higher costs as part of the implementation. The team decided not to act on this restraining force.

Staff inflexibility -5

The team expects the purchasing staff will be reluctant to accept the change. The old system rewarded purchasers for keeping inventory levels high. The integration team recommends dropping the old incentives and creating new ones.

Gwen's integration team decided to try to weaken the impact of the strongest restraining force. Studies show that diminishing the power of restraining forces is the most effective way to increase acceptance of change.

Then Gwen and Chance, another member of the integration team, discussed the team's next move.

Chance: If we develop new sources for raw materials, that should reduce the chances of a supply interruption, right?

Gwen: That's right. Now assume we can do that. How should we change the weight of that restraining force?

Chance: How about changing it to zero? That definitely swings the balance in our favor. We can wrap this up right now.

Gwen: Hold on, now. It's easy to just change the numbers until we like them. But will we really be able to eliminate this restraining force altogether?

Chance: Well, no. Not really. But I think we can cut the risk in half. So I say we should reduce the weight to a 4. And if we can work out a new bonus plan for the purchasing specialists, we can reduce the weight of that restraining force to a 2.

Gwen: Sounds good. Now, let's see whether there's a way for us to change the driving forces in our favor.

Chance: Do you think we should? After all, we've always found that reducing resistance is the smart way to go.

Gwen: That's true. But let's see if we can give ourselves just a little bit more of an advantage.

Chance is right. Working to reduce the strength of restraining forces is the smarter strategy. Trying to increase the strength of driving forces often has an unanticipated result: More force creates more resistance.

But Gwen is also right. The team shouldn't quit without examining the driving forces. Which driving force do you think the team can alter most favorably?

See each driving force to learn more.

Reduced Inventory +9

"Our budgeting department explored this issue thoroughly. The change will save the company $865,000 the first year. But there's nothing our team can do to change that number or increase its strength as a driving force for change."

Alternative sources +5

"We need to develop new sources to reduce supply interruptions. That has another positive benefit. Our purchasing specialists will gain more leverage in negotiating delivery times. We'll add another point to the weight of this driving force."

While the team discussed the driving forces on the diagram, Chance realized they had overlooked another important driving force.

See this driving force for his explanation.

Increased flexibility +3

"If we reduce the quantity of raw materials we keep on hand, we'll be purchasing more frequently. We'll be able to react quickly when prices fluctuate. We can add this as an additional driving force. I suggest giving it a weight of 3."

When the team finished examining the driving and restraining forces, it had agreed on three important priorities. It decided the company needed to cultivate new sources for raw materials, create a new incentive plan for purchasing specialists, and prepare to purchase more frequently.

If the team can include these priorities in its implementation plan, the weight of driving forces increases to 17. The weight of restraining forces decreases to 9. The increased difference indicates a higher probability of success.

Case Study: Question 1 of 3

Scenario:

Kira manages the inventory control department of a children's clothing retailer. She's working with an integration team to change the way the company counts merchandise during its annual inventory. The company wants to begin counting the merchandise by using computer scanners to read the bar codes on price tickets. The team has developed a force-field analysis.

Reduces costs +8

By using scanners, the annual inventory count can be accomplished with fewer people. As a result, the cost of counting will drop by more than 60 percent. The savings will be spent upgrading the company's computer equipment.

Equipment requirements -5

The new method of counting will require an investment in expensive new equipment that will rarely be used. Many of the company's employees may object to the money being used for equipment purchases instead of increased pay.

Reduces errors +5

In the past, people made many counting mistakes by failing to distinguish between similar products. Using bar code scanners will eliminate these errors for a more accurate count.

Exception handling -2

When employees counted the merchandise by hand, they were able to identify and count merchandise with missing price tickets. Changing to scanners means that exceptions will be more difficult to handle.

Manager skepticism -4

Many senior managers in the company are comfortable with the existing inventory process. They are skeptical of the benefits of making this change. Their opinions shape the attitudes of the rest of the company.

Question:

Kira's integration team completes the force-field analysis and analyzes the resulting chart. It recommends moving forward without making changes to alter the influence of driving and restraining forces. Is this the correct decision, based on the data given?

Options:

1. Yes, because the driving forces outweigh the restraining forces.
2. Yes, because the driving and restraining forces are near equilibrium.
3. No, because altering the driving and restraining forces can make acceptance of the change more likely.
4. No, because there are more driving forces than restraining forces.

Answer:

Actually, even though the driving forces outweigh the restraining forces, Kira's team can still tilt the balance more in favor of acceptance of the change.

Option 1: Incorrect. If restraining forces are almost equal to the driving forces, there will still be significant resistance to change.

Option 2: Incorrect. In order to successfully implement a change and have it accepted, it is best to have the driving forces noticeably outweigh the restraining forces.

Option 3: Correct. The driving forces are almost equal to the restraining forces. It is preferable to have a greater disparity between the two forces, with more weight on the side of the driving forces.

Option 4: Incorrect. It is desirable to have the driving forces significantly outweigh the restraining forces. This ensures a smoother transition.

Case Study: Question 2 of 3

Kira suggests preparing an analysis that shows how the cost of the new equipment will be recovered through increased productivity. She wants to make this the team's first priority. Is she making a good decision based on the information in the force-field analysis?

Options:

1. Yes, because costs represent the strongest restraining force.
2. Yes, because she's increasing the weight of the strongest driving force.
3. No, because the other restraining forces can be eliminated entirely with the right strategy.
4. No, because she needs to add an additional driving force to make both sides equal.

Answer:

Actually, the most effective way to proceed is to reduce the weight of the strongest restraining force.

Option 1: Correct. Reducing the weight of the restraining forces is the most effective way to modify the force-field diagram to indicate that the change will be successfully implemented.

Option 2: Incorrect. It is more effective to reduce the weight of the restraining forces than to increase the weight of the driving forces.

Option 3: Incorrect. Studies show that diminishing the power of restraining forces is the most effective way to increase acceptance of change. Eliminating them altogether is not a good strategy.

Option 4: Incorrect. It is not necessary to have an equal number of driving forces and restraining forces. The most effective method is to reduce the weight of the restraining forces, rather than increase the weight of the driving forces.

Case Study: Question 3 of 3

One member of the integration team works in the data processing department. She points out that the results of the inventory count can be completed in two days when the counts are scanned. Using the previous method, her department needed a week to complete the job. Kira suggests making this information known to the senior managers and adding this fact as a driving force in the force-field analysis. Is she using the force-field analysis method correctly?

Options:

1. Yes, because adding an additional driving force is an appropriate way to increase the acceptance of change.
2. Yes, because she's offsetting the effect of the strongest restraining force.
3. No, because reducing the strength of restraining forces is the most effective way to alter the balance.
4. No, because her strategy fails to increase the strength of the strongest driving force.

Answer:

Actually, trying to increase the strength of existing driving forces often meets with increased resistance. However, adding more driving forces is frequently an effective strategy.

Option 1: Correct. After working to reduce the weight of the restraining forces, the next step is to try to increase the weight of the driving forces.

Option 2: Incorrect. While this new information will make a strong addition to the weight of the driving forces, it does not directly apply to the strongest restraining force.

Option 3: Incorrect. This statement may be true, but it doesn't apply to the question. Kira is correct in adding the information as a new driving force because it is a factor that will alter the balance and increase management's acceptance of change.

Option 4: Incorrect. It is preferable to add another driving force rather than strengthen the existing ones. The overall effectiveness will be greater.

Kira and her team used the force-field analysis effectively. They created a presentation to show how the cost of the new equipment would be recovered quickly. They also developed a demonstration to prove the accuracy of scanning the inventory instead of counting it by hand.

By using the force-field analysis correctly, the integration team set priorities that facilitated the implementation process.

Creating and analyzing a force-field analysis isn't a scientific process. The diagram is a tool to help integration teams identify key issues in the implementation process. In this topic, you learned to create a force-field analysis diagram, and then analyze it by:

- estimating the probability of a successful implementation,
- examining the restraining forces,
- examining the driving forces.

The grass-roots analysis diagram

When people say, "Somebody should do something about that," who are they usually talking about?

Many companies have one person who seems to be able to get things done. But should a company rely on one person to implement a major decision? That's a heavy load for anyone to carry, especially if the decision will affect people throughout the company. Convincing a group of people with differing priorities to work together toward a single goal is time-consuming and difficult. That's why some people compare leading a committee to herding cats. The job seems nearly impossible.

Question

Successful team leaders know that getting results depends on their ability to delegate responsibility among the members of the team.

Think about the teams you've observed in the past. Which of the following methods of delegating responsibilities was more successful?

Options:

1. team members received broad, general assignments and made their own decisions about the details
2. team members received detailed, specific assignments with predetermined deadlines

Answer:

Successful teams usually assign each member detailed, specific tasks. Without clearly defined assignments, people duplicate each others' efforts or work toward conflicting deadlines.

Option 1: Incorrect. If assignments are too general, the results are likely to differ from the goals.

Option 2: Correct. This is an effective method of delegating responsibilities because when tasks are divided into smaller, more defined parts, the results closely match the desired outcome.

In this topic, you'll learn how to create and use a simple diagram that can help your integration team map the detailed steps required to reach a major goal. The diagram is called a "grass-roots analysis." To create a grass-roots diagram, follow these four steps:

- Write the main objective on one side of the diagram.
- Break the objective into three or more branches or sub-objectives.
- Break each branch into root actions.
- Eliminate duplicate roots and set priorities.

Tyler is a product manager for a snack foods manufacturer. The company's brand of tortilla chips is losing sales to competing brands. Customer surveys reveal that people who buy tortilla chips perceive the company's brand as both bland and expensive.

Tyler receives the assignment of improving the image of the company's chips in an effort to reverse the recent losses.

Tyler assembles an integration team to implement this decision. He realizes that he must translate a broad goal--improving the brand's image--into specific actions. The team begins its work by performing a grass-roots analysis. For the sake of brevity, you'll see only part of the analysis.

First, Tyler put a concise statement of the team's primary goal on the left side of the diagram.

Next, the team discussed how it planned to accomplish this goal. It agreed on three major branches or subgoals: develop new flavors of chips, design a more appealing package, and increase the use of discount coupons.

The team continued to break down each of these branches into specific tasks, or root actions. Root actions are narrow enough to be assigned to one person on the team with a specific deadline.

Question

How many branches do you think a team should create from its original objective?

Options:

1. two to four
2. eight to ten
3. 20 or more

Answer:

Option 1: In most situations, three or four branches are optimal because you can get lost with too much detail. If that's not sufficient for your needs, try narrowing the scope of your current project and creating separate additional projects.

Option 2: In most situations, three or four branches are optimal because you can get lost with too much detail. If that's not sufficient for your needs, try narrowing the scope of your current project and creating separate additional projects.

Option 3: In most situations, three or four branches are optimal because you can get lost with too much detail. If that's not sufficient for your needs, try narrowing the scope of your current project and creating separate additional projects.

After each of the branches had been broken down to root actions, the team refined the results.

See each of Tyler's comments to learn more about this process.

Comment 1

"We reviewed all of the root actions and eliminated duplicates. We decided to conduct one set of customer focus groups to test recipes and package designs."

Comment 2

"We examined the roots to see which actions were most important. We prioritized the actions that had to be completed first."

Question

Performing a grass-roots analysis helps an integration team identify the actions needed to implement a decision. Which statements describes the steps of performing a grass-roots analysis?

Options:

1. Examine the root actions to eliminate duplicates and set priorities.
2. Eliminate root actions that may delay the implementation past its deadline.

3. Create at least three statements that describe how the objective will be achieved.

4. Decide which team member or members will assume responsibility for each major branch.

5. Describe the objective in a short, concise statement.

6. Break each major branch into smaller objectives to reach the root actions.

Answer:

State the objective, then create at least three major "branches" by describing how the objective will be reached. Break each branch into smaller actions until you've identified root actions. Eliminate duplicates and set priorities.

Option 1: Correct. This is the final step in conducting a grass-roots analysis.

Option 2: Incorrect. Setting deadlines is not among the four steps of conducting a grass-roots analysis."

Option 3: Correct. It is ideal to create three or four branches from the original objective. This is the second step in performing a grass-roots analysis.

Option 4: Incorrect. Assigning tasks to people takes place in the root action phase of a grass-roots analysis. That is when the tasks have been broken down into small enough parts for one person to perform them.

Option 5: Correct. The objective that you identify will provide you with an attainable goal.

Option 6: Correct. Dividing each major branch into smaller parts allows you to create tasks in the root actions that are small enough for one person to do.

When Tyler's integration team finished creating the grass-roots analysis chart, it had compiled a list of several dozen root actions needed to improve the image of the company's product.

Listing the root actions is only half the job. Next, the team analyzed the resulting list of root actions to begin creating an implementation strategy.

First, the team examined all of the root actions to determine whether some tasks depended on the completion of other tasks. They discovered that the root actions can be sequentially interdependent, simultaneously interdependent, or independent of other actions.

See each kind of root actions for Tyler's explanation.

Sequentially interdependent

"When one task must be completed before another can begin, sequential interdependency exists. We have to develop test recipes before we can conduct customer focus groups to test those recipes. We also have to select which recipes we'll produce before we can print newspaper coupons."

Simultaneously interdependent

"When two tasks have to be completed at the same time, those two actions have simultaneous interdependency. We plan to design a new package for our product, and we want to print coupons on that package. Performing these tasks simultaneously will be more efficient."

Independent

"Some tasks aren't dependent on other tasks. These are frequently the root actions that need to be performed to set the rest of the implementation in motion. For example, developing recipes for new chip flavors is an independent action and the first step we need to accomplish."

After Tyler's integration team determined which root actions contained interdependencies, it was able to set timelines for the project.

See each of Tyler's comments for an explanation of how the timelines were developed.

Comment 1

"Every project includes a few tasks with long lead times. We had to design the package and allow six weeks lead time for printing."

Comment 2

"We had a general idea of when we needed to finish the project. We worked backward from that date to fill out the rest of the timeline.

Of course, you won't always be able to accurately set completion dates for all of the root actions. Unknown factors may require you to put in estimated completion dates until you have more information.

Go ahead and fill in estimated completion dates to make sure the rest of the timeline is consistent and realistic. But be sure to clearly indicate which dates are estimated. Failing to do so may cause embarrassment or confusion later in the project.

With the tasks defined, it was time to decide who would be responsible for each one. Tyler discussed assignments with Mae, an integration team member.

Tyler: Mae, since you're representing the marketing department on this project, would you like to take charge of placing coupons in newspaper ads?

Mae: Sure, I'd be glad to. Just tell me how much of a discount we're going to offer, and I'll take it from there.

Tyler: Actually, I was hoping you'd talk to the budgeting department to figure out what the most effective discount has been in the past. Can you do that?

Mae: That's a little out of my department. But I'll see what I can do.

Tyler: Now, the coupons will be one of the last tasks on our list. Until then, I was wondering if you'd be willing to help Carl from product development. He's going to be in charge of developing the test recipes.

Mae: That sounds like fun, but I don't have any experience at all in that area. Why do you want me to be involved?

Tyler: You can help Carl choose flavors that will appeal to younger customers. Your last survey showed that they're the customers who are most likely to prefer our competitors' products.

Mae: Makes sense to me. I'll help any way I can.

Notice that Tyler didn't assign major branches of actions to a single department. He recruited members of the integration team from a variety of departments to share responsibility for root actions in different branches.

Tyler and his integration team kept careful records of task assignments and timelines. They created a calendar and updated it frequently. The calendar proved to be the best way for the integration team to communicate with:

- managers and supervisors,
- workers in affected departments,
- members of the integration team.

Tyler's integration team decided to send out updates to its calendar once a week throughout the life of the project. Why? The team wanted the rest of the company to be aware of its progress. It also wanted to be able to adjust the document as the project progressed. The grass-roots analysis usually won't provide a perfect picture of an implementation. Rather, the analysis is open to continuing discussion and change.

Tyler's team used its grass-roots analysis to set its project in motion. The team was able to develop new varieties of the company's product, a new package for the product, and new incentives to get customers to sample the product. Through careful implementation of a business decision, it increased the company's share of the market along with sales and profits. The team used the grass-roots diagram to identify the actions that needed to be taken then analyzed the results to:

- identify interdependencies,
- establish timelines,
- assign root actions,
- communicate with the rest of the company.
- **Case Study: Question 1 of 2**

Scenario:

Tim directs the technical support department for a computer manufacturer that specializes in low-priced computers. Answer the questions in order.

Question:

The integration team decides to create a timeline for each of the three branches of action. Team members from each department receive assignments for actions across all three major action branches. Tim and the team members agree on deadlines for each of the three branches. They publish their timelines in a single document which Tim presents to the senior managers. Did Tim and the integration team make the best use of the grass-roots analysis?

Options:

1. Yes. The team created effective timelines, assigned actions, and communicated goals.
2. Yes. The team created shared responsibilities, assigned actions, and produced separate timelines for each major goal.
3. No. The team created timelines and created shared responsibilities but failed to identify interdependencies.
4. No. The team created timelines and shared responsibilities but failed to assign major goals to a single department.

Answer:

Actually, the team could have used the grass-roots analysis more effectively by taking the time to check the root actions in each branch to see if any depended on the completion of other actions.

Option 1: Incorrect. Without the first step of identifying interdependencies, the team will not know how the root actions relate with each other.

Option 2: Incorrect. While the team did all these steps, they did not perform the first step of identifying the interdependencies among the root actions.

Option 3: Correct. The team did not perform the first step towards analyzing the results of their grass- roots diagram. It is important to analyze the relationships among the root actions.

Option 4: Incorrect. The team assigned the actions in the correct manner, but they did not examine the interdependencies among the root actions.

Case Study: Question 2 of 2

Tim presents the team's timelines and other plans to the senior managers. The vice president of strategic development tells Tim that the company plans to introduce a new product, a video game console. Technical support for the new product will be provided by Tim's staff using the same policies that are being implemented for computer customers. What should Tim do to include this new information in his team's grass-roots analysis?

Options:

1. add appropriate actions under each major branch and distribute a revised analysis to the integration team
2. create a fourth major branch to the analysis but wait until the next team meeting to discuss appropriate deadlines
3. keep the analysis in its original form and perform a separate analysis for the new product
4. keep the existing action roots but revise the timeline to allow time to assess the effect of the new product launch

Answer:

Actually, the grass-roots analysis is very flexible. If new information arises that make the team's original assumptions unworkable, it's perfectly acceptable to make changes. Just be sure to keep your team informed.

Option 1: Correct. It is important for Tim to incorporate new information into his grass-roots analysis and communicate any changes necessary to those involved with the project.

Option 2: Incorrect. The new information should be included in the grass-roots analysis, but it should be integrated into the existing branches. Any revisions should be communicated immediately.

Option 3: Incorrect. The grass-roots diagram is intended to be flexible. The new information should be integrated into the existing analysis.

Option 4: Incorrect. Any new tasks must be incorporated into the existing analysis. One of the advantages of using a grass-roots analysis is that it allows for this kind of flexibility.

The grass-roots analysis provides an integration team with a strong, structured method for planning an implementation without sacrificing flexibility.

In this topic, you learned how to create a grass-roots analysis diagram and how to use the diagram to create an implementation strategy.

Managing the Action

Will farmers be successful if they merely plant seeds and leave the rest up to nature?

No. In fact, those who neglect their agricultural responsibilities will likely spend harvest time on the couch instead of in the fields. Their decisions to plant the seeds will bear no fruit whatsoever unless they manage the crops afterward.

When it comes to business decisions, don't be a couch potato. Manage the implementation of your decisions with as much care and attention as possible. Your career success will grow in lock step with that of your organization.

It's often said that "Two heads are better than one." But when it comes to implementing a business decision, you want to engage more than your colleagues' brainpower: You want their hearts behind the decision as well.

When you make others feel strongly about your decision's merit, they'll probably include their practical efforts in its implementation as well. Get ready to learn how to obtain stakeholder involvement during the implementation of your business decision by:

- involving important "gatekeepers" first,
- bringing in "know-how",
- championing the decision.

"When you come to a roadblock, take a detour." --Mary Kay Ash, founder of Mary Kay Cosmetics

Implementation roadblocks aren't your enemy. Your faulty reaction to them is. In this topic, you'll discover several ways to effectively cope with adjustments during decision implementation:

- Remember that no decision is final.
- Make needed adjustments promptly.
- Examine any new training requirements.

"Hear one side and you will be in the dark. Hear both and all will be clear." --Thomas C. Haliburton, Canadian author

Keep this in mind while reading on: You should manage resistance. And you should lead people. In this topic, you'll learn to apply these strategies to manage resistance to a business decision:

- holding one-on-one meetings with resistance leaders,
- setting up a concrete feedback loop.

Successfully managing the implementation of a business decision

Will farmers be successful if they merely plant seeds and leave the rest up to nature?

No. In fact, those who neglect their agricultural responsibilities will likely spend harvest time on the couch instead of in the fields. Their decisions to plant the seeds will bear no fruit whatsoever unless they manage the crops afterward.

When it comes to business decisions, don't be a couch potato. Manage the implementation of your decisions with as much care and attention as possible. Your career success will grow in lock step with that of your organization.

Katrina, a sales manager, can vouch for the importance of guiding business choices to their successful completion.

See each benefit Katrina gains from being a conscientious custodian of her decisions.

Engendering greater support

"I pay as much attention to decision making as I do to decision management. The two activities truly go hand in hand.

Colleagues appreciate the active role I take in the guidance of my decisions and, in turn, lend me their added support."

Saving time

"Few things frustrate me more than wasting time on conflict that results from ill-managed business decisions. By being a good decision manager, I'm able to reduce any interpersonal strife that erupts and spend the saved time on more productive matters."

Harnessing potential

"I make business decisions based on the promise they contain. In order to get the most from those choices and realize the potential they hold, I need to implement them in a thoughtful and skillful manner. That's what being a manager is all about."

Question

A business decision that's not effectively implemented is no decision at all. Select the statements that illustrate the value of successfully managing the implementation of a business decision.

Options:

1. You'll spend less time embroiled in time-consuming conflicts.
2. You'll explain your reasoning behind making the decision.
3. You'll obtain added support from colleagues and co-workers.
4. You'll reap the most benefit from each business decision.

5. You'll determine the origin of future decision complications.

Answer:

Actually, you'll engender greater support from colleagues, reduce time spent on conflict resolution, and harness the full potential of each decision. Explaining your reasoning and determining the cause of complications are separate issues.

Option 1: Correct. By managing the implementation of business decisions, you will be able to reduce interpersonal strife and focus your time on more productive matters.

Option 2: Incorrect. Exhibiting your rationale is not part of implementing your decision. Implementation deals with moving forward with the steps necessary reach the desired goal.

Option 3: Correct. Your colleagues and co-workers will want to lend you their support because of the active role you take in managing your decisions.

Option 4: Correct. It takes thoughtful consideration, but managing your decisions will help you to reach your goals effectively.

Option 5: Incorrect. While it can alert you to potential complications, proper management of a decision will help you gain support, save time, and reach for your potential.

Your decisions affect everyone around you. As you saw in the previous exercise, the value of effectively managing the implementation of a business decision applies to both you and your organization.

In this lesson, you'll learn how to keep decision stakeholders engaged in the decision implementation, guide yourself through implementation adjustments, and manage initial resistance to your decision follow-through.

Strategies applied to involve stakeholders

It's often said that "Two heads are better than one." But when it comes to implementing a business decision, you want to engage more than your colleagues' brainpower: You want their hearts behind the decision as well.

When you make others feel strongly about your decision's merit, they'll probably include their practical efforts in its implementation as well. Get ready to learn how to obtain stakeholder involvement during the implementation of your business decision by:

- involving important "gatekeepers" first,
- bringing in "know-how",
- championing the decision.

Question

So what do you think a "stakeholder" is?

Options:

1. A stakeholder is a manager or supervisor whose role is to assess your effectiveness at implementing a business decision.

2. A stakeholder is anyone who has a business or personal interest in the effective implementation of a business decision.

Answer:

Your manager or supervisor almost always holds this status, but the title of stakeholder also applies to anyone who has even a passing interest in the productive implementation of your business decision.

Option 1: Incorrect. The stakeholder has a vested interest in the successful outcome of the implementation of the decision. This includes, but is not limited to, management.

Option 2: Correct. A stakeholder is someone who stands to benefit from the successful implementation of the decision.

Henry Ford once remarked, "Coming together is a beginning, staying together is progress, and working together is success." When decision stakeholders work with you to ensure a smooth implementation, you'll usually progress from a promising start to a very successful end.

The first strategy for making sure stakeholders are engaged is involving important "gatekeepers" first. Gatekeepers are influential colleagues whose opinions and ideas carry significant weight within your organization.

Lynn, a systems administrator, enlisted the involvement of Stephen and Patty, two influential operations managers.

Lynn: Hey, thanks for speaking with me, Stephen and Patty. As you've heard, I decided to implement several new databases to facilitate our internal record keeping. I wanted to first explain my intentions to you both. People in our company value your opinions, and I would love to see you engaged with this project.

Stephen: Thanks for the compliment, Lynn. I read your decision report and found it persuasive. You'll need to work out a few kinks, but I generally agree with your thinking.

Lynn: Excellent. How about you, Patty?

Patty: I'm not as efficient as Stephen is; I haven't had the chance to review the report yet. I've heard about your decision though, and my initial thought is that I'm behind you as well.

Lynn: Let me know if you have any questions after getting the details, Patty. And read the report with this in mind: I truly want not only your collective support, but I'd also like you to take active roles in implementing the new databases. Your involvement will motivate other stakeholders to work with me toward a successful integration.

Patty: I like your directness, Lynn. I also like your emphasis on teamwork. Stephen and I will check back with you after we've thought more about the actual implementation. By the way, it's really nice of you to include us in this process.

Lynn: You bet. Together, I think we'll make this work.

Notice that Lynn explicitly requested Stephen and Patty's support and involvement.

She realized that to get everyone on board and participating, it was first up to her to lower the ladder for her most important decision navigators: her organization's gatekeepers.

After her meeting, Lynn used the next strategy for involving stakeholders in her database decision by bringing in "know-how." Know-how refers to experts, inside or outside your company, who have direct experience with the subject matter of your business decision.

Lynn lined up several experts to meet privately with stakeholders and to make a presentation to the entire organization regarding the proposed databases.

See each of Lynn's comments, in order, to discover how she mustered her army of experts.

Comment 1

"Richard, a co-worker, used these same databases at a previous job. I enlisted his help in talking to the various stakeholders about the program's features. Richard's explanations kept my colleagues informed and enthusiastic."

Comment 2

"I even called one of the original system designers and persuaded her to make an appearance at my company. Her direct experience lent credence to my decision. She did a great job clarifying the roles co-workers would take in the implementation."

Comment 3

"I covered my bases. With Richard meeting one-on-one with stakeholders, those people were able to receive advice and input tailored to their individual needs."

Comment 4

"On the flip side, Meredith, the systems designer, made a presentation to the entire company during our weekly meeting. Her comments, based on her relevant qualifications, made others feel secure and motivated in their involvement."

Comment 5

"It's great to have both internal and external experts help promote the implementation, but it's not always feasible. That's OK. I simply make sure some amount of know-how is available to all decision stakeholders."

Question

Select valid strategies for involving stakeholders in the implementation of a business decision.

Options:

1. Directly ask for the support and involvement of your organization's gatekeepers.
2. Bring in external experts to speak with decision stakeholders only as a last resort.
3. Make sure your experts have direct experience with or knowledge about your subject matter.
4. Release information about your decision incrementally so that colleagues aren't overwhelmed.

Answer:

In fact, valid strategies include making an explicit request for gatekeeper support and involvement and using only qualified experts. Don't hesitate to rely on external experts. Your release of information will depend on the circumstance.

Option 1: Correct. Gatekeepers are people in the organization with a lot of influence. Enlisting their support is the first step towards making sure the other stakeholders are engaged.

Option 2: Incorrect. It is always a good idea to bring in an external source of information. The stakeholders' confidence in the decision will increase.

Option 3: Correct. Because using experts is designed to instill confidence in the stakeholders, it is imperative that their experience is direct and that they are knowledgeable.

Option 4: Incorrect. It is important to avoid actions, such as holding back information, that would undermine the confidence stakeholders have in your decision. Instead, enlist the help of experts to instruct stakeholders in all aspects of the decision.

The strategies discussed thus far result in interactions that take place at specific times. But there's also something you can do to involve stakeholders during the entire implementation process.

You can execute the third strategy and champion the decision. You do this by promoting and fighting for your business choice every step of the way, using both word and deed.

Lynn championed her database decision by exuding optimism whenever discussing her plan. At the same time, she touted the benefits of her decision to all listeners.

Select each of Lynn's comments to find out how she sparked the involvement of stakeholders by also making herself available for questions and concerns.

Comment 1

"I constantly stressed that the databases would save the company money. They would also save each stakeholder time and increase his productivity."

Comment 2

"During meetings with stakeholders, I emphasized that I encouraged their input. I held voluntary meetings at which I fielded questions about the new databases."

By being optimistic, touting the decision benefits, and being available to stakeholders, Lynn proved herself to be a real champ at ensuring the involvement of others.

So how can you be sure you, or other colleagues, have been effective at using strategies to involve stakeholders in the execution of a business decision? Be inquisitive. Ask yourself questions.

Select each of the areas Lynn considered when she assumed the role of detective and investigated her own effectiveness to learn more about how she did it.

Gatekeepers

"I always ask whether I requested the involvement of my organization's gatekeepers in an explicit manner. There's no use beating around the bush. Was I upfront when asking for their engagement in my decision's implementation?"

Experts

"I want to involve others who possess immediately relevant knowledge about or experience in my business decision. Did I enlist the help of experts whose credentials lend themselves directly to the issue at hand?"

Benefits

"Did I involve stakeholders by emphasizing the benefits of my decision and their involvement with it?"

Coercion

"I'm sometimes tempted to twist arms and make threats. This practice will come back to haunt me though. Did I avoid using coercion of any sort to obtain active stakeholder involvement in my decision's implementation?"

Case Study: Question 1 of 2

Scenario

For your convenience, the case study is repeated with each question.

Earl, the operations manager for a company that manufactures automated teller machines, decided to incorporate retina scan technology into his products. Earl felt this user identification technology would give his company a competitive advantage. However, he needed to keep the decision stakeholders involved in the implementation to ensure success.

1. Involving gatekeepers

Earl first met with several influential managers. He stressed the importance of their involvement with the retina scan implementation and directly asked for their support. He got some initial resistance but remained optimistic throughout the meeting.

2. Bringing in know-how

Earl also brought in three ophthalmologists who hadn't worked with the technology but were familiar with the theory behind it. The scientists presented their supportive opinions during an all-staff meeting.

3. Championing the decision

Earl spoke optimistically about the benefits of the retina scan decision, including greater market share and market image enhancement. Earl also emphasized that he was available at all times for questions or concerns.

Question:

Was Earl effective at using strategies to involve stakeholders in the implementation of his retina scan decision?

Options:

1. Earl was effective because he championed the retina scan decision, engaged influential gatekeepers, and invited experts to speak about the enhancement.
2. Earl was ineffective because he had ophthalmologists speak about the technology but failed to overcome initial gatekeeper resistance to the retina scans.

3. Earl was ineffective because he involved gatekeepers and touted the benefits of the retina scans but failed to bring in experts who had direct experience with the scans.

4. Earl was effective because he engaged important gatekeepers, emphasized the retina scan's benefits, and made himself available for any questions.

Answer:

Actually, Earl used several strategies properly. But he was ultimately ineffective because the ophthalmologists he invited to speak to employees had no direct knowledge or experience with the retina scan technology.

Option 1: Incorrect. While Earl did a good job with involving gatekeepers and championing his idea, the experts he brought in did not have the necessary direct experience with the new retina technology.

Option 2: Incorrect. The meeting Earl held with the influential managers he chose as gatekeepers was considered successful. The real weakness lay in the lack of experts brought in who had direct experience with the new technology.

Option 3: Correct. The two areas of involving gatekeepers and championing the idea were successfully completed by Earl, but he needed to find experts with direct experience with the retina scan technology he was trying to implement.

Option 4: Incorrect. This question emphasizes the success Earl had at choosing influential gatekeepers and championing his idea, but the necessary component of enlisting experts with direct experience was missing.

Case Study: Question 2 of 2

What questions did you ask to determine whether Earl was effective at using strategies to involve stakeholders in the implementation of his teller machine enhancement?

Options:

1. Did Earl avoid using coercion to secure stakeholder involvement with the retina scan implementation?
2. Did Earl make it a point to explicitly ask gatekeepers for their support in the enhancement implementation?
3. Did Earl overcome all initial resistance to the retina scan idea by promising to review the idea before acting on it?
4. Did Earl emphasize the benefits of the retina scan technology in a positive and upbeat manner?
5. Did Earl invite experts who had direct experience with the technology to speak to stakeholders?

Answer:

In fact, you should have asked if Earl explicitly requested the support of stakeholders, brought in experts with direct knowledge or experience, touted the enhancement benefits, and avoided using coercion to involve stakeholders.

Option 1: Correct. It is imperative to avoid using coercion because of the negative side effects associated with it.

Option 2: Correct. By directly asking the gatekeepers for their participation, Earl will be more able to gain their support.

Option 3: Incorrect. This action was not in the scenario. Earl didn't promise to review his idea in order to overcome resistance.

Option 4: Correct. If Earl is enthusiastic about the benefits of this project, he will find that his enthusiasm has an impact on others. Excitement for the project will be heightened.

Option 5: Correct. Bringing in experts who are directly involved with similar projects will strengthen Earl's efforts to implement the new technology.

Had Earl invited truly qualified experts to speak with his colleagues, support for and involvement with his decision would have likely been more pronounced.

You can't go it alone. You need the active involvement of your organization's stakeholders to productively implement any business decision. In this topic, you learned to effectively involve stakeholders in the implementation of a business decision by:

- involving important gatekeepers first,
- bringing in know-how,
- championing the decision.

Effectively coping with adjustments

"When you come to a roadblock, take a detour." -- Mary Kay Ash, founder of Mary Kay Cosmetics

Implementation roadblocks aren't your enemy. Your faulty reaction to them is. In this topic, you'll discover several ways to effectively cope with adjustments during decision implementation:

- Remember that no decision is final.
- Make needed adjustments promptly.
- Examine any new training requirements.
- **Question**

Think about five business decisions, trivial or significant, you've made during the past few months.

How many of those decisions did you implement verbatim, without altering your plans in any way?

Options:

1. one
2. two
3. three

4. four
5. five

Answer:

Option 1: A business decision implemented strictly as planned represents an exception to the rule. By being prepared for and skillfully coping with inevitable change, you'll adhere to the rules of business success.

Option 2: A business decision implemented strictly as planned represents an exception to the rule. By being prepared for and skillfully coping with inevitable change, you'll adhere to the rules of business success.

Option 3: A business decision implemented strictly as planned represents an exception to the rule. By being prepared for and skillfully coping with inevitable change, you'll adhere to the rules of business success.

Option 4: A business decision implemented strictly as planned represents an exception to the rule. By being prepared for and skillfully coping with inevitable change, you'll adhere to the rules of business success.

Option 5: A business decision implemented strictly as planned represents an exception to the rule. By being prepared for and skillfully coping with inevitable change, you'll adhere to the rules of business success.

It's said that "The best-laid plans of mice and men oft go astray." Nowhere does this idiom hold more true than in the realm of business decisions.

So when coping with implementation adjustments and modifications, always remember that no decision is final. This first step of change management will keep you both flexible and anchored.

Jean, a meteorologist for a large agribusiness, knows all too well that adjustments in decision implementations are usually inevitable.

See Jean's comments, in order, to find out how she avoided being blown away by the winds of change.

Comment 1

"Based on long-range weather forecasts, I decided to recommend my company scale back feed corn production schedules. It turned out my decision needed adjusting."

Comment 2

"It wasn't a huge deal. Because I prepared my colleagues for potential adjustments beforehand, they and I adapted to the situation much more readily."

The realization that you need to adjust your decision's implementation often arrives as a gut feeling or hunch. After studying the potential change rationally and deciding in its favor, take the second coping measure and make the needed adjustments promptly.

Have you ever gotten a pebble caught in your shoe? It soon feels like a boulder unless you take measures to remove it.

Neglecting to make needed adjustments during decision implementation will put you between a rock and hard place.

On the other hand, setting those required adjustments into motion usually results in:

- a revitalized course of action,
- a savings of time and money,
- the respect and admiration of your colleagues.

Lastly, you should cope with adjustments during decision implementation by examining any new training requirements that result from your change of plans.

Select each training aspect Jim considered while thinking about the ramifications of a recent implementation change to learn more about it.

Input on training

"When I decided to adopt a more complex employee time-reporting software package than originally planned, I knew some added training was required. I instructed the various department supervisors to determine how many people needed guidance and what form they thought it should take."

Training content

"The new system mirrored the one employees were already being trained on but included several new features. I decided the existing training should continue, with the additional content addressed at the end of the training regimen."

Training timetable

"An entirely new reporting system would have called for wholesale changes to the training timetable. Fortunately, in the present case, I just extended the time frame by a few days. Timing is everything. Had I not considered it, my decision change may have caused a lot of scheduling hassles."

Question

The only constant in business, as in life, is change. Identify valid strategies for effectively coping with adjustments during decision implementation.

Options:

1. Bear in mind that no decision is unchangeable.
2. Institute only noncontroversial adjustments.
3. Take any training modifications into account.
4. Implement decision adjustments without delay.

Answer:

In fact, you recognized that no decision is final, that you must act on adjustments promptly, and that you need to examine the new training requirements. On the other hand, you can't always avoid controversial decision modifications.

Option 1: Correct. Flexibility is the key to dealing with changes that may be encountered in the implementation process.

Option 2: Incorrect. People are always reluctant to accept change. You should prepare the stakeholders to be flexible throughout the implementation process.

Option 3: Correct. After the change has been noted, it is necessary to examine the effect of that change on current training initiatives.

Option 4: Correct. Beginning immediately to make any necessary changes has many benefits, including saving time and money.

According to an ancient Chinese proverb, "The wise adapt themselves to circumstances, as water molds itself to a pitcher."

When you use the strategies covered in the previous exercise, you'll effectively manage even the mightiest flood of decision adjustments.

In this topic, you learned several valuable ways to cope with adjustments during decision implementation: remember there are no final decisions, act on necessary adjustments promptly, and examine any new training requirements.

Strategies to manage resistance

"Hear one side and you will be in the dark. Hear both and all will be clear." --Thomas C. Haliburton, Canadian author

Keep this in mind while reading on: You should manage resistance. And you should lead people. In this topic, you'll learn to apply these strategies to manage resistance to a business decision:

- holding one-on-one meetings with resistance leaders,
- setting up a concrete feedback loop.

Ted began making homemade ice cream at an early age. He later turned his childhood hobby into a thriving business and distributed his frozen treats across the country. Ted decided to diversify his business by entering the ultracompetitive chocolate chip cookie market.

As he expected, his decision left a bad taste in a few of his employees' mouths.

Ted immediately employed the first strategy for managing resistance to his business decision.

He held one-on-one meetings with the resistance leaders.

A resistance leader is a dissenting colleague who is either particularly vocal or whose opinion carries significant weight within your organization. In Ted's company, two influential colleagues expressed strong reservations about his decision to market the cookies.

See each method Ted used to manage George and Emily's initial resistance to his plan to learn more about it.

Encouraging directness

"As in my meeting with George, I encouraged Emily to offer her thoughts in an honest and direct way. Emily, an operations manager, usually spoke up. But she often did it in a way that minimized the strength of her feelings. I emphasized that I wanted to know exactly how she felt."

Finding out the root causes of resistance

"A dissenting colleague like Emily typically has several intertwined reasons for resisting a decision, some minor and some significant. The more important reasons usually supersede the less crucial ones. That's why I asked both George and Emily to tell me what was really driving their resistance."

See each of Ted's comments to learn more about how he dug below the surface in an effort to find out the root cause of the resistance leaders' discontent.

Comment 1

"Resistance leaders usually have several reasons they don't endorse your decision. I told George and Emily to tell me about the most significant ones."

Comment 2

"George resisted my decision to enter the cookie market because he didn't think it was lucrative. Emily felt we would need to hire too many new skilled employees."

Question

Select valid strategies to manage resistance to a business decision while conducting one-on-one meetings with resistance leaders.

Options:

1. Strongly encourage resistance leaders to be upfront about their feelings.
2. Gently explain the consequences of failing to back your business decision.
3. Try to determine the real reason that resistance leaders hesitate to endorse your choice.
4. Explain to the resistance leaders that you prize their input and opinions.

Answer:

In fact, you should encourage resistance leaders' directness, value their input, and determine the root cause of their resistance. Talking about the consequences of nonconformity will serve only to enhance the person's resistance.

Option 1: Correct. Encouraging an honest account of the resistance leaders' feelings communicates that you value their opinion.

Option 2: Incorrect. Your aim is to generate support and avoid coercion. You shouldn't be presenting consequences for failing to back your decision.

Option 3: Correct. By identifying the real reasons for resistance, you will be able to directly manage the issue. This will lead to the quickest resolution.

Option 4: Correct. This will generate respect and maximize your chances of gaining the leaders' support for the needed modifications.

Using the strategies covered in the previous exercise during your private meetings will help stem the tide of resistance. But it's important to carry that momentum over into the proceeding weeks and months.

Ted maintained his inertia of goodwill by using the second strategy to manage resistance to a business decision: setting up a concrete feedback loop. Ted ensured that anyone with concerns or questions could contact him by establishing predetermined channels through which colleagues provided input.

See each method Ted used to encourage feedback to learn more about it.

Follow-up meetings

"At the end of my discussions with resistance leaders, I said I wanted to talk to them again at a follow-up meeting after they'd thought more about the situation. This way, I underscored my openness and was able to monitor their resistance levels."

Web-based survey

"To keep the lines of communication with all employees open, I sent out e-mail invitations to participate in a Web-based survey. The survey allowed colleagues to respond with their thoughts about the cookie decision anonymously."

Suggestion boxes

"I went so far as to put suggestion boxes in the employee cafeteria and reception area."

Available to talk

"I also let people know I'd be in my office Tuesdays, from 1 p.m. to 2 p.m., with the express purpose of talking about the decision to anyone who wanted to drop by. I emphasized the "office hours" would continue throughout the decision implementation."

The resistance to Ted's decision didn't simply evaporate. But the strategies Ted adopted enabled him to manage that resistance and diminish its potentially harmful effects. The resistance leaders may have had slight disagreements with Ted, but they certainly didn't find his handling of the situation half-baked.

In this topic, you learned how to apply these strategies to manage resistance to your business decision: Hold one-on-one meetings with resistance leaders and set up a concrete feedback loop.

Evaluating the Action

Have you ever suffered from hay fever? One of the most frustrating things about this allergy is that you require constant medication to reduce the symptoms. Otherwise, your sneezing and itching problem never lets up.

It can be the same with business decisions. You must take measures to evaluate and reduce potential problems in order to stay symptom-free. On the bright side, you don't require a doctor to write you that prescription for success.

Every decision you make, trivial or monumental, affects the way you conduct business. So the first step in assessing the outcome of a business decision is to examine the negative objective consequences of the action. Objective consequences denote measurable adverse effects resulting from your choice.

Some of the most precise individuals at gymnastic competitions aren't the gymnasts. They're the judges.

They look for flaws in the competitors' routines and then rate their overall success.

After implementing a business decision, you need to switch roles from competitor to judge. Done smartly, this maneuver won't require you to bend over backward.

"You don't drown by falling in water: You drown by staying there." --Edwin Louis Cole, motivational expert

When decisions fail, as some inevitably do, take action. Colleagues will expect you to do so. Your success and their confidence in your abilities hang in the balance.

Constantly evaluating business decisions

Would you be concerned if the pilot of your plane failed to monitor the instruments at all times?

Question

You'd certainly have reason to worry if that was the case. As would your decision-making colleagues if they knew you weren't monitoring the success of your business choices on a frequent basis.

How about you? How often do you make strategic choices at work, refocus your attention on other matters, and lose sight of the outcome of your original decision?

Options:

1. never
2. rarely
3. half the time
4. sometimes
5. always

Answer:

Making a decision and failing to evaluate it thoroughly is like taking one step forward and two steps back. By finishing what you start, you're more likely to see yourself through to business success.

Have you ever suffered from hay fever? One of the most frustrating things about this allergy is that you require constant medication to reduce the symptoms. Otherwise, your sneezing and itching problem never lets up.

It can be the same with business decisions. You must take measures to evaluate and reduce potential problems in order to stay symptom-free. On the bright side, you don't require a doctor to write you that prescription for success.

The benefits of frequently monitoring the effectiveness of your business decisions are like a breath of fresh air.

See each aspect of monitoring business decisions to find out how Lewis, the owner of a large fitness machine manufacturer, exercises decision vigilance at all times.

Potential problems

"Only by staying on top of the progress of my business decisions am I able to recognize and counteract potential problems."

Previous mistakes

"Plus, I'm better able to learn from my previous mistakes. And that makes me more confident in the ultimate success of my business decisions."

Question

When it comes to decision making, it pays to be vigilant.

Select benefits of constantly evaluating business decisions.

Options:

1. You'll feel more confident in the success of your business decisions.
2. You'll be able to demonstrate the logic behind your business decisions.
3. You'll be less likely to repeat any errors you've committed in the past.
4. You'll be more assured you're heading off potential decision problems.

Answer:

In fact, you'll be more confident in your decision's success, be more assured you're reducing potential problems, and enjoy an increased ability to learn from the past. Demonstrating your logic doesn't really concern decision evaluation.

Option 1: Correct. Knowing that you are continually on the alert for problems that arise and exercising the tools to solve those problems results in feeling confident about the ultimate success of your business decisions.

Option 2: Incorrect. Constantly evaluating business decisions has definite benefits, such as learning from past mistakes and providing a feeling of confidence in the success of the business. Business logic does not readily apply.

Option 3: Correct. Constant evaluation of your business decision allows you to learn from past mistakes and thereby avoid similar errors in the future.

Option 4: Correct. Constant vigilance allows a level of awareness that prevents unforeseen problems from occurring.

Do the benefits covered in the previous exercise sound appealing? They're yours to be had when you constantly evaluate your business decisions. In this lesson, you'll learn how to:

- assess the merits of your business choices;
- take the first steps in recovering from decision failure.
-

Ways to assess a decision outcome

His friends gave Evan a nickname: "Grip." As an ace news reporter, Evan never let a story slip through his hands. He wanted to know exactly how the event in question turned out.

You'll make the decision-making headlines if you follow Evan's example. Never leave a business decision behind until you've thoroughly evaluated its end result.

In this topic, you'll learn how to assess a business decision by:

- examining adverse objective consequences of the action,
- examining adverse social consequences of the action,
- determining the degree to which you solved your business problem.

Question

What do you think? When can you consider a business decision truly complete?

Options:

1. A business decision is truly complete after you've made up your mind and decided exactly how to solve a problem.
2. A business decision is truly complete after it has been thoroughly implemented and its corresponding effects have been taken into account.

Answer:

Actually, a business decision qualifies as complete only after it has been put into action and its effectiveness has been fully evaluated.

Option 1: Incorrect. A successful business decision is completed in stages, and requires input and feedback from many sources.

Option 2: Correct. A successful business decision is complete when all of the stages of implementation have been completed and evaluated.

Every decision you make, trivial or monumental, affects the way you conduct business. So the first step in assessing the outcome of a business decision is to examine the negative objective consequences of the action. Objective consequences denote measurable adverse effects resulting from your choice.

See each aspect Suzanne, a marketing specialist for a large backpack manufacturer, considered when she took stock of a recent business decision.

Finances

"To increase sales, I opted to market backpacks with built-in waterproof rainflies. I wanted to know how productive this option proved, so I looked at an objective measure of its success: the bottom line. The new line of packs surpassed projections--no adverse consequences here."

Materials

"We made the rainflies with a special nylon laminate. We had some difficulty obtaining enough of that laminate to meet demand. We had to put some packs on backorder. Of course, this was a great problem to have, but I still had to take it into consideration in order to really assess my decision outcome."

Company image

"I also wanted to determine whether I met my goal of enhancing our products' image. I sent out a survey to both retailers and end-users asking them if, and how, they perceived our products in a different light after this design upgrade. I looked for any signs of dissatisfaction with the rainflies."

After evaluating the more measurable adverse consequences of the rainfly implementation, Suzanne used the next strategy to assess her decision outcome. She examined the negative social consequences of her action.

When you consider adverse social consequences of your decision, you target people within your own organization. How did your choice affect their ability to do, and feelings about, their jobs?

See each of Suzanne's comments to learn how she took the social pulse of her colleagues.

Comment 1

"I asked around to see whether the new rainflies placed more demand on expected employee production time than first assumed."

Comment 2

"I also tried to determine whether colleagues were in any way disgruntled about working with the new materials. Had my decision adversely affected morale?"

Overall, Suzanne noted few negative ramifications, objective or social, resulting from her rainfly decision.

Lastly, she sought to put the finishing touches on her assessment, so she determined the degree to which she solved the business problem.

Suzanne did this by assigning her decision a "success rating." This rating entails some degree of subjectivity. But by giving your business decision such a designation, you're able to learn from past mistakes and focus on avenues of improvement in the future.

See each step, in order, Suzanne performed in order to rate her success.

1. Consider the adverse consequences

"I first considered all the adverse consequences, objective and social, that I uncovered using the first two assessment strategies. I hadn't found many, but it was important to assess their total effect."

2. Review expectations and goals

"Then I reviewed my expectations and goals regarding the benefits of incorporating rainflies into our backpacks. To what extent did I meet sales goals? To what degree did I succeed in enhancing our product image?"

3. Assign a success rating

"Based on the relative lack of negative consequences, the full achievement of sales goals, and the results of my product-image survey, I assigned the rainfly decision a success rating of 90 on a scale from 0 to 100."

4. Focus on ways of increasing the effectiveness of action

"In other words, I found the decision highly successful. That success rating enabled me to then focus my attention on ways I could have made the action 10 percent more effective."

Question

You can learn a lot from a backward glance. Identify ways to assess a decision outcome.

Options:

1. Establish to what extent you solved your business problem.

2. Determine whether discarded options may have proved more effective.

3. Consider any negative effects your decision had on others.

4. Examine adverse objective ramifications of your decision.

Answer:

Actually, you should determine to what degree you solved the problem and examine both the adverse social and objective decision consequences. Reviewing discarded options doesn't help you assess the present situation.

Option 1: Correct. After gathering information on the objective and social effects of your decision, the last step in assessing a decision outcome is to determine a "success rating" for that decision.

Option 2: Incorrect. All the focus in assessing a decision outcome should be on the effects of the actual decision. It is inappropriate to re-examine discarded options because that doesn't help you to evaluate the current outcome.

Option 3: Correct. It is necessary to evaluate all the social effects of your decision.

Option 4: Correct. The effects of a decision that can be measured are the first ones to be evaluated.

When you make business decisions and fail to assess the outcomes, it's like starting a campfire and leaving it unattended.

Keep your decision-making future burning bright by practicing the strategies covered in the previous exercise.

In this topic, you learned how to evaluate a decision outcome by determining to what extent you solved your business problem and analyzing any undesired objective or social consequences resulting from the decision implementation.

Strategies used to evaluate a decision outcome

Some of the most precise individuals at gymnastic competitions aren't the gymnasts. They're the judges. They look for flaws in the competitors' routines and then rate their overall success.

After implementing a business decision, you need to switch roles from competitor to judge. Done smartly, this maneuver won't require you to bend over backward.

In this topic, you'll learn how to analyze the effectiveness of strategies used to evaluate a business decision.

The strategies you'll study are: examining adverse objective consequences of the decision, examining adverse social consequences of the decision, and determining the degree to which the business problem was resolved.

First, how familiar are you with the term "consequence" as it pertains to business decisions?

See each variety of negative decision effects to learn more about it.

Adverse objective consequences

Negative objective consequences concern organizational drawbacks resulting from a business decision that are measurable and quantifiable.

For example, lower-than-expected revenue figures, larger output reductions than anticipated, and a decline in customer satisfaction that you establish by compiling survey results.

Adverse social consequences

Negative social effects are harmful interpersonal consequences suffered by colleagues within your own organization.

For example, a resulting inability of a colleague to perform his job efficiently, an increase of interpersonal conflict among employees, and a decrease in the amount of productive communication among co-workers.

Question

Match the type of decision consequence to one or more descriptions.

Options:

A. adverse objective consequences

B. adverse social consequences

Targets:

1. customer opinion surrounding the business decision

2. negative impacts on employees' abilities to do their jobs

3. drawbacks of the decision that are concrete and measurable

Answer:

Actually, adverse objective consequences involve measurable drawbacks, including fluctuation in customer opinion. Adverse social effects are suffered by people within your own organization.

Because this effect is measurable and quantifiable, (when determined by a customer survey) it is an objective consequence.

This is a description of an effect on interpersonal relations within the company. These effects are referred to as adverse social consequences.

Objective consequences are the effects of business decisions that can be counted and measured, and do not change.

Casey, the owner of a uniform manufacturing company, decided to increase the durability of his products beyond what the industrial specifications called for. Although initially more expensive, Casey believed this increased durability added value and would eventually cause demand for his uniforms to soar. He also believed his company's rather stale image would be enhanced. After the beefed-up uniforms had been on the market for several weeks, Casey decided to assess the durability of his original decision.

Casey formed a cross-departmental team and gave it the task of evaluating the durability decision. After team members executed their evaluation strategies, Casey analyzed the results.

See each method Casey use to analyze the team's effective use of the first evaluation strategy, examining the adverse objective consequences of the decision.

Summarized progress

"I made sure my team checked revenue levels, supply costs, and production output and compared them to estimates. We concretely summed up our progress thus far."

Sent out customer surveys

"We sent out customer surveys quantifying their pre- and post-uniform decision attitudes to the change. The results helped us be objective about our success"

After analyzing the team's use of the first evaluation strategy, Casey then scrutinized its examination of the negative social effects of the durability decision. Casey proceeded one analytical step at a time, covering all his bases.

Casey explained to Michelle, his human resources manager, how he judged the team's job at assessing the negative social effects of the decision.

Casey: The team did a great job, Michelle. They spoke to each of the department supervisors and asked them whether their employees suffered any negative personal effects from the decision. After all, working with the more durable materials required them to adjust their work habits considerably.

Michelle: What do you mean by "personal effects," Casey?

Casey: I'm talking about reductions in their ability to do their jobs, or any interpersonal conflict that may have accompanied the adjustment to the heavier materials.

Michelle: From what I've heard, employees are actually enjoying the challenge and change of pace.

Casey: Apparently, you're right, Michelle. The decision evaluation team also monitored the time reports employees turn in each week, another great way to assess the results of our uniform decision. Production efficiencies actually increased.

Michelle: Great news.

Casey: I agree. According to my analysis, the evaluation team performed its social assessment like real pros.

After speaking with Michelle, Casey added the final piece to his analysis puzzle.

He investigated his evaluation team's performance of the last assessment tool: determining the degree

to which the uniform marketing problem was solved.

See each step that Casey performed to sum up the team's effectiveness on this last evaluation step to learn more about it.

Step 1

"I ensured that the team assigned an appropriate success rating to the uniform-materials decision."

Step 2

"I verified that team members arrived at this figure by considering both the adverse objective consequences of the decision, which were few, and the nonexistent negative social effects."

Step 3

"Then I checked to see if the team members combined these factors with the feedback they received from all employees regarding their current morale levels. Did employees feel upbeat or frustrated from working with the new uniform materials?"

Step 4

"Based on these three factors, the team assigned the decision a success rating of 90 on a scale from 0 to 100. I deemed that figure appropriate."

Step 5

"More important, it's crucial to use that rating to consider ways in which the original decision could have been improved."

Step 6

"It pleased me that team members spent considerable time devising strategies to use on a similar business decision that would lift its success rating from 90 to 100. For example, would better decision timing have boosted our effectiveness?"

After assessing the team's use of the third evaluation technique, Casey asked himself several other questions in order to finish his analysis of the team's effectiveness. You should ask the same questions when you wish to analyze your, or someone else's, decision success.

See each aspect of assessing a business decision to find out the thoughts that ran through Casey's mind during his evaluation.

Adverse objective consequences

"I always ask whether the decision makers examined the measurable negative objective consequences stemming from their business choices. After all, these types of drawbacks are called "objective" for a reason."

Adverse social consequences

"When scrutinizing the adverse social effects of a decision, did the decision makers target people within their own organization?"

Degree to which the problem was solved

"Say a decision maker assigned the success of his decision a rating of 70. Did he then use that rating to examine ways in which he could have improved his original business decision by the 30 points found lacking?"

Case Study: Question 1 of 2

Scenario:

Joanne managed the operations department of a company that manufactured water filtration systems. It sold the majority of its products to governmental agencies in Third World countries. To boost flagging sales, Joanne decided to market the products in countries once deemed too politically unstable.

Answer the questions in order.

Question:

Was Joanne effective at using strategies to evaluate her marketing decision?

Options:

1. Joanne was effective because she used the first two strategies to assess her decision by examining consequences internal to her organization and basing her success rating on feedback regarding morale.

2. Joanne was ineffective because she examined the adverse objective consequences and negative social effects of her risky marketing decision but failed to use her success rating to think about ways in which she could have improved her original marketing decision.

3. Joanne was effective because she studied adverse objective consequences of her marketing choice that were measurable and examined the adverse social effects on colleagues within her organization.

Answer:

In fact, Joanne examined both the adverse objective and social consequences properly but was ultimately ineffective in her evaluation because she didn't use her decision success rating to study ways she could have improved her choice.

Option 1: Incorrect. Both of these methods deal with the adverse social consequences. Joanne also evaluated the adverse objective consequences and assigned a success rating, but she failed to use her success rating to determine ways to improve.

Option 2: Correct. The real value afforded by the decision success rating comes when it is used to generate ways to improve the decision.

Option 3: Incorrect. Both of these strategies were sound ones, but the third strategy, creating a decision success rating, was not completed. Joanne needed to use the success rating to determine ways the decision could have been improved.

Case Study: Question 2 of 2

What questions did you ask to determine whether Joanne was effective at using strategies to evaluate her risky marketing decision?

Options:

1. Did Joanne use her success rating to examine ways she could have improved her bold marketing decision?

2. Did Joanne study concrete and measurable adverse objective consequences of her marketing decision?

3. Did Joanne consider the negative social consequences of her business choice by focusing on people within her own company?

4. Did Joanne quantify the long-term possibilities that the unstable countries would not be able to pay for the water filtration systems?

Answer:

Actually, you should have asked if Joanne examined measurable adverse objective consequences, examined adverse social effects on her own colleagues, and used her success rating to study ways to have improved her decision.

Option 1: Correct. This is one of the important questions to ask when making this determination. The success rating is much more helpful if it is used to find ways to improve decisions.

Option 2: Correct. This is one of the three questions to ask to determine if an evaluation is effective. Objective consequences are only concerned with the effect of the decision on the organization and the company performance.

Option 3: Correct. The negative social consequences are important to consider because they have impact on employee morale and productivity. A thorough evaluation will report on these consequences.

Option 4: Incorrect. Predictions of long-term effects of the decision is not one of the things that Joanne is expected to have evaluated. Her level of effectiveness will not be affected by whether or not she did this research.

Take a cue from Joanne. Be sure to use the success rating you assign your next decision to examine ways you could have improved your original choice. By doing so, you'll likely filter out impurities in your decision-making habits.

After completing this topic, your analytical abilities should be sharper than ever. In this topic, you learned how to analyze the effectiveness of strategies used to evaluate a business decision:

- examining adverse objective consequences of the decision,
- examining adverse social consequences of the decision,

- determining the degree to which the business problem was resolved.

Strategies for addressing a failed decision

"You don't drown by falling in water: You drown by staying there." --Edwin Louis Cole, motivational expert

When decisions fail, as some inevitably do, take action. Colleagues will expect you to do so. Your success and their confidence in your abilities hang in the balance.

In this topic, you'll learn how to effectively address decision failure by using these strategies: don't sugarcoat the situation, divorce the failure from the people involved, and form a decision review team.

Chris, a highly effective portfolio manager at a national bank, made a faulty investment decision that negatively affected profits. After reminding himself that failure is often a key ingredient in eventual success, he prepared himself to explain the setback to his co-workers.

See each perspective Chris took when explaining to his co-workers to find out how he used the first strategy--don't sugarcoat the situation--to address his decision failure.

Explaining realistically and honestly

"Sugarcoating the situation never works. Instead, I explained the circumstances in a realistic, honest manner."

No downplaying

"I didn't downplay the extent of the financial loss. I simply and briefly told the people involved what had happened."

By being straightforward about the nature of the failure and not sugarcoating the situation, Chris exuded a positive attitude and avoided sounding defensive.

In fact, many co-workers let him know afterward that his honesty and forthrightness actually bolstered his credibility.

The truth be told, Chris didn't make the flawed decision alone. He based his final investment choice on the input of colleagues. With that in mind, Chris also used the second strategy for addressing decision failure: He divorced the failure from the people involved.

Chris reminded himself of a quote from business author William D. Brown: "Failure is an event, never a person." Taking this maxim to heart, Chris pointed fingers only at the circumstances surrounding the investment choice and never at others. You, too, should divorce the failure from the people involved by:

- not thinking in terms of "blame",
- not using colleagues' names and the reasons for failure in the same breath,
- remembering that many failed decisions result from pure chance or bad luck.

After not sugarcoating the decision failure and divorcing the circumstances from the colleagues involved,

Chris knew the next step in recovering from the shortcoming lay just ahead. He implemented the last strategy for addressing failure and formed a decision review team.

See each aspect of forming a decision review team to find out how Chris revived his chances for investment success.

Members

"I composed my review team of the people most directly affected by the poor investment strategy. Naturally, I included those colleagues originally involved in the decision. But I also invited Nathan, our accountant, who had to track the losses. Several other people attended as well."

Purpose

"During our proceedings, we examined the events that led up to the decision. Each of us volunteered speculations about why we made an error in judgment. We determined the root cause of the failure and intended to learn from our mistake."

Action

"Not only did we record our findings in a report file, but we also discussed how to best implement our pre-established backup plan. By the time the meeting ended, we had put the original investment failure behind us and looked forward to an impressive rally."

Notice that Chris didn't retreat from failure. Rather, he advanced toward success by addressing the faulty decision in a level-headed, strategic way. Chris may have lost an investment battle. But by effectively addressing decision failure, he eventually won the war of success.

Never take decision failure personally. Instead, use the techniques covered in the previous exercise to ensure that you quickly get back on track and engineer an effective recovery. In this topic, you discovered those strategies:

- avoiding sugarcoating the situation,
- divorcing the failure from the people involved,
- assembling a review team.

CHAPTER SIX

Group Problem Solving and Decision Making

How to Spot an Ineffective Problem-solving Group

What does it mean to be prepared to solve problems and make decisions? It means you're ready to take full advantage of the time your team is allowed to reach its goals.

Repeating the mistakes made by other teams amounts to lost time and opportunity. Eliminate those errors, and you'll be prepared to make the most of your time on the "problem-solving clock."

Which is more frustrating: spending huge amounts of time in meetings or, in those meetings, arriving at decisions that ultimately fall short of your goals?

Both situations anger most business people. You can avoid such outcomes by understanding the causes of group inadequacies. In this topic, you'll learn common characteristics of ineffective problem-solving and decision-making groups:

- generating an incomplete problem definition,
- seeking a limited number of potential solutions,
- failing to develop contingency plans.

Scientists refer to animal ecosystems as "webs." That's because when the fortunes of one species suffer, or if that species becomes extinct, the outcome reverberates throughout the entire food chain.

Problem-solving and decision-making teams mirror ecosystems.

Learning from mistakes

Todd's competitors on the game show had completed most of the word puzzle before eventually faltering. Fortunately, their mistakes revealed enough of the puzzle to allow Todd to win the "lightning round."

Question

Todd built on the successes of his opponents. More important, he learned from their mistakes and was therefore able to clinch the prize.

How about you? When solving problems and making decisions with others, how often do you consider and avoid the mistakes other teams have made in the past?

Options:

1. never
2. rarely
3. sometimes
4. often
5. always

Answer:

In today's frenzied business world, it's tempting to move quickly from one decision to the next. But unless you pause and absorb the lessons from other team failures, you may get stuck on a problem-solving treadmill that goes nowhere.

What does it mean to be prepared to solve problems and make decisions? It means you're ready to take full advantage of the time your team is allowed to reach its goals.

Repeating the mistakes made by other teams amounts to lost time and opportunity. Eliminate those errors, and you'll be prepared to make the most of your time on the "problem-solving clock."

Sheila, a publishing company manager, takes history to heart. She realizes that the value of learning from the mistakes of other problem-solving and decision-making teams extends beyond mere time savings.

See confident and career success for Sheila's insights.

Confident

"I'm confident I'm not committing the same blunders I've witnessed in the past. That means I'm more confident in the ultimate success of the decisions I make."

Career success

"And because I've avoided making those same errors, I've been able to parlay the results into enhanced career success."

Question

History teaches valuable lessons. Which statements reflect the value of learning from the mistakes of other ineffective problem-solving and decision-making groups?

Options:

1. You'll lose fewer work hours making up for poor preparation.

2. You'll flawlessly implement all of your future business decisions.

3. You'll bolster your confidence in the ultimate success of the decision.

4. You'll be able to enhance the success of your career.

Answer:

Actually, you'll avoid wasting time because of poor preparation, increase your confidence in your decision's success, and enhance your career prospects. Flawlessly executing all business decisions is unrealistic.

Option 1: This is a correct choice. When you understand the snags other groups ran into in the past, you can steer clear of those time-wasters. Your preparation is more likely to be on target.

Option 2: This is an incorrect choice. Looking at the mistakes past groups made doesn't mean that your group will never make any mistakes. Learning history can help you avoid pitfalls. It doesn't make you perfect.

Option 3: This is a correct choice. When you see the errors that people made in the past, it builds confidence that your team can at least avoid those same mistakes.

Option 4: This is a correct choice. Top managers are impressed when they see that certain employees are able to avoid common mistakes--and that can lead to more responsibility.

You value your time and your career.

As you saw in the previous exercise, learning from the mistakes of other problem-solving teams adds value to both. In this lesson, you'll explore reasons problem-solving teams sometimes fall short of their business goals. You'll also learn how to eliminate interpersonal group problems that hinder maximum productivity.

Ineffective problem-solving and decision-making groups

Which is more frustrating: spending huge amounts of time in meetings or, in those meetings, arriving at decisions that ultimately fall short of your goals?

Both situations anger most business people. You can avoid such outcomes by understanding the causes of group inadequacies. In this topic, you'll learn common characteristics of ineffective problem-solving and decision-making groups:

- generating an incomplete problem definition,
- seeking a limited number of potential solutions,
- failing to develop contingency plans.

Frederick's sales team became mired in the decision-making mud. Team members wanted to alleviate the company's flagging sales, but each had different notions of what the problem actually was. Frederick's team displayed the first characteristic of ineffective problem-solving and decision-making groups: It had generated an incomplete problem definition.

Select each attribute in order to discover how Frederick worked to help team members generate a complete problem definition.

Brevity

"Problem definitions need to be focused and succinct. We were tempted to include every aspect of our circumstances in our problem definition. I urged team members to set priorities and concentrate on the most pivotal concerns instead of dwelling on every detail."

Clarity

"Upon further analysis, we realized that domestic sales were stable but international sales were plummeting. By zeroing in on this sector specifically, we kept our problem definition short and clear."

Definable performance measurement

"Once we were focused on the same issue, we tightened our problem definition even further. After more discussion, we agreed that our problem could be defined as the need to increase international sales by 25 percent within eight months."

Question

What started as a morass of contradictory opinions ended up as a unitary problem definition that was brief, clear, and contained a definable measure of performance. This enabled the team to proceed as a cohesive unit.

With a focused problem definition in hand, Frederick's team then turned its attention to attacking the sales problem. Suppose you were a member of his group. What advice would you give the team about generating solutions?

Options:

1. Limit solutions to a manageable number to avoid being overwhelmed.
2. Generate as many potential solutions as possible, regardless of their initial feasibility.

Answer:

Actually, generating a large quantity of potential solutions almost always results in selecting from a larger pool of quality alternatives during later problem-solving stages. Limiting alternatives often translates into limited success.

Option 1: This is an incorrect choice. You don't want to eliminate the perfect solution right from the start just because it represents one too many ideas. Consider every possibility at the onset of a project.

Option 2: This is the correct choice. If you only seek a limited number of solutions, you are making your team less effective. Innovation comes from finding non-obvious solutions.

Did you provide wise counsel to Frederick's team in the previous exercise? Sound advice would have stopped the team from falling prey to the second characteristic of ineffective groups: seeking a limited number of solutions.

See each action to learn how Frederick addressed the issue of a limited number of solutions.

Develop solutions

"I made sure I set aside plenty of time to develop potential solutions to our international sales problem."

Do not censor

"When team members offered solutions, I never censored them. Instead, I wrote down each idea, regardless of its feasibility."

Frederick fostered an atmosphere that encouraged people to volunteer as many solutions as possible. At decision time, his team realized that it's much more productive and enjoyable to choose from many viable options than from only a few.

Finally, Frederick reminded himself that inefficient problem-solving and decision-making groups fail to develop contingency plans. After all, solid backup plans enable you to recover from decision failure.

Squirrels don't bury all of their acorns in one spot.

Similarly, Frederick and his team devised contingency plans so they would know exactly what to do if their primary sales solution failed to perform as planned.

Question

Few things frustrate group problem solvers more than arriving at inadequate decisions. Identify the characteristics of ineffective problem-solving and decision-making groups.

Options:

1. Ineffective groups pay too much attention to others' feedback.
2. Ineffective groups compose an incomplete problem definition.
3. Ineffective groups generate too few potential solutions.
4. Ineffective groups don't develop backup plans.

Answer:

In fact, ineffective groups generate incomplete problem definitions, seek a limited number of potential solutions, and fail to develop a contingency plan. Feedback from others should always be taken into account.

Option 1: This is an incorrect choice. Paying attention to the feedback of others is a good way to refine and improve decisions, which can only make your group more effective.

Option 2: This is a correct choice. Without a focused problem definition in hand, it's very difficult for a team to effectively attack the problem. Generating an incomplete problem definition is a common characteristic of ineffective groups.

Option 3: This is a correct choice. To come up with a large pool of quality alternatives, a group needs to generate a large quantity of potential solutions.

Option 4: This is a correct choice. An inefficient group may not develop contingency plans. This is a mistake, because solid backup plans could help the group recover from decision failure.

In this topic, you discovered the characteristics of ineffective problem-solving and decision-making groups. They generate an incomplete problem definition, they seek a limited number of potential solutions, and they fail to develop contingency plans.

Group dynamics problems

Scientists refer to animal ecosystems as "webs." That's because when the fortunes of one species suffer, or if that species becomes extinct, the outcome reverberates throughout the entire food chain.

Problem-solving and decision-making teams mirror ecosystems.

A group's chance of success falls sharply when group dynamics--the personal relationships among members--aren't ideal.

In this topic, you'll learn how to spot common problems with group dynamics: inefficient communication flow, improper group size, and a lack of group cohesiveness.

Meg owned a regional advertising agency. She assembled a cross-departmental team to develop branding strategies for a major client. Meg wanted to ensure that her team didn't fall prey to the first group dynamics problem: an inefficient communication flow.

See each method to find out how Meg made sure her group didn't experience an inefficient communication flow.

Don't focus on titles

"I consider the content of a book to be much more important than its title. When it comes to problem-solving teams, members often focus on corporate titles rather than the content of each member's input."

Titles inhibit inclusion

"For example, higher-status group members often have a bad habit of talking to one another rather than including lower-status members in the discussion."

Titles create unhealthy team dynamics

"Lower-status members, on the other hand, usually direct their statements to higher-status members. As a result, lower-status members may do some 'talking to,' but they're rarely 'spoken with.'"

Emphasize equality

"That's why, at the team's first meeting, I urged members to set aside corporate titles. I emphasized the equality of the group members and then guaranteed it by redirecting any individual conversations to the entire team."

Question

Meg's actions unleashed an impressive flow of group communication after she stressed that she wanted the full participation of all team members.

Think back to the productive decision-making teams you've participated in. On average, how many people were on those effective teams?

Options:

1. two or three

2. five to ten
3. 11 or more

Answer:

Working in decision-making groups is like attending a dinner party: too few diners and the conversation may stagnate. On the other hand, too many attendees often results in a lack of food.

Most experts believe problem-solving groups of between five and ten people are the most effective. Numbers above or below this range may result in the second group dynamics problem: improper group size.

See each team size to find out why Meg agrees with those experts.

Fewer than five

"I've found that teams with fewer than five members don't offer enough different perspectives to generate the original insights I'm after."

More than ten

"When teams have more than ten people, some members' opinions may never be aired. More isn't necessarily merrier for problem-solving teams."

The last group dynamics problem is a lack of cohesiveness. When a group fails to cohere, it doesn't hold or stick together, either in thought or in deed.

See each problem to find out the pitfalls of group cohesiveness that Meg focused on.

Lack of a clear purpose

"A problem-solving team without a clear purpose rarely makes effective decisions. I define the specific business problem to be addressed early in the process, usually before the group meets for the first time."

Lack of clear expectations

"In the same vein, a lack of clear expectations produces confusion and wastes time. I always provide an idea of the problem-solving activities to be undertaken. I also specify a rough time frame in which I'm looking for a decision."

Improper use of rewards

"Finally, handing out rewards and holding celebrations for problem solving success must be handled in the right manner. Rewarding individuals instead of the group only strains relationships. We function as a team, so we celebrate as one too."

Question

A machine may break down if there's a problem with any of its parts. Select the typical group dynamics problems.

Options:

1. A group has an improper size because it contains more than ten members.
2. Group communication suffers because higher-status members talk only among themselves.
3. A group has an improper size because it's composed of only seven people.
4. A group lacks cohesiveness because individuals are rewarded instead of the team.

Answer:

In fact, group dynamics problems result when you have more than ten members, when higher-status members speak only to one another, and when individuals are rewarded instead of the team. Seven members is within the desirable range.

Option 1: This is a correct choice. Having five to ten members in a problem-solving group ensures different perspectives and that all ideas will be heard.

Option 2: This is a correct choice. Communication flow is crucial, and it's important to get everyone in the mix. When higher-status members only speak to one another, other members of the group feel ignored or overlooked.

Option 3: This is an incorrect choice. Keeping the number of members to between five and ten will enhance group dynamics by encouraging full participation.

Option 4: This is a correct choice. Handing out rewards for problem-solving success must be handled in the right manner. Rewarding individuals instead of the group only strains relationships.

If you eliminate the problems covered in the previous exercise, your team stands a much better chance of making effective business decisions. In this topic, you learned to recognize these group dynamics problems:

- improper group size,
- inefficient communication flow,
- lack of group cohesiveness.
-

General Strategies for Improving Group Success

To harness the power of teamwork, you first need to set the stage for making team business decisions. You must prepare people to take on the issues at hand. Maintaining a team's effectiveness throughout the problem- solving process requires willpower. But rest assured--your role as leader will pay off.

You'll discover you can do this by holding short, productive meetings; identifying progressive, meaningful milestones; and celebrating your team's successes.

The first strategy for maintaining team engagement is to hold short, productive meetings. Too often, meeting time is monopolized by activities that could be handled more effectively outside the meeting.

In this topic, you'll learn how to enhance group communication. You'll make the right call by promoting full participation, encouraging and protecting minority opinions, and keeping opinions separate from the opinion holders.

Here's the unfortunate truth: In almost every decision-making group you take part in, you'll run across someone who gets under your skin.

You probably want to stay out of his way, but you certainly shouldn't let him run you over. In this topic, you'll learn how to apply these strategies to handle a difficult team member:

- Show you're listening.
- Demonstrate patience.
- Redirect the conflict.

Establishing and maintaining an effective problem-solving group

"If I could solve all the problems myself, I would." -- Thomas Edison, inventor, when asked why he had a team of 21 assistants

Question

For all of his brilliance, Edison realized he simply couldn't go it alone.

How would you assess your problem-solving and decision-making ability? Consider the business obstacles you've overcome. What percentage of those problems did you solve without input from others?

Options:

1. 0 percent
2. 25 percent
3. 50 percent
4. 75 percent
5. 100 percent

Answer:

If two heads are indeed better than one, think of the benefits you'll reap by including the problem- solving efforts of others. Teamwork works.

To harness the power of teamwork, you first need to set the stage for making team business decisions. You must prepare people to take on the issues at hand. Maintaining a team's effectiveness throughout the problem- solving process requires willpower. But rest assured--your role as leader will pay off.

See each benefit in order to find out why Shawn, an accountant, believes in the group problem-solving process.

Enhanced individual attitudes and job satisfaction

"When a problem-solving team starts off on the right foot and keeps going until it meets its goals, you can see the satisfaction on each member's face. People's attitudes really receive a huge boost."

Enhanced organizational morale

"Have you ever noticed that organizations have distinct personalities? That aura is determined by a group's success at solving business problems. When employees set out to accomplish those objectives, company morale skyrockets."

More confidence in a successful outcome

"Combine those two factors--enhanced individual and corporate morale--and you end up being much more confident that your team decisions will produce lasting results."

Question

Strive to establish productive problem-solving momentum, and then maintain that effectiveness. Choose the benefits of establishing and maintaining an effective problem-solving group.

Options:

1. You'll be more confident that your decision will produce desirable results.

2. You'll be able to enhance the overall morale of your organization.

3. You'll enjoy knowing that individuals are happier about their jobs.

4. You'll be able to eliminate any potential resistance to your team's decisions.

Answer:

In fact, you'll not only be more confident in a successful decision outcome, but you'll also bolster individual and organizational morale. Eliminating all resistance to your business decisions is an unrealistic goal.

Option 1: This is a correct choice. When you have good group dynamics, you can be more confident in the ultimate success of the decisions you make.

Option 2: This is a correct choice. Good decisions help the whole organization. When you consistently make good choices to resolve business problems, company morale skyrockets.

Option 3: This is a correct choice. When you prepare people to take on issues and maintain the team's effectiveness until it meets its goals, you enhance attitudes and job satisfaction.

Option 4: This is an incorrect choice. Eliminating all resistance to your business decisions is an unrealistic goal.

As you just learned, the benefits flow naturally when you establish and maintain effective problem-solving teams. In this lesson, you'll learn the following strategies for improving group success:

- keeping your problem-solving team's interest piqued,
- ensuring the unimpeded flow of group communication,
- reducing harmful team conflict.

Maintaining a team's engagement

The art gallery caught Helen's eye. She was in a hurry but checked it out anyway. On impulse, she bought a colorful painting that she intended to hang in her kitchen.

The painting held her attention for the first few weeks. But then the novelty of her hasty purchase wore off. It just didn't engage her anymore. In this topic, you'll learn how to avoid waning enthusiasm and instead maintain a team's engagement while it resolves a business problem.

You'll discover you can do this by holding short, productive meetings; identifying progressive, meaningful milestones; and celebrating your team's successes.

The first strategy for maintaining team engagement is to hold short, productive meetings. Too often, meeting time is monopolized by activities that could be handled more effectively outside the meeting.

See do and don't to find out how Claude holds short, productive meetings.

Don't

"Don't waste time merely reporting team activities. Circulate these details prior to the meeting. Save your time for more important matters, such as solving problems."

Do

"Use meetings to harness the team's brainpower. Reserve this time for brainstorming, problem solving, and discussing options."

Almost any activity done repeatedly tends to lose some attraction over time. For example, seasoned runners must take measures to avoid burnout and to keep their workouts fresh and invigorating.

Claude realized that one of the leading causes of corporate boredom centers around unproductive meetings, so he took measures to cut the fat out of his meetings.

The second strategy you can use to maintain team engagement is to identify progressive, meaningful milestones.

To reach most business objectives, several intermediate goals must be accomplished along the way. These progressive milestones present opportunities to mark your team's progress.

These intermediate milestones also should be meaningful. In other words, fulfilling them should signify specific, crucial accomplishments along the road to problem-solving success.

Case Study: Question 1 of 2

Scenario:

Melanie has been assigned the task of solving a major processing problem for a credit card company. She created a team of colleagues from various departments who have very busy schedules.

Answer the following questions in order.

Question:

Melanie is preparing the agenda for her second team meeting. Select appropriate topics and times that will help keep the group engaged while it resolves the credit card processing issue.

Options:

1. introduce new members--15 minutes
2. progress reports--15 minutes
3. progress report questions--5 minutes
4. identify processing issues--10 minutes
5. processing problem-solving session--45 minutes

Answer:

Actually, Melanie should only spend a brief time on questions about the progress reports before she moves on to identifying the issues and then spending the bulk of the meeting time on brainstorming activities. That's an effective meeting.

Option 1: This is an incorrect choice. Introducing new members for 15 minutes is a sure way to start team members dozing before the meeting even gets started.

Option 2: This is an incorrect choice. Looking backwards always seems redundant, and it isn't a good tactic to grab your team's attention or get them focused on the issues.

Option 3: This is a correct choice. It's OK to devote a brief time to catching up on the issues and answering questions about progress, but don't devote too much time to this activity.

Option 4: This is a correct choice. Identifying issues is the first step towards resolving them, and it's a good way to get the participants focused on problem solving.

Option 5: This is a correct choice. The bulk of the time in a meeting should be spent on the real purpose of the meeting--resolving identified problems.

Case Study: Question 2 of 2

Melanie and the team are seeking to define the project's milestones. Choose the individual milestones that should keep the team engaged with its problem-solving purpose.

Options:

1. Identify all the card-processing problems the company is experiencing.
2. Develop three viable potential solutions for each processing problem.
3. Get the go-ahead from the executive staff to initiate proposed processing solutions.
4. Specify when group morale starts to slide in order to take corrective measures.

Answer:

Actually, fully identifying the problems, developing viable solutions, and receiving approval to implement them are all significant milestones. Tracking team morale is an ongoing concern, not an accomplishment per se.

Option 1: This is a correct choice. Identifying the issues is an important first step to get the meeting off on the right track.

Option 2: This is a correct choice. Developing viable solutions is a significant milestone in the problem-solving process. Coming up with several solutions will help broaden thinking and expand options.

Option 3: This is a correct choice. When you get to the point where you can seek executive approval to implement your ideas, that is an accomplishment that gives everybody on the team reason to celebrate.

Option 4: This is an incorrect choice. It's important to maintain a team's effectiveness throughout the problem-solving process, so the group doesn't ever become discouraged or demoralized.

The third strategy to maintain your group's engagement while it resolves a business problem is to celebrate your team's successes.

You've probably heard the old saying "Everyone loves a party."

But don't leave anyone out. Rewarding the team as a team goes a long way toward securing the collective enthusiasm of all group members.

Start small, perhaps with a furnished breakfast the morning after the first accomplishment. Then cap things off with a more elaborate celebration after the team meets its ultimate goal.

Question

Regina wants to keep her team engaged with the task of developing new discount pricing structures for her company's services. Identify strategies Regina should use to maintain her team's engagement while it resolves its business problem.

Options:

1. Regina should limit her meetings to a half hour. She should spend a few minutes on updates and 25 minutes developing the discount pricing plans.

2. Regina should keep all group members current on the team's progress by urging them to spend more time reading messages on the electronic bulletin board.

3. Regina should celebrate the completion of each milestone, starting with bagels after the first one and a company party after the project conclusion.

4. Regina should divide the task into sections: proposing discount options, determining the leading options, and making the final decision.

Answer:

Actually, Regina can keep the team's interest by celebrating successes, identifying meaningful milestones, and holding short, productive meetings.

Option 1: This is a correct choice. Spending a brief time on progress reports and then quickly moving on to brainstorming activities is a good way to run an effective meeting.

Option 2: This is an incorrect choice. Reading messages on an electronic bulletin board is not a good way to keep the team's interest.

Option 3: This is a correct choice. Scheduling milestone celebrations, perhaps by throwing small parties when each goal is reached, is a good way to avoid waning enthusiasm and maintain a team's engagement.

Option 4: This is a correct choice. When Regina divides the task into sections, she can identify the skills required to work on each section, and assign activities appropriately.

Use the strategies covered in the previous exercise, and your engaged team will likely achieve problem-solving success. In this topic, you learned to maintain the engagement of your team while it resolves a business problem by:

- holding short, productive meetings,
- identifying progressive, meaningful milestones,
- celebrating your team's successes.

Strategies to enhance group communication

Say you're on vacation and you want to call a friend back home to rub in the fact that your feet are in the sand instead of in hard shoes.

Do you think constructing a telephone from tin cans and string would be sufficient for conveying your information?

That device wouldn't exactly enhance your ability to communicate. And if solving problems is your goal, you'd better upgrade not only your technology but your interpersonal communication strategies as well.

In this topic, you'll learn how to enhance group communication. You'll make the right call by promoting full participation, encouraging and protecting minority opinions, and keeping opinions separate from the opinion holders.

Kristen, the leader of a decision-making team within a lobbying firm, worries about her group members' unwillingness to speak up. She wants to inspire not only more conversations but also better ones.

See each method to find out how Kristen employs the first strategy to enhance group communication: **promoting full participation**.

Call on people in turn

"Whenever I want team members' input but it isn't forthcoming, I call on each person in turn. I ask that member to express his or her thoughts to the rest of the group. Once that person is finished, I prompt the next person, and the next, and so on."

Request more input

"After each team member speaks up at my request, I ask the group for additional feedback. Once people get in the habit of offering input, communication is much easier to maintain."

Summarize positions

"At the close of each meeting, I request that team members summarize their ideas and opinions in an e-mail. This reinforces the notion that I value their input and engenders the habit of participating fully in the group's problem-solving processes."

Kristen encourages input every chance she gets. Calling on people in turn shows she is interested in every member's thoughts. The team members' summaries engage their thinking and inspire them to be active communicators.

But what if someone's thoughts don't exactly inspire agreement from other team members?

That's a good thing. Opposing ideas provoke lively, healthy communication. To keep your group communication in good shape, use the second enhancement strategy and encourage and protect minority opinion. See recap and elaborate to learn how Kristen encourages and protects minority opinion.

Recap

"I recap both majority and minority opinions at the beginning and end of each meeting. I don't make an elaborate display of it; I just review the group's thinking."

Elaborate

"Sometimes I'm a little sneaky. I'll periodically tell one of the dissenters that I don't understand her idea. I'll then ask her to elaborate on it for the group."

Whenever Kristen's team comes close to arriving at a decision, she reminds everyone of any contradictory opinions circulating through the group. The majority members have no choice but to continue the discussion.

Question

Practice what you've learned. Identify effective strategies for enhancing group communication.

Options:

1. When members refuse to speak up, call on them in turn to elicit their thoughts.
2. Ask team members to send you an e-mail containing their opinions.
3. Coerce group members to participate by pointing out potential repercussions.
4. Ask dissenters periodically to elaborate on their thinking for the team.

Answer:

Actually, you can promote full participation by calling on members in turn when discussion dies down, have them summarize their thoughts in an e-mail, and protect minority opinions by having dissenters elaborate on their ideas.

Option 1: This is a correct choice. Just because team members don't offer their opinions freely doesn't mean they don't have them. Giving them a chance to speak up will make them feel like part of the team and may elicit valuable contributions.

Option 2: Correct. This is a good way to organize feedback for group discussions. It can give the leader and everyone else a heads-up on what members are thinking about a problem.

Option 3: This is an incorrect choice. Intimidation is never a good strategy to increase communication. It will only build resentment and bad feelings.

Option 4: This is a correct choice. Team members who don't think the group is making the right decision probably have different perspectives and concerns that should be taken into consideration.

Question

Among students of communication, Marshall McLuhan is known for his opinion that "the medium is the message." But is McLuhan's opinion the same thing as McLuhan the man?

In other words, do you think it's fair to say that an individual's opinions and ideas are the same thing as the person who holds them?

Options:

1. They're very different.
2. I'm neutral.
3. They're the same.

Answer:

Option 1: Try going out to dinner with "trickle down economics." You can't dine with ideas or opinions, and they won't tip the waiters. In all seriousness, opinions and opinion holders are two entirely different things. Relay this fact to your team.

Option 2: Try going out to dinner with "trickle down economics." You can't dine with ideas or opinions, and they won't tip the waiters. In all seriousness, opinions and opinion holders are two entirely different things. Relay this fact to your team.

Option 3: Try going out to dinner with "trickle down economics." You can't dine with ideas or opinions, and they won't tip the waiters. In all seriousness, opinions and opinion holders are two entirely different things. Relay this fact to your team.

If you don't practice the third strategy to enhance group communication and keep opinions separate from opinion holders, interpersonal conflict may get in the way of your group's communication.

Select people and opinions to discover how Kristen artfully draws the distinction between opinions and opinion holders.

People

"I assign names to ideas and refer to them by title instead of by the holder's name. I use phrases like "our lobbying idea" or "the influence diagram" instead of "Joanie's lobbying idea" or "Raul's influence diagram."

Opinions

"As you can see, I not only give ideas titles, but I also refer to them in the collective sense: our idea, not his or her opinion."

Erect a fence. Keep team members on one side and opinions on the other. That separation will keep people talking and allow their ideas to roam freely.

How did Kristen know whether her team, or another team within her company, was effective at using strategies to enhance group communication?

Kristen assumed the role of detective and revisited the team's communication.

See each aspect to find out how Kristen knew whether her team, or another team within her company, was effective at using strategies to enhance group communication.

Communicate

"Did the team leader push people to communicate if information and ideas weren't forthcoming? Did the leader use 'generic' language to divorce ideas from their sources?"

Minority opinions

"Did the leader make special efforts to bring minority opinions into the open and actually emphasize them?"

Case Study: Question 1 of 2

Scenario:

Isaac led a sometimes uncommunicative marketing team. His company manufactured waterproofing products for shoes and clothing. The team's goal was to decide whether to expand operations into other countries. However, Isaac worried that group discussion lacked both the quality and quantity it needed to move forward effectively.

Full participation

To prompt members to freely volunteer ideas, Isaac called on them in turn during meetings, requesting their input. He encouraged all ideas, no matter how crazy. He even asked them to e-mail a summary of their opinions to him.

Minority opinions

Brittany alone wanted to focus strictly on the Asian market. Isaac ensured that her idea wasn't swept under the rug by asking her to restate the idea several times and reminding members about it at the close of the meeting.

Opinions and opinion holders

Isaac felt strongly that people should be responsible for their choices. Whenever the team discussed an idea, Isaac reminded the group who "owned" that opinion to inspire pride in the opinion holder.

Question:

Was Isaac effective at using the strategies to enhance communication on his waterproofing products marketing team?

Options:

1. Isaac was ineffective because, although he called on marketing team members in turn and emphasized team responsibility, he placed too much emphasis on Brittany's marketing idea.

2. Isaac was effective because he called on members in turn using generic language, encouraged Brittany's participation, and made sure people were held accountable for their marketing ideas.

3. Isaac was ineffective because, although he prompted full participation on his team and protected Brittany's dissenting opinion, he failed to divorce marketing opinions from the opinion holders.

Answer:

Actually, Isaac was ineffective. He promoted full participation and protected Brittany's minority opinion, but he didn't divorce opinions from opinion holders. Accountability is important, but enhanced communication takes precedence here.

Option 1: This is an incorrect answer. The problem wasn't that Isaac placed too much emphasis on Brittany's idea, but that he reminded the group that Brittany "owned" that opinion.

Option 2: This choice is incorrect. If Isaac holds people accountable for the ideas they present, he will likely not hear many innovative suggestions. He should divorce marketing opinions from the opinion holders.

Option 3: This is the correct choice. Whenever Isaac mentioned potential solutions, he shouldn't have identified the people who devised them. Divorcing opinions from opinion holders is important to encourage frank communication.

Case Study: Question 2 of 2

What questions did you ask to determine whether Isaac was effective at using the strategies to enhance group communication on his team?

Options:

1. Did Isaac use impersonal language to divorce marketing ideas from the waterproofing marketers?

2. Did Isaac chide the group if it didn't generate enough waterproofing marketing solutions?

3. Did Isaac endeavor to protect and emphasize Brittany's dissenting marketing opinion regarding Asian markets?

4. Did Isaac force team members to speak out if marketing ideas weren't being volunteered?

Answer:

In fact, you should have asked whether Isaac pushed for people's input, protected and emphasized minority opinion, and used generic language when discussing members' marketing ideas.

Option 1: This is a correct choice. It's important to use generic language to divorce ideas from their sources. This will keep people talking and encourage them to express their ideas freely.

Option 2: This choice is incorrect. Making the group feel inadequate or unproductive won't promote full participation or encourage creativity.

Option 3: This is a correct choice. Keeping opinions separate from opinion holders helps prevent interpersonal conflict from getting in the way of group communications.

Option 4: This is a correct choice. Since Isaac's marketing team tends to be uncommunicative, it's important for Isaac to prompt members to volunteer ideas and provide input.

Avoid Isaac's mistake and inspire your group to new heights of communication excellence. In this topic, you learned to establish effective group communication by using these strategies:

- Promote full participation.
- Encourage and protect minority opinions.
- Keep the opinions separate from the opinion holders.

Handling a difficult team member

Here's the unfortunate truth: In almost every decision-making group you take part in, you'll run across someone who gets under your skin.

You probably want to stay out of his way, but you certainly shouldn't let him run you over. In this topic, you'll learn how to apply these strategies to handle a difficult team member:

- Show you're listening.
- Demonstrate patience.
- Redirect the conflict.

Matt, a member of your problem-solving team, has a knack for being offensive and pitiful at the same time. He expects you to meet his every need but acts like a sad puppy when you tell him you're busy. Then he explodes. To deal with Matt's outbursts, the first thing you should do is show him you're listening. If a colleague like Matt feels ignored, his insensitivity and anger will only fester.

When he accuses you of letting him down, ask him clarifying questions like "When did I do this?" and "What are you referring to?" These questions indicate you're willing to hear him out and that you're interested in a peaceful resolution.

Art, another member of your group, has a lot of experience handling interpersonal conflict. Select each tactic to find out what further advice Art has on being a good listener.

Defuse

"The last thing you want to do is grin sarcastically or laugh in Matt's face. Remember, you want to defuse the conflict, not heighten it."

Repeat

"Repeat things he's said to show you're taking him seriously. Use short phrases like "You think I made a mistake?" or "I think I understand how you feel."

First, try to assume as neutral a stance as possible when dealing with difficult team members. If you appear either aggressive or defensive, you may provide them with justification to prolong their tirades.

Second, defuse the tension by demonstrating patience. You can do this by refusing to provoke the other person, trying to understand him or her, and sticking to the real issue at hand.

Business moves at breakneck speed. So does the wrath of difficult people like Matt. You'll find it's worth taking the time to neutralize his outbursts.

See each tactic to learn how Art demonstrates patience.

Remain calm

"Remember, the result you're after is to defuse the conflict. Even if Matt called you a lying loser, don't be lured into his trap. Don't challenge him with references to his authority or attack his character. Remain calm."

Try to empathize

"If you understand why Matt is upset, try empathizing with him. This doesn't mean giving in to Matt; it means showing you understand how he came to his conclusions. Say something like "I can see why you'd think that, Matt."

Focus on the real issue

"Nasty people with burrs in their sides lose sight of the real issue. Guide their attention back to the heart of the matter. This enables you to refocus their thoughts on potential ways to resolve the conflict."

Slow things down

"It really all boils down to slowing the pace of the conversation. Remember the saying "When you laugh, the world laughs with you"? You may not inspire many chuckles from Matt, but he'll respond to your relaxed attitude."

Question

Art gave you some handy advice. Find out whether you heeded it. Identify effective ways to handle a difficult team member.

Options:

1. Show you're listening by repeating her statements back to her.
2. Question whether the difficult team member has the right to complain.
3. Ask clarifying questions like "Why do you feel that way?"
4. Don't get sidetracked; bring her attention back to the real problem.

Answer:

In fact, you should repeat her statements back to her, ask clarifying questions, and stick to the issue. Questioning her authority may just spur her to indignation.

Option 1: This is a correct choice. When difficult team members believe that their opinions are being heard, they tend to be less disruptive and more reasonable.

Option 2: Incorrect. If a team member is being difficult, questioning his right to express himself or herself is likely to backfire. The team member is likely to become even more obtrusive.

Option 3: This is a correct choice. Getting team members to explain a negative response or comment will determine the validity of their opinions and help defuse difficult situations.

Option 4: This is a correct choice. Sometimes team members waste the team's time by harping upon issues that really have nothing to do with the team's mission, and it's important to steer them back towards the immediate problem.

The strategies you were just tested on would be great ways to deal with Matt. By showing Matt you're listening and you're being patient, you strip him of the motivation to turn your confrontation into a brawl. And you'll gain credibility with your fellow team members as well.

At the same time, you don't want the title "doormat" emblazoned on your forehead. Save face by using the third strategy for handling a difficult team member: Redirect the conflict.

Redirecting the conflict amounts to bringing the confrontation to an amicable close. In a nutshell, you convey to the difficult team member that it's time to move on.

See each tactic to learn how Art redirects conflict.

Issue a simple apology

"One way to do this is to "apologize" for the "misunderstanding" and return to your work. You may not actually feel sorry. But when you briefly mention you regret the circumstances, it gives the difficult team member a reason to back off."

Hold your ground

"Sometimes you just have to look the other person in the eye and say in no uncertain terms that you've received the message. This should let him know you're ready to move past the problem."

Agree to disagree

"Other times, ask him whether he'll agree to disagree. This gives him a choice, and it has the effect of wrapping up the conversation."

Irritating people like Matt have the capacity to vent for hours unless you redirect the conflict toward a resolution.

Bring the confrontation to a halt so Matt can redirect his energy--and you can get back to producing solid results for your decision-making team.

You'll receive a blue ribbon from your team when you use the strategies you just learned to handle a difficult team member. You'll win that award if you:

- listen,
- demonstrate patience,
- redirect the conversation.
-

Effective group problem-solving techniques

Should your decision-making team engage in a tug-of-war contest? Or should it pull together as a group?

The answer is simple: Combine your forces. You can do that by relying on effective group problem-solving techniques. If you don't, your decision-making team will lack structure and focus. But when you employ productive group techniques, you and your team will:

- be more assured you've fully identified the issue,
- capitalize on the synergy created by group interaction,
- receive more enjoyment from the problem-solving process.

Hugh's team pushed to get the product released in time for the new quarter. It had to do that by making numerous strategic decisions - and quickly. The team members didn't know where to start. Hugh suggested using several specific and dynamic group decision-making techniques. Within no time, the group was off and running.

See each technique to learn how Hugh's team worked productively together.

We identified the obstacle

"At first, we didn't even realize what our obstacles were. By using concrete problem diagnostic techniques, like the alternative worldview method, we got a handle on that very quickly."

We felt the synergy

"I knew that properly formed and managed groups often outperform their best members. The result is called "synergy." And that's exactly what we achieved after harnessing the power of group decision-making strategies."

We enjoyed the experience

"Our company president claims that "synergy is the first cousin of happiness." She's right. Because the specific strategies we relied on provided a sense of confidence and purpose, we all really enjoyed the experience."

Question

Problem-solving teams often resolve dilemmas more quickly than individual decision makers. Select the benefits of using effective group problem-solving techniques.

Options:

1. You'll have more assurance that you've completely identified the business problem.

2. You'll be able to harness the synergy created by your problem-solving group.

3. You'll defuse resistance to your choices because many people made the decision.

4. You'll find the problem-solving process to be increasingly enjoyable.

Answer:

Actually, you'll be more assured you've identified the problem, be able to capitalize on group synergy, and enjoy the problem-solving process to a greater degree. Defusing all resistance to a choice, even a group decision, is unrealistic.

Option 1: This is a correct choice. When people with different backgrounds and experience look at an issue, they provide different perspectives, which helps pinpoint the problem.

Option 2: This is a correct choice. Properly formed and managed groups often outperform even their best members.

Option 3: This is an incorrect choice. It doesn't matter how many people were involved in the decision-making process. Acceptance depends upon the quality of the solution.

Option 4: This is a correct choice. When groups rely upon effective strategies, it provides a sense of confidence and purpose, which can be an enjoyable experience.

Those benefits are yours when you take full advantage of group decision-making opportunities.

In this lesson, you'll discover powerful group decision-making strategies to diagnose business problems, brainstorm solutions, and negate the harmful effects of groupthink.

You'll also explore how to make decisions using the nominal group technique and learn how to conduct an effective decision follow-up meeting.

Better Group Decision Making

Should your decision-making team engage in a tug-of-war contest? Or should it pull together as a group?

The answer is simple: Combine your forces. You can do that by relying on effective group problem-solving techniques. If you don't, your decision-making team will lack structure and focus. But when you employ productive group techniques, you and your team will:

- be more assured you've fully identified the issue,
- capitalize on the synergy created by group interaction,
- receive more enjoyment from the problem-solving process.

Doctors today increasingly practice what's termed "holistic medicine." These healers incorporate a variety of techniques from diverse medical traditions to keep their patients healthy.

Like those medical professionals, your problem-solving team should diagnose business problems using a variety of approaches. Therein lies the prescription for decision-making success. In this topic, you'll learn to employ the alternative worldview method to diagnose your group's business problems by:

- breaking into two groups,
- diagnosing the problem based on opposing worldviews,
- debating and evaluating the results.

"The best way to get a good idea is to get a lot of ideas." --Linus Pauling, U.S. chemist

Group brainstorming, the collective generation of numerous potential solutions, kicks up the winds of business opportunity. In this topic, you'll learn how to weather the storm of group decision-making and use this technique by:

- generating as many ideas as possible,
- initially withholding judgment on those ideas,
- developing ideas that piggyback on other ideas.

Have you ever participated on a decision-making team that others described as "aggressively mediocre"?

If so, your team probably succumbed to the sinister effects of "groupthink." And you probably succumbed to frequent bouts of extreme frustration. In this topic, you'll learn how to be a real leader and employ techniques to overcome groupthink by:

- initially downplaying the strength of your own opinions,
- assigning a rotating devil's advocate to the team's ideas,
- seeking feedback from an external expert.

When it comes to the nominal group technique, however, that key word means just the reverse. The results you'll receive by employing this strategy are anything but trivial.

In fact, the nominal group technique is one of the oldest and most revered group problem-solving techniques. In this topic, you'll learn how a team effectively performs the four steps of the nominal group technique by:

- anonymously voting on initial favored solutions,
- recording the votes in a round-robin fashion,
- clarifying any confusing ideas,
- evaluating the final solutions.

If you remove your car's rearview mirror, the police will probably pull you over because of your poor decision.

Car mirrors aren't only recommended; they're required by law. And the law for group problem solving is to look where you've been and review the decisions your team has reached. In this topic, you'll learn how to conduct a decision follow-up meeting in which you:

- focus specifically on the long-term consequences of a decision,
- revisit discarded options,
- play devil's advocate to the chosen option.

The alternative worldview method

Doctors today increasingly practice what's termed "holistic medicine." These healers incorporate a variety of techniques from diverse medical traditions to keep their patients healthy.

Like those medical professionals, your problem-solving team should diagnose business problems using a variety of approaches. Therein lies the prescription for decision-making success. In this topic, you'll learn to employ the alternative worldview method to diagnose your group's business problems by:

- breaking into two groups,
- diagnosing the problem based on opposing worldviews,
- debating and evaluating the results.

It's a big world out there. And in this diverse world, and throughout time, people have pondered the major issues of existence using differing mind-sets and attitudes.

Whether the subject is religion, philosophy, or the economy, people hold an array of opinions. It's this variety of thought that powers the wheels of progress.

Decision-making groups often make the mistake of adopting only one point of view when diagnosing the real causes of their business problems. By taking a cue from society's historical diversity of attitudes and behaviors, these groups receive fresh insight into problem-solving possibilities.

Stiff competition had eaten away at the sales of Sandra's pesticide manufacturing company. To address the situation, Sandra called a meeting of employees from various departments. She wanted to fully diagnose the sales problem before generating potential solutions.

See each diversity aspect to learn how Sandra used the first step of the alternative worldview method and separated the employees into two groups.

Diverse backgrounds

"I determined beforehand which employees would be on each team. When it comes to fashion, you should "mix and match." I did the same thing in this situation by placing members from different departments on the same teams."

Diverse opinions

"Henry thought we should expand our marketing efforts into hardware stores. I knew Meredith disagreed. I placed these two employees on the same team. I also made sure the other team was composed of members whose ideas and diagnostic opinions varied."

Because the groups were composed of members with diverse backgrounds and opinions, Sandra increased the likelihood that their follow-up analysis wouldn't merely cover the same old, familiar ground.

After the groups assumed their places, Sandra told them how to use the crucial element of this diagnostic To accomplish this step, your team groups should examine the business problem from a strict vantage point. They should speculate on root causes of the problem according to the respective mind-set they've been instructed to adopt.

See each aspect to discover how Sandra adjusted the attitudes of her groups' members.

Meredith's Team

"First, I told Meredith's team to assume the internal worldview. The team should specify possible internal reasons for the pesticide sales drop. In other words, what were we doing wrong?"

Ali's Team

"I assigned the external worldview to Ali's group. Its task was to list reasons the cause of the sales problem originated outside the company. What was happening in the external market to adversely impact revenue?"

Listing All Causes

"I instructed both groups to devise an exhaustive list of causes based on their respective outlooks. They wrote their ideas down on a sheet of paper. It was then time to switch the worldviews of both teams."

Meredith's Team's New View

"I told Meredith's group to look at the sales problem from a human standpoint. How could the sales deficiency be explained in terms of people's actions, inside or outside the company?"

Ali's Team's New View

"Ali's group looked at the situation from a process worldview. The team devised reasons the sales dip was caused by nonhuman factors, such as technology, pesticide composition, and economic conditions."

Finding Parallels and Ranking Causes

"Afterward, I had each group re-examine both lists of causes. Did they see parallels between the results emanating from the various worldviews? I also had them rank the potential causes from most to least likely."

In essence, Sandra forced a shift in perspective by manipulating the attitudes and outlooks of the people in the two groups. She negated the possibility of stale, bland thinking.

Question

Practice what you've learned. Identify valid strategies for employing the first two steps of the alternative worldview method to diagnose business problems.

Options:

1. Break the team into two groups composed of members from diverse backgrounds or holding diverse opinions.
2. Have the team adopting the internal worldview examine problem causes stemming from factors within your company.
3. Break the team into two groups composed of members from similar backgrounds or holding similar opinions.
4. Have the team adopting the human worldview examine problem causes stemming from technological and economic factors.

Answer:

Actually, you want two diverse, dissimilar groups employing the alternative worldview method. The internal worldview examines causes within your company.

Option 1: This is a correct choice. Breaking the members into two groups will help diagnose the problem, since each group can diagnose the problem from different worldviews.

Option 2: This is a correct choice. When one group diagnoses the situation using internal company factors, it helps determine what the company is doing wrong.

Option 3: This is an incorrect choice. Similar backgrounds and similar opinions will produce similar solutions. For a broad range of diverse, creative solutions, you want people with different backgrounds and solutions.

Option 4: This is an incorrect choice. The team adopting the human worldview needs to look at human resources and how the problem affects workers on a personal level.

Many early birds find the first light at the break of dawn refreshing and inspiring. Don't sleepwalk through uneventful problem diagnoses. Among others, use the strategies covered in the previous exercise to wake up your team members.

After finishing its intellectual journey, Sandra's team capped off its use of the alternative worldview method.

It debated and evaluated its findings. Sandra made a special effort to focus on the shifts in diagnostic perspectives emanating from the changing worldviews.

See new outlooks and team discussion to find out how Sandra stimulated her team's debate and evaluation of its findings.

New outlooks

"Several team members ended up with different notions about why our pesticide sales were infested. I asked them to explain their new outlooks."

Team discussion

"This spurred even more team discussion. Getting members to talk about their mind-changing processes cleared the way for an array of new ideas."

Sandra, against the team's wishes, had to adjourn the meeting on time even though the discussions among members just started to heat up. The team would have a lot to talk about during the next get-together.

When analyzing whether your team effectively diagnosed its business problem using the alternative worldview method, ask yourself several questions.

See each aspect to discover Sandra's questioning technique.

Diverse groups

"Did I compose each group with members coming from different backgrounds or having different opinions? After all, if they agreed in the first place, the alternative worldview method probably wouldn't change any minds. And changed minds can be a very good thing."

Alternative worldviews

"Did we diagnose the problem using both sets of opposing worldviews? These clashes of perspectives usually promote novel insights into the business problem."

Unchanged opinions

"And did we revisit our initial diagnoses if no one's opinions changed after employing the method? I expect ideas to change. If they don't, it's a possible sign that either people misunderstood the process or they weren't thinking divergently enough."

Case Study: Question 1 of 2

Scenario:

Lora worked for an espresso machine manufacturer that experienced little luck placing its products in cafe franchises. Lora's cross-departmental team met to diagnose the real problem.

Question:

Was Lora's team effective at using the alternative worldview method to diagnose its espresso machine marketing problem?

Options:

1. Lora's team was ineffective because, although it broke into two groups composed of members with different ideas and diagnosed the marketing problem from the two sets of worldviews, it failed to revisit its initial diagnoses after final agreement.
2. Lora's team was effective because it examined the espresso machine problem from internal, external, human, and process worldviews using groups of diverse opinions and several members altered their initial marketing diagnoses.
3. Lora's team was ineffective because, although it arrived at novel diagnoses of its espresso machine problem and debated those diagnoses using diverse groups, it failed to utilize enough alternative worldviews to clarify its marketing problem.

Answer:

In fact, Lora's team was ultimately effective because it diagnosed its problem in diverse groups using both sets of alternative worldviews, and several members altered their original diagnoses of the espresso machine situation.

Option 1: This is an incorrect choice. Revisiting the initial diagnoses is only necessary if no one's opinions changed after employing the method.

Option 2: This is the correct choice. Lora's problem-solving team diagnosed the business problem using a variety of approaches. Therein lies the prescription for decision-making success.

Option 3: This is an incorrect choice. Lora's team diagnosed the marketing problem from internal, external, human, and process worldviews. That was enough alternative worldviews.

Case Study: Question 2 of 2

What questions did you ask to determine if Lora's team was effective at using the alternative worldview method to diagnose its espresso machine marketing problem?

Options:

1. Did Lora's team break into groups composed of members with diverse backgrounds or opinions?
2. Did Lora's team review its initial diagnosis of the marketing problem if opinions were unchanged?
3. Did Lora's team generate numerous ideas for placing the company's espresso machines in franchise cafes?
4. Did Lora's team diagnose the marketing problem from internal, external, human, and process worldviews?

Answer:

Actually, you should have asked whether Lora's team broke into groups composed of diverse members, diagnosed the marketing problem from both sets of alternative worldviews, and revisited the diagnoses if opinions were unchanged.

Option 1: This is a correct choice. A team will ultimately be more effective if it diagnoses its problem using groups of diverse opinions.

Option 2: This is a correct choice. If no one's opinions changed, it's a possible sign that either people misunderstood the process or they weren't thinking divergently enough.

Option 3: This is an incorrect choice. Lora's team was focused on diagnosing its business problem, not on brainstorming potential solutions.

Option 4: This is a correct choice. Diagnosing the problem using opposing worldviews usually promotes novel insights into the business problem.

Lora effectively removed the haze from her team's diagnostic vision and prompted new perspectives on its marketing problem. In this topic, you learned how to diagnose group business problems using alternative worldviews. This technique involves:

- breaking into two diverse groups,
- diagnosing the problem based on opposing worldviews,
- debating and evaluating the results.

Effective group brainstorming strategies

"The best way to get a good idea is to get a lot of ideas." --Linus Pauling, U.S. chemist

Group brainstorming, the collective generation of numerous potential solutions, kicks up the winds of business opportunity. In this topic, you'll learn how to weather the storm of group decision-making and use this technique by:

- generating as many ideas as possible,
- initially withholding judgment on those ideas,
- developing ideas that piggyback on other ideas.

Question

Consider the last business problem you needed to solve. Did you have many options at your disposal?

In a perfect world, how many potential solutions would you have enjoyed choosing from?

Options:

1. just one
2. two to five

3. five to nine
4. ten to 20
5. as many as possible

Answer:

Most people want as many options as possible, not only when shopping for groceries, but when solving business problems as well.

Have you ever had difficulty deciding which restaurant you and your colleagues should choose for lunch? You're much more likely to find culinary satisfaction if the area has many restaurants.

In the same vein, having numerous ideas allows a problem-solving group to achieve business success. That's why the first strategy for effective group brainstorming is generate as many ideas as possible.

When generating potential solutions, your group should first shoot for quantity over quality. Group members should volunteer as many ideas as they can.

Select each of Jane's tactics to discover how she ensured that her team developed an impressive output of ideas by using the second brainstorming strategy: Initially withhold judgment on those ideas.

Welcome all possible solutions

"My team welcomes all possible solutions, no matter how wacky or impractical. In fact, sometimes the craziest ideas end up being the most dynamic and successful."

Censor criticism

I make sure the sparks of creativity fly by censoring any criticism of the proposed solutions. That way, group members remain spontaneous and inspired.

Jane's team members, employees of a company that manufactured high-end ski poles, received a mandate from the executive staff. They were instructed to think of ways to make the poles more appealing to "extreme" backcountry skiers. Jane instructed the team to develop as many ideas as it could and to withhold judgment on those potential solutions.

See each team member's idea to find out how Jane had people employ the third group brainstorming strategy: Develop ideas that piggyback on other ideas.

Ron's Idea

"Ron came up with the notion of manufacturing an "intelligent ski pole" that knew where it was on the mountain and could point the skier in the right direction. That may have sounded crazy at first, but I told others to just run with that idea."

Patty's Idea

"Ron's idea inspired Patty to think of hollowing out a section of the poles where maps of the ski resort trails could be kept."

Amelia's Idea

"Amelia then mentioned that the hollow section could be just below the pole handle. In other words, the skier would screw off the handle to access the map. The bottom end of that handle would be a great place to mount a small compass."

One Last Idea

"I thought this idea had run its course. But then Ron chimed in with another thought: The top of the removable handle would be an ideal spot to include a tripod mount for a camera."

Question

Frank wanted his team to generate as many potential solutions to its sales problem as possible. Select the effective group brainstorming strategies Frank should employ.

Options:

1. Frank should urge his team to develop 30 ideas or more.

2. Frank should talk with the senior staff about implementing ideas.

3. Frank should urge team members to delay judgment of ideas.

4. Frank should encourage the team to expand on proposed ideas.

5. Frank should reward his team after solving its sales problem.

Answer:

In fact, Frank should urge his team to devise numerous possible solutions, to initially withhold judgment on all ideas, and to expand on the solutions after they've been volunteered.

Option 1: This is a correct choice. It's important for Frank to urge his team to generate a large number of potential solutions during the first brainstorming meeting.

Option 2: This is an incorrect choice. Talking with the senior staff about implementing ideas is not part of the group brainstorming process.

Option 3: This is a correct choice. When Frank's team comes up with a number of potential solutions, Frank should instruct them to withhold all judgment of ideas. That may impede creativity and also reduce the number of potential solutions.

Option 4: This is a correct choice. Once a team member submits an idea, Frank should have the other team members use it to base additional ideas on, and to inspire other related solutions.

Option 5: This is an incorrect choice. Rewarding the team may be part of Frank's strategy for maintaining team engagement, but it really isn't part of the group brainstorming process.

As you participate in or lead brainstorming sessions, remember to help others generate many ideas, refrain from judgment, and develop potential solutions that piggyback on other ideas.

Have you ever participated on a decision-making team that others described as "aggressively mediocre"?

If so, your team probably succumbed to the sinister effects of "groupthink." And you probably succumbed to frequent bouts of extreme frustration. In this topic, you'll learn how to be a real leader and employ techniques to overcome groupthink by:

- initially downplaying the strength of your own opinions,
- assigning a rotating devil's advocate to the team's ideas,
- seeking feedback from an external expert.

What is groupthink? Groupthink is the tendency of group members to allow conformity and team loyalty to guide their decisions. When a team falls prey to groupthink, it:

- censors dissenting opinions,
- seeks unanimity at any cost,
- fails to seek other solutions.

Groupthink also inspires a sense of invulnerability, as if the team's decisions will be, now and forever, infallible.

When problem-solving disaster threatens, the "groupthinkers" suddenly go blind. And in the last inning, when disaster actually strikes, even a decision-making home run won't be enough to save the game.

When leading a problem-solving team, you should employ the first strategy to overcome groupthink: Initially downplay the strength of your own opinions.

Underselling your own ideas seems to contradict the principles of lively debate, does it not? At first glance, yes.

See each tactic, for an explanation from Corbin, who manages a decision-making team within a company that sells organic enzymes used to clean up oil spills.

My objective

"Essentially, our product eats and digests petroleum. That's not the only possible use for it, however. I wanted to motivate my team to come up with and act on other enzyme applications."

I downplayed my ideas

"While guiding my team toward strategic decisions, I kept in mind that my opinions carry weight. I didn't want to force others to adopt my ideas. Instead, I encouraged open disagreement and diverse solutions."

I didn't repeat my ideas

"Initially, I wanted to market the enzymes to those 10-minute oil change businesses, as well as auto repair shops. I mentioned that possibility to the group. I didn't, however, re-emphasize the idea. Repetition may have been perceived as a mandate."

I wasn't persuasive

"I also trimmed my language of persuasion and subtle coercion. By doing so, I didn't exert a conforming influence on the group. Rather, I opened the door to more stimulating debate of colleagues' other possible enzyme uses."

By not repeating his opinions and forsaking persuasive language, Corbin assumed a role opposite to that of a judge. He would have preferred a hung jury to a mindless, unanimous verdict.

Corbin also employed another contradictory role. He used the second strategy for overcoming groupthink and assigned a rotating devil's advocate role to members of his group.

The devil's advocacy technique received its name from a traditional practice within the Roman Catholic Church.

Before a church member was elevated to sainthood, the College of Cardinals appointed an official to investigate and express all the reasons the candidate's canonization should not be approved.

The engine beneath the hood of today's business world is the push and pull of friendly competition. Similarly, the give and take among problem-solving team members powers truly dynamic business decisions.

See each action to discover how Corbin guided his group's exchange of ideas.

I let them brainstorm

"The group brainstormed an array of potential enzyme applications. No one criticized potential ideas at that stage."

I appointed a devil's advocate

"In the next meeting, I told Gayle to be the devil's advocate and dispute the options we discussed. For example, Max wanted to market the enzymes as a driveway cleaner. Gayle provided reasons that idea might not work."

Everyone had a turn

"During follow-up decision meetings, I assigned the devil's advocate role to other colleagues. Because the responsibility rotated during each meeting, members never took the role for granted. And there was always a dissenting voice to counter conformity."

By including the presence of at least one contradictory opinion, Corbin defused the adverse effects of groupthink.

The devil's advocate ensured that no sense of group infallibility occurred on the team.

Finally, Corbin employed the third strategy to keep groupthink at bay: He sought feedback from an external expert.

Decision-making groups can become insulated, conformity-seeking units if they spurn input on their choices from outside sources.

See each factor to discover how Corbin counteracted groupthink with help from Vicki, an external expert.

The decision-making process

"I had breakfast with my chemist pal, Vicki. I told her about the process my team undertook to avoid making conformist, overconfident enzyme decisions."

The tentative decisions

"The group decided to pursue a couple of novel marketing paths. I relayed these tentative choices to Vicki."

The expert's knowledge

"First, I confided in Vicki because she was familiar with the chemical structure and potential applications of the organic enzymes."

The expert's motivation

"Second, I knew Vicki had no vested interest in the actions of my team. She worked for a pharmaceutical company. Neither Vicki nor her organization would benefit in any way from knowing about our intentions."

Corbin asked what Vicki thought about not only his team's decision-making process but about its potential solutions as well.

She approved of both. Had she not, Corbin would have reconsidered the possibility that groupthink had short-circuited his team's effectiveness.

To analyze his or another group's effectiveness at employing strategies to overcome groupthink, Corbin asked himself several questions.

See each strategy to find out what Corbin expects a team leader should do to avoid groupthink.

Devil's advocate

"I always ask if the leader undersold her own ideas by not repeating them. Also, did she rotate the devil's advocate responsibility?"

External expert

"Finally, did the team leader speak with an external expert who had no vested interest in the team's decision?"

Case Study: Question 1 of 2

Scenario:

Reginald's company helped e-Businesses incorporate streaming video into Web sites. He organized a team to determine novel uses of the technology.

Question:

Was Reginald effective at employing the techniques to overcome groupthink in his streaming video team?

Choose only one answer.

Options:

1. Reginald was ineffective because, although he de-emphasized his own feelings about the video solutions and consulted an external expert, he didn't assign more than one person to the devil's advocate role.

2. Reginald was effective because he sought the input of Virginia, an uninvolved expert, he didn't persuade others to implement his video ideas, and he assigned a rotating devil's advocate to the members' solutions.

3. Reginald was ineffective because, although he had Bo play devil's advocate to Lucinda's video solution, he didn't guide the team toward adopting his own idea nor did he ask Virginia how to negate the effects of groupthink.

Answer:

Actually, Reginald was effective because he de-emphasized his own opinions about the streaming video and assigned a rotating devil's advocate. He also consulted an external expert, Virginia, who had no vested interest in the outcome.

Option 1: This is an incorrect choice. Reginald only has to ensure that at least one group member plays the role of devil's advocate at all times, so no potential solution goes unchallenged.

Option 2: This is the correct choice. These steps helped Reginald contend with competing interests among the participants and steer the team away from the adverse effects of groupthink.

Option 3: This is an incorrect choice. Reginald should keep the strength of his opinions to himself and, as team leader, it's his job to steer the panel away from the adverse effects of groupthink.

Case Study: Question 2 of 2

What questions did you ask to determine if Reginald was effective at employing the techniques to overcome groupthink?

Options:

1. Did Reginald avoid repeating his own opinions concerning the use of the company's streaming video?
2. Did Reginald ensure that team members took periodic meeting breaks to refresh their minds?
3. Did Reginald make sure he had a rotating devil's advocate so that no members took the role for granted?
4. Did Reginald seek the feedback of an expert outside the video team who had no vested interest in the decision?

Answer:

In fact, you should have asked if Reginald initially de-emphasized his own opinions, assigned a rotating devil's advocate role, and consulted an external expert. Periodic meeting breaks have little effect on groupthink.

Option 1: This is a correct choice. When leading a problem-solving team, the first strategy Reginald should employ to overcome groupthink is to initially downplay the strength of his own opinions.

Option 2: This is an incorrect choice. Taking periodic breaks might be refreshing, but to diminish the harmful effects of groupthink, Reginald needs to downplay his own opinions, assign a devil's advocate, and seek feedback from an external expert.

Option 3: This is a correct choice. The devil's advocacy technique is very useful to consider and express all the reasons the team's decision or solution should not be approved. It's always good having a dissenting voice to counter conformity.

Option 4: This is a correct choice. Decision-making groups can become insulated, conformity-seeking units if they don't ask an outside experts to review their decision-making processes and potential solutions.

As a group, think together. But don't let groupthink neutralize your ability to devise original, even nonconformist, business decisions. In this topic, you learned to employ techniques to overcome groupthink by:

- underselling your opinions initially,
- rotating the role of devil's advocate,
- getting second opinions from an external expert.

Techniques to overcome groupthink

Have you ever participated on a decision-making team that others described as "aggressively mediocre"?

If so, your team probably succumbed to the sinister effects of "groupthink." And you probably succumbed to frequent bouts of extreme frustration. In this topic, you'll learn how to be a real leader and employ techniques to overcome groupthink by:

- initially downplaying the strength of your own opinions,
- assigning a rotating devil's advocate to the team's ideas,
- seeking feedback from an external expert.

What is groupthink? Groupthink is the tendency of group members to allow conformity and team loyalty to guide their decisions. When a team falls prey to groupthink, it:

- censors dissenting opinions,
- seeks unanimity at any cost,

- fails to seek other solutions.

Groupthink also inspires a sense of invulnerability, as if the team's decisions will be, now and forever, infallible.

When problem-solving disaster threatens, the "groupthinkers" suddenly go blind. And in the last inning, when disaster actually strikes, even a decision-making home run won't be enough to save the game.

When leading a problem-solving team, you should employ the first strategy to overcome groupthink: Initially downplay the strength of your own opinions.

Underselling your own ideas seems to contradict the principles of lively debate, does it not? At first glance, yes.

Select each tactic, for an explanation from Corbin, who manages a decision-making team within a company that sells organic enzymes used to clean up oil spills.

My objective

"Essentially, our product eats and digests petroleum. That's not the only possible use for it, however. I wanted to motivate my team to come up with and act on other enzyme applications."

I downplayed my ideas

"While guiding my team toward strategic decisions, I kept in mind that my opinions carry weight. I didn't want to force others to adopt my ideas. Instead, I encouraged open disagreement and diverse solutions."

I didn't repeat my ideas

"Initially, I wanted to market the enzymes to those 10-minute oil change businesses, as well as auto repair shops. I mentioned that possibility to the group. I didn't, however, re-emphasize the idea. Repetition may have been perceived as a mandate."

I wasn't persuasive

"I also trimmed my language of persuasion and subtle coercion. By doing so, I didn't exert a conforming influence on the group. Rather, I opened the door to more stimulating debate of colleagues' other possible enzyme uses."

By not repeating his opinions and forsaking persuasive language, Corbin assumed a role opposite to that of a judge. He would have preferred a hung jury to a mindless, unanimous verdict.

Corbin also employed another contradictory role. He used the second strategy for overcoming groupthink and assigned a rotating devil's advocate role to members of his group.

The devil's advocacy technique received its name from a traditional practice within the Roman Catholic Church.

Before a church member was elevated to sainthood, the College of Cardinals appointed an official to investigate and express all the reasons the candidate's canonization should not be approved.

The engine beneath the hood of today's business world is the push and pull of friendly competition. Similarly, the give and take among problem-solving team members powers truly dynamic business decisions.

See each action to discover how Corbin guided his group's exchange of ideas.

I let them brainstorm

"The group brainstormed an array of potential enzyme applications. No one criticized potential ideas at that stage."

I appointed a devil's advocate

"In the next meeting, I told Gayle to be the devil's advocate and dispute the options we discussed. For example, Max wanted to market the enzymes as a driveway cleaner. Gayle provided reasons that idea might not work."

Everyone had a turn

"During follow-up decision meetings, I assigned the devil's advocate role to other colleagues. Because the responsibility rotated during each meeting, members never took the role for granted. And there was always a dissenting voice to counter conformity."

By including the presence of at least one contradictory opinion, Corbin defused the adverse effects of groupthink.

The devil's advocate ensured that no sense of group infallibility occurred on the team.

Finally, Corbin employed the third strategy to keep groupthink at bay: He sought feedback from an external expert.

Decision-making groups can become insulated, conformity-seeking units if they spurn input on their choices from outside sources.

See each factor to discover how Corbin counteracted groupthink with help from Vicki, an external expert.

The decision-making process

"I had breakfast with my chemist pal, Vicki. I told her about the process my team undertook to avoid making conformist, overconfident enzyme decisions."

The tentative decisions

"The group decided to pursue a couple of novel marketing paths. I relayed these tentative choices to Vicki."

The expert's knowledge

"First, I confided in Vicki because she was familiar with the chemical structure and potential applications of the organic enzymes."

The expert's motivation

"Second, I knew Vicki had no vested interest in the actions of my team. She worked for a pharmaceutical company. Neither Vicki nor her organization would benefit in any way from knowing about our intentions."

Corbin asked what Vicki thought about not only his team's decision-making process but about its potential solutions as well.

She approved of both. Had she not, Corbin would have reconsidered the possibility that groupthink had short-circuited his team's effectiveness.

To analyze his or another group's effectiveness at employing strategies to overcome groupthink, Corbin asked himself several questions.

See each strategy to find out what Corbin expects a team leader should do to avoid groupthink.

Devil's advocate

"I always ask if the leader undersold her own ideas by not repeating them. Also, did she rotate the devil's advocate responsibility?"

External expert

"Finally, did the team leader speak with an external expert who had no vested interest in the team's decision?”

Case Study: Question 1 of 2

Scenario:

Reginald's company helped e-Businesses incorporate streaming video into Web sites. He organized a team to determine novel uses of the technology.

Question:

Was Reginald effective at employing the techniques to overcome groupthink in his streaming video team?

Choose only one answer.

Options:

1. Reginald was ineffective because, although he de-emphasized his own feelings about the video solutions and consulted an external expert, he didn't assign more than one person to the devil's advocate role.

2. Reginald was effective because he sought the input of Virginia, an uninvolved expert, he didn't persuade others to implement his video ideas, and he assigned a rotating devil's advocate to the members' solutions.

3. Reginald was ineffective because, although he had Bo play devil's advocate to Lucinda's video solution, he didn't guide the team toward adopting his own idea nor did he ask Virginia how to negate the effects of groupthink.

Answer:

Actually, Reginald was effective because he de-emphasized his own opinions about the streaming video and assigned a rotating devil's advocate. He also consulted an external expert, Virginia, who had no vested interest in the outcome.

Option 1: This is an incorrect choice. Reginald only has to ensure that at least one group member plays the role of devil's advocate at all times, so no potential solution goes unchallenged.

Option 2: This is the correct choice. These steps helped Reginald contend with competing interests among the participants and steer the team away from the adverse effects of groupthink.

Option 3: This is an incorrect choice. Reginald should keep the strength of his opinions to himself and, as team leader, it's his job to steer the panel away from the adverse effects of groupthink.

Case Study: Question 2 of 2

What questions did you ask to determine if Reginald was effective at employing the techniques to overcome groupthink?

Options:

1. Did Reginald avoid repeating his own opinions concerning the use of the company's streaming video?
2. Did Reginald ensure that team members took periodic meeting breaks to refresh their minds?
3. Did Reginald make sure he had a rotating devil's advocate so that no members took the role for granted?
4. Did Reginald seek the feedback of an expert outside the video team who had no vested interest in the decision?

Answer:

In fact, you should have asked if Reginald initially de-emphasized his own opinions, assigned a rotating devil's advocate role, and consulted an external expert. Periodic meeting breaks have little effect on groupthink.

Option 1: This is a correct choice. When leading a problem-solving team, the first strategy Reginald should employ to overcome groupthink is to initially downplay the strength of his own opinions.

Option 2: This is an incorrect choice. Taking periodic breaks might be refreshing, but to diminish the harmful effects of groupthink, Reginald needs to downplay his own opinions, assign a devil's advocate, and seek feedback from an external expert.

Option 3: This is a correct choice. The devil's advocacy technique is very useful to consider and express all the reasons the team's decision or solution should not be approved. It's always good having a dissenting voice to counter conformity.

Option 4: This is a correct choice. Decision-making groups can become insulated, conformity-seeking units if they don't ask an outside experts to review their decision-making processes and potential solutions.

In your next group decision-making effort, do as Reginald did. Use techniques to overcome groupthink in a way that eliminates its unfavorable presence.

As a group, think together. But don't let groupthink neutralize your ability to devise original, even nonconformist, business decisions. In this topic, you learned to employ techniques to overcome groupthink by:

- underselling your opinions initially,
- rotating the role of devil's advocate,
- getting second opinions from an external expert.

The nominal group technique

Marketers like to use the phrase "at a nominal fee" to describe various add-on services that accompany their primary products. "Nominal" in this case implies a trivial amount.

When it comes to the nominal group technique, however, that key word means just the reverse. The results you'll receive by employing this strategy are anything but trivial.

In fact, the nominal group technique is one of the oldest and most revered group problem-solving techniques. In this topic, you'll learn how a team effectively performs the four steps of the nominal group technique by:

- anonymously voting on initial favored solutions,
- recording the votes in a round-robin fashion,
- clarifying any confusing ideas,
- evaluating the final solutions.

Using the nominal group technique allows groups to arrive at effective business decisions because it limits an individual's input to short explanations and relies on anonymous voting to choose among potential solutions.

The technique negates the persuasive effects that dominant or overbearing team members may have on others. It helps ensure that fair, unbiased business decisions are made.

Paul owned a nationwide recycling company that specialized in processing industrial scrap metal. He and his team of managers established a goal of increasing the sales of the company's recycled metals by 15 percent within the next nine months. After generating more than 20 potential solutions to increase its sales, the team met to choose which idea, or ideas, it would implement.

In the meeting, Paul passed around a checklist detailing the potential solutions the team had generated. He then instructed each member to take the first step in the nominal group technique: anonymously vote for his or her initial favored solutions.

Before Paul noted the ideas he favored--expanding into the international market and focusing on more government contracts--he passed out notecards on which team members could write their preferences.

See each of Paul's methods for team members to vote on favored solutions to learn more.

Writing down solutions

"I told team members to write down their preferred two or three solutions to our sales crisis."

Anonymous voting

"By keeping the voting anonymous, Bruce and Lauren weren't able to bully the others into adopting only the solutions they favored."

After team members jotted down their votes, Paul took the next step in the nominal group technique and recorded the votes in a round-robin fashion.

See each action to learn how Paul recorded the votes in a round-robin fashion.

I use a projector or dry erase board

"I usually bring an overhead projector or dry-erase board to the meeting. It's important that all team members see the voting results as they're recorded. We'll revisit them after this step."

I recorded the first person's vote

"I'm left-handed. Maybe that explains why I always start by asking the person on my left to announce his or her first preferred solution. In this case, Monica endorsed the possibility of shifting our attention to international markets. I wrote that idea on the overhead."

I recorded the rest of the votes

"After Monica finished, I asked the person next to her for his vote. When I recorded the idea, I simply wrote down a description of that solution. I then moved to the next person, and then the next person, and so on."

I recorded each idea only once

"After Monica voted for selling to international clients, other team members who had voted for and written down that idea weren't allowed to revote for that solution. Instead, they simply said "pass," and the next member took the floor and announced a new idea."

This round-robin voting continued until all the ideas had been written down. Paul duly recorded each and every suggestion on the overhead.

If a member voted for a solution unpopular with other members, Paul didn't censor or eliminate the offering.

With the initial votes accounted for, Paul moved on to the next step of the nominal group technique and instructed group members to clarify any confusing ideas.

See each factor to find out how Paul instructed group members to clarify any confusing ideas.

Need for clarification

"Our company primarily sells recycled metal to commercial shipbuilders. Nathan wanted some clarification on the potential solution to capture government contracts."

Brevity of clarification

"Emily had been the first to vote on it. I told her to briefly clarify and explain that proposed solution. She gave Nathan the high-level version of the governmental business idea. I didn't allow Emily to elaborate on the details."

Lack of persuasion

"I made it perfectly clear that whenever a team member clarified an idea for another, there would be no "selling" involved. This didn't please some members, but persuasion has no place in the nominal group technique."

Final understanding

"When the questions died down, I asked if anyone required further clarification on any of the solutions. There was no use continuing to the next stage if everyone wasn't on the same page."

Several of Paul's team members felt the urge to push their ideas on the others when clarifying them. But Paul stood firm and stymied those attempts.

By clarifying any confusing ideas, Paul cleared the way for the next step, in which his team evaluated the final solutions.

The nominal group technique often produces ten or more possible solutions. Paul told team members to reconsider each idea on the overhead. He then distributed notecards on which each person voted for his or her top two final choices.

These notecards were, in effect, secret ballots. Paul disallowed any further discussion. After team members passed the ballots back to Paul, he evaluated the final solutions by:

- assigning each first place vote a score of 2,
- assigning each second place vote a score of 1,
- tallying the final scores,
- announcing the results.

Paul and his team decided that international markets held the most sales appeal. His company may have sold its products primarily to domestic shipbuilders, but it was about to set sail for deeper waters.

You should ask the same questions posed by Paul, the metal recycler.

Check each factor to learn how Paul analyzed a team's effectiveness at putting the nominal group technique to work.

You should ask the same questions posed by Paul, the metal recycler.

See each factor to learn how Paul analyzed a team's effectiveness at putting the nominal group technique to work.

anonymity

"I always ask whether team members anonymously voted on the solutions they initially favored. Otherwise, they may bias the entire process."

recording ideas

"I make sure that team members announce their votes in a round-robin fashion and pass on solutions if they were already mentioned. In other words, was each nominated solution only announced once?"

clarification, not persuasion

"Also, I ask if all unclear ideas were clarified by the supporting parties, but not in a persuasive way. Salesmanship has no place in the nominal group technique."

secret ballot

"Lastly, did the team vote on its final ideas using a secret ballot? Again, this technique defuses the influence of dominant team members."

Case Study: Question 1 of 2

Scenario:

Michael, a manager for an automobile insurance company, noticed a recent drop in employee morale. He formed a cross-departmental team to generate solutions to the problem and choose the best one or two ideas.

Step 1

"We developed an array of potential solutions to our employee morale problem. A few of them were upgrading the employee health plans, holding a company party, increasing vacation time, and offering performance-based monetary incentives."

Step 2

"Each team member anonymously nominated two or three favored ideas. I recorded those ideas after the members expressed their preferences. The party idea received several initial votes and looked like a strong solution in the early rounds."

Step 3

"A few team members were unclear about how the performance-based incentives would be used. That was Ann's solution, so I gave her a minute or two to clarify that idea but not persuade others to endorse it."

Step 4

"Afterward, we voted on the final decision via a secret ballot. Just as I suspected, the company party option won, with the health plan enhancements placing a close second. In the end, we decided to adopt both solutions."

Question:

Was Michael's team effective at using the nominal group technique to make a decision regarding the employee morale problem?

Options:

1. His team was ineffective because, even though all voting took place anonymously, Michael allowed the company party idea to receive more votes than allowed in this procedure.
2. His team was effective because members anonymously voted on their initial morale-enhancement ideas, clarified but didn't sell those solutions, and effectively arrived at a final decision.
3. His team was ineffective because, even though it used a secret ballot to vote on the final morale-enhancement solutions, Michael failed to encourage enough discussion in the initial voting stage.

Answer:

Actually, even though Michael's team effectively used most aspects of the nominal group technique, the company party idea was counted more than once after the initial anonymous voting. This mistake made its procedure ineffective.

Option 1: This is the correct choice. When recording the votes in a round-robin fashion, each idea should get only one vote. This ensures that the team nominates many potential solutions and remains unbiased toward any single idea.

Option 2: Incorrect. The team was ineffective because the company party idea got more than one vote when the initial votes were recorded in a round-robin fashion. Round-robin is necessary to nominate many ways to solve the problem.

Option 3: This is an incorrect choice. Michael should begin by having each member anonymously vote for two or three preferred solutions, without any general discussion.

Case Study: Question 2 of 2

What questions did you ask to determine whether Michael's team was effective at using the nominal group technique to make a decision regarding the employee morale problem?

Options:

1. Did Michael's team employ a secret ballot to settle on the best strategies to enhance employee morale?
2. Did Michael's team insist on making a final decision after generating several new solutions?
3. Did Michael's team merely explain and clarify unclear morale-enhancement solutions instead of using persuasion?
4. Did Michael's team record all of its initial morale-enhancement ideas and not remove any from consideration?
5. Did Michael's team nominate its initial two or three morale-enhancement solutions anonymously?

Answer:

In fact, you should have asked if the initial voting as well as the final ballot were anonymous, if all initial ideas were included for consideration, and if team members clarified ideas rather than sold them.

Option 1: This is a correct choice. When group members vote for their preferred solution, it's important to use a secret ballot to eliminate peer pressure.

Option 2: Incorrect. After nominating solutions, those ideas need to be clarified for other team members--providing enough information so they understand the concepts.

Option 3: This is a correct choice. Team members can briefly explain their solutions, but they shouldn't try to sell them or persuade the others of their merits.

Option 4: This is a correct choice. The fist step in the nominal group technique is for team members to look over a complete list of potential solutions.

Option 5: This is a correct choice. It's important to nominate two or three favored ideas anonymously. Otherwise, it can skew the final opinions of all team members.

In the previous exercise, Michael may have allowed bias to enter his team's proceedings. When a potential solution receives more attention than others when it's recorded, it can skew the final opinions of all team members.

On the other hand, using the nominal group technique properly translates into business decisions that tip the scales in your favor. In this topic, you learned how to use the nominal group technique to make a team business decision:

- Anonymously vote on initial favored ideas.
- Record them in a round-robin fashion.
- Clarify the confusing solutions.
- Evaluate the final ideas.

Strategies for decision follow-up meetings

If you remove your car's rearview mirror, the police will probably pull you over because of your poor decision.

Car mirrors aren't only recommended; they're required by law. And the law for group problem solving is to look where you've been and review the decisions your team has reached. In this topic, you'll learn how to conduct a decision follow-up meeting in which you:

- focus specifically on the long-term consequences of a decision,
- revisit discarded options,
- play devil's advocate to the chosen option.

After your team makes a business decision, members may immediately move on to the next pressing matter, to the next "fire" that needs to be extinguished.

The team's decision, however, takes on a life of its own. Like any good parent, your responsibility lies in nurturing that decision by periodically reviewing its effectiveness.

That's why, in your decision review meeting, your group should focus specifically on the long-term consequences of the chosen option. Team members should ask these questions:

- What decision results do we expect to see in six months?
- What ramifications may result from the decision one year down the line?
- What will be the outcome of the choice two years after it's been implemented?

After examining the long-range decision consequences, you can put down your team binoculars and take out a microscope. You'll use this tool to practice the next decision follow-up strategy: Closely study your discarded options.

A few months back, Carla's team of portfolio analysts reviewed its decision to invest in Eurodollar futures contracts. True, the transactions had already been executed; however, by revisiting previously discarded investment ideas, Carla's team could derive inspiration for redirecting those funds if necessary.

See each factor to find out how Carla instructed the group to closely study the discarded options.

Internal expectations

"Our revenue expectations had changed since we originally made the Eurodollar decision. By examining other investment options we considered but then discarded, we got ideas for redistributing the underperforming contracts if we needed to."

External relationships

"Also, our clients had become a little more skittish about the Eurodollar contracts. The investment options we didn't pursue may have been more to their liking."

Economic factors

"Economic forecasts at the time of our decision follow-up meeting indicated a shift to currency contracts. We wanted to be prepared, so we re-examined our forsaken investment solutions to see if we had researched the currency market. We might be able to use those findings."

After revisiting discarded options, Carla instructed the team to use the third meeting strategy and play devil's advocate to the chosen option.

Carla: OK, everybody. For the most part, we seem to be pleased with the decision to invest in the Eurodollar futures market. I'd like to try to uncover reasons our investment choice won't pan out. I want each of you to play devil's advocate to the Eurodollar strategy.

Stan: How exactly should we do that?

Carla: Be a critic. Write down two or three reasons you imagine the funds should have been funneled elsewhere. In other words, why shouldn't we have invested in other areas?

Marti: I can think of several right off the bat.

Carla: Good, Marti. We can't ignore them. Only by factoring in what could possibly go wrong with our decision can we really evaluate its potential.

Stan: I guess if we come up with several convincing reasons the Eurodollar futures won't meet our goals, we can take steps to improve our chances of success.

Carla: Exactly. What's the purpose of reviewing a decision if we're afraid to improve it?

At Carla's decision follow-up meeting, team members decided to hold their investment ground for the time being. They scheduled another follow-up meeting for next month to re-evaluate the situation again.

Should corrective action need to be taken, Carla's team was one step ahead of the game.

Question

Practice what you've learned about summing up team decisions. Identify effective strategies to use during a decision follow-up meeting.

Options:

1. Concentrate on long-term decision ramifications in particular.
2. Make sure you always invite customers to your review meeting.
3. Re-examine the potential solutions you initially rejected.
4. Try to imagine reasons your decision won't prove effective.

Answer:

Actually, you should focus on long-term decision consequences, revisit discarded options, and play devil's advocate to the chosen option. It's not mandatory, nor always wise, to invite customers to this type of meeting.

Option 1: This is a correct choice. Your group should focus specifically on the long-term consequences of the chosen option, because the team's decision will take on a life of its own.

Option 2: This is an incorrect choice. Customers have no role in a company's internal decision-making process except, perhaps, to provide information.

Option 3: This is a correct choice. Closely studying your discarded options can help your team derive inspiration for improving the chosen solution as implementation proceeds.

Option 4: This is a correct choice. Playing devil's advocate to the chosen option will help you really evaluate its potential and--if necessary--take steps to improve your chances of success.

Don't let business decisions wither on the vine.

Use the strategies covered in the previous exercise during your next decision follow-up meeting and you'll reap the rewards.

In this topic, you learned how to use these decision follow-up meeting strategies: Focus specifically on the long- term consequences of the decision, revisit discarded options, and play devil's advocate to the chosen option.

Now that you've arrived at the end of this course, think back to what you've learned. It's not enough to wait for

the perfect opportunity to use your newfound knowledge. Only your relentless effort to apply that understanding- -today--will influence your group's success.

In this course, you learned how to avoid inefficient group problem solving practices. And along the way, you discovered how to apply several specific group problem-solving and decision-making techniques.

GLOSSARY

Glossary

A

acronym - A shortened form derived from the initial letters of the words that make up the complete form. Acronyms are pronounced as words (for example: ZIP Code, OSHA, and scuba).

anchoring - A mental shortcut in which you use a certain idea as a starting point and adjust your perception of the new event away from that anchor.

assumptions - Factors about a problem that are taken for granted, often mistakenly.

attributions - Assigning the cause of an event to another thing – a person or situation.

availability heuristic - The tendency to most easily recall those events that are the most "available" or vivid in memory.

B

bias - A mental leaning or inclination that can distort thinking.

C

causation - A situation with one variable being the sole cause of an event.

chunking - A memory device in which you group a long series of numbers into more manageable segments.

confirmation bias - The tendency to seek out and acknowledge evidence that confirms your beliefs while ignoring evidence that runs counter to them.

consistency bias - The psychological tendency to maintain consistent social actions.

contrast effect - The comparison of two different situations where each one distorts your perception of the other one.

correlation - A relationship or association between two variables.

critical thinking - Thought that places a premium on logic and analytical reasoning.

E

egocentric bias - The tendency to assume that other people experience events the same way you do.

F

fundamental attribution error - The tendency to overlook the influence of a situation on others' behavior and to overemphasize personal traits instead.

H

heuristic - A mental shortcut that may or may not facilitate effective thinking.

hindsight bias - The tendency to falsely believe you could have predicted a past event or result more accurately than you really did.

I

initialisms - A shortened form derived from the initial letters of the words that make up the complete form. Initialisms are pronounced letter by letter (for example: IBM, FBI, and CT scan).

M

method of loci - A memory device in which you mentally place objects you want to remember in familiar locations – or "loci" – so that you can later revisit that place in your mind and more easily recall the targeted objects.

mnemonic device - Any device for aiding the memory. The principle is to create in the mind an artificial structure that incorporates unfamiliar ideas or, especially, a series of dissociated ideas that by themselves are difficult to remember.

R

rationalize - The working out of superficially rational or plausible explanations.

representativeness heuristic - A mental shortcut in which people classify something according to how similar it is to a typical instance.

S

selective perception - The perception of what you expect and hope to see rather than what is true and accurate.

self-serving bias - The excessive attribution of your success to your own traits or disposition and attributing your failures to circumstance. When making attributions about others, it's doing just the opposite.

REFERENCES

References

The Problem Solving Journey: Your Guide for Making Decisions and Getting Results - 2000, Hoenig, Christopher W., Perseus Press

Sources of Power: How People Make Decisions - 1999, Klein, Gary, MIT Press

Creative Solution Finding - 1999, Nadler, Gerald, and Shozo Hibino, Prima Publishing

Decision Traps: Ten Barriers to Brilliant Thinking and How to Overcome Them - 1990, Russo, J. Edward, Fireside Press

Decision Making and Problem Solving in Management - 2000, Vaughn, Robert H., Williams Custom Publishing

Psychology - 1999, Fernald, L. Dodge, Prentice-Hall College Division

The Problem-solving Journey: Your Guide to Making Decisions and Getting Results - 2000, Hoenig, Christopher W., Perseus Press

Serious Creativity - 1992, de Bono, Edward, Harper Business

Printed in Great Britain
by Amazon

79160167R00304